Journal for the Academic Study of Magic

ISSN 1479-0750

ISBN 1869928 962

Published by Mandrake of Oxford, PO Box 250, Oxford, OX1 1AP, UK. http://www.mandrake.uk.net

In association with the Society for the Academic Study of Magic,
c/o Dep't of Historical Studies, University of Bristol,
13 Woodland Road, Bristol, BS8 1TB, UK
http://www.sasm.co.uk/index.html

Bibliographic conventions: please cite as: David Evans (Ed.), *The Journal for the Academic Study of Magic,* 2, (Mandrake, Oxford, 2004)

Copyright of individual articles remains with the author(s), while editorial, style, layout etc of the Journal is © SASM, JSM and Mandrake of Oxford 2006.

All rights reserved. No part of this Journal may be reproduced or utilized in any form or by any means, electronic or mechanical including photocopying, recording or by any information storage and/or retrieval system, without express prior permission in writing from the Publishers.

Short extracts may be reproduced for review purposes. A copy of the review, and notification of where and when it appeared would be appreciated, sent to SASM please.

Contents

Editorials 5

News 12

Obituaries 14

Book Review Policy: 18

A Technical Note for Prospective Authors: 19

Editorial Board 20

JSM3 Contributors list, in Alphabetical Order: 21

Buffy and Beyond:
Language and Resistance in Contemporary Teenage Witchcraft
Hannah E. Sanders 25

A Language of Her Own:
Witchery as a New Language of Female Identity
Amy Lee 61

Discovering the Witch's Teat:
Magical Practices, Medical Superstitions in The Witch of Edmonton
Mary Hayes 78

The Re-enchantment of the Medical:
an examination of magical elements in healing.
Penny Lowery 109

Apparitions, Ghosts, Fairies, Demons and Wild Events:
Virtuality in Early Modern Britain
Dr. Jonathan Paul Marshall 141

'A half-choked meep of cosmic fear': Is there esoteric symbolism in H.P.Lovecraft's The Dream-Quest of Unknown Kadath?
David Geall 176

Creative Revolution: Bergsonisms and Modern Magic
Dave Green 212

Becoming a Sorcerer: Jean-Pierre Bekolo's Quartier Mozart and the Magic of Deleuzian and Guattarian Becoming
Susan Gorman 248

Living the Mystery: Sacred Drama Today
K. A. Laity 263

Book Reviews 277

Journal for the Academic Study of Magic, Issue 3.

Editorials

Editorial 1

A warm welcome to Issue 3 of the JSM. Now that we have, so to speak, 'found our feet' I am happy to write that our audience is growing, and we have received some very useful and world-wide feedback about what we are achieving with this publication. I'm very pleased to see the diversity of submissions continue to cover many disciplines, historical periods and geographical areas.

It may appear to be doing things in reverse, but now we are up and running I feel it appropriate to write about the founding of the Journal, as it has some bearing on where we are going today in the study of magic within academia.

In June 2002, during my doctoral studentship, after way too much coffee and too much bemoaning of the paucity of possible publishing outlets for magical-themed academic writings it was my great privilege to be co-founder (with my friends and colleagues Dr. Alison Butler, Dr Dave Green and Dr Owen Davies) of a new peer-reviewed annual academic publication, which you now hold in your hands, published by a firm previously known largely for their intelligent 'hands-on' occult practitioner books; Mandrake of Oxford. The Journal was first produced in spring 2003, in parallel with a marvellously diverse international conference, *Magical Practice and Belief 1800-2000*, held at Bristol University, with a second, larger issue of the Journal, produced by a larger editorial board comprising a mixture of 'name' academics and new doctoral-level researchers, following around a year later.

In many cases the founding of the JSM has personally led to growing friendships and research alliances between academics and magicians around the world, some of which alliances and friendships are my own, and which continue to be of immense academic value and personal pleasure. The shrewd business sense and general enthusiasm of the proprietor of Mandrake, Mogg Morgan, who is both author and magician, appears to have seen a niche needing this kind of publication, and it has been well received by both magical and academic communities *in general*. There has been some resistance from both the magical and academic world, however. It would be churlish to provide names of the opposition parties, but one 'name' academic told me (comments paraphrased) that 'it was a waste of time doing the thing, as nothing the journal could print would be any good, as 99% of supposed quality academic work published on magic was rubbish'. Their own work on the subject always falling into the one per cent of excellence, of course....

On the neo pagan front, one occultist posted a fabricated and utterly baseless defamatory quote that was purported to be taken directly from the Journal website (a website which I solely authored) on an Internet magical forum, *and before a copy of the Journal had ever appeared in print*, to the effect that

"Authors attempting to put forward theories of cosmology, metaphysics, psychology, etc., at variance with accepted academic theories will not be published. In particular, theories proposing the existence of types of energy which cannot be detected and measured by currently existing scientific instruments, or which propose the existence of non-biological forms of life (including but not limited to gnomes, sylphs, salamanders, undines, devas, elves, angels, archangels, gods, etc.), or which imply the existence of any form of deity or divine being (whether male, female, or dual-gendered), or which propose the existence of any sort of divine plan for the universe, will be considered 'un-academic'...".[1]

and it was only after several 'difficult' emails that I persuaded the author of the slur that a public retraction was in order, which they eventually made in December 2002. The first Issue of the Journal was released four months later. There have been other similar criticisms from the neo pagan world, almost invariably from those who have also obviously not seen the journal, which is ironically precisely the kind of censorial and omniscient attitude that neo pagans themselves often criticise some members of the Christian Church for holding about all areas of occultism.

They do have a point, however, so far as the history of much of such research is concerned, since there have been 'betrayals of trust'. For example the researcher Andy Letcher wrote that Tanya Lurhmann's anthropological work on modern magicians in London has "ignited considerable debate… her *a priori* assumption is that the practice of magic is irrational… the wording of her central question reasserts the dominant academic discourse of secular atheism, her question shaping the answer".[2] The reductionist approach that plagued academia for centuries is that, for example, when a subject tells a researcher they have had an experience X, if the researcher does not personally believe that experience X is possible, then their interview subject is pathologised in some way, or simply taken to be totally mistaken. It may yet take decades of 'good research' in this field to undo the harm caused by a century of arrogant assumption and denial. The researcher should aim to produce "value-free descriptions", not value-*less* ones.[3] This Journal allows a voice to a diversity of magical approaches under study; there are often no 'right answers' in the academic study of magic; if someone says X, Y and Z happened after a ritual, then for them it did. If an academic observer says that to the contrary that A, B and C happened for them within the same ritual, then it did for them. The representation of multiple voices allows for a broad spectrum of research and considering all the viewpoints is perhaps the most inclusive way forward. This is not to say that "everyone was won and all must have prizes",[4] but rather to indicate that methodologically, the finest mesh net allows for catching the most fish, and from those the most representative can be chosen, and an interpretive viewpoint can be reached having examined as much evidence as could be found.

We simply do not have the right tools yet, so research into magic is sometimes carried out in the frame of mind of 'lets try to make some alternative methods' and 'let's try to make things happen with what we've got as methods'. These methods are alternative both in the meaning of 'choice', and in some forms, of 'opposition', to a science that would perhaps try to define magic by measuring the electrical changes in a magician's brain in the midst of a ritual that had so much more data present, such as smell, sounds, objects, movements, words, lights and a rich 'tradition' or paradigm. As Robert Wallis writes "a compartmentalising, positivist and empirical interpretative framework does not seem to be the ideal tool for gaining entry to spiritual aspects"[5] and although metaphor is understood by Westerners to be a purely literary tool, in the study of magic "'metaphor' may remain a useful tool for explaining alien… experiences in terms understandable to Westerners".[6]

A future article by one of our editorial board, hopefully to appear in JSM4 will address the matter of whether magic can be properly studied from within academia at all.

On a personal note, having co-founded the JSM in 2002 with Alison Butler, and now steered it to the pre-publication stage of Issue 3, I am now taking a back seat and passing the general editorship on to other members of our current board, to allow myself time to do other things, including work on the publication of my own PhD thesis. I have hugely enjoyed the process of starting this venture from scratch, and while I will not miss the fundamentalist hate mail that occasionally arrives and I will certainly not miss the vicious academic and neo-pagan back-biting that sometimes rears up from outside influences who do not consider magic to be a subject worthy of study (or who find the JSM to be 'too UK-centric', or too academic…. both of which are simply nonsense), I will surely miss corresponding with many of our 'regulars'; who have been quite superb and warm supporters of this venture. Please continue in that positive vein with the new general editors.

As a sign-off, the JSM admin and start-up costs were financed to a large part by a bequest made to me by my aunt, Sylvia Evans-Billings, who was a lifelong advocate of education and international co-operation (if not necessarily this subject area), so this volume is dedicated to her memory.

Dave Evans

Notes

1 The quote from 'David' has been rendered anonymous and is left unsourced here out of pity.

2   Andrew Letcher, *The Role of the Bard*, unpublished PhD thesis, p 13-15.

3   *Ibid.*, p 12, which quotes Smart, *The science of religion and the sociology of knowledge*, Princeton, Princeton University Press, 1973, p 21.

4   The quote comes from the 'Dodo bird' in Lewis Carroll, *Alice's adventures in wonderland,* New York, Random House, 1999, p 28, Original 1865. It has famously been used as the title for a paper analysing many comparative (and competing) psychological approaches where to the consternation of the researchers, all seemed to have pretty much equal merit. Lester Luborsky, *et al*, Comparative studies of psychotherapies: Is it true that "Everyone has won and all must have prizes"? *Archives of General Psychiatry*, 1975, 32, 995-1008.

5   Wallis, Sociopolitics of Ecstasy, *Taliesin's Trip*, p 1

6   *Ibid.*, p 16

Editorial 2

My name is Dave Green from The University of the West of England, UK, and I have been charged with taking over the final stages of production of JSM 3, after a brief hiatus, and the much tougher task of following in Dave Evans' shoes as one of two co-editors of future issues of the JSM. First of all I would like to start with a big thank you to Dave whose time, commitment and energy not only has made this journal possible, but has quickly established it as an innovative and scholarly publication of high repute in such a short period of time. Thank you Dave.

Also, at the risk of this sounding too much like a bad Oscar acceptance speech, a big thank you must also go to Mogg Morgan of Mandrake, publisher of the JSM, who has been patient whilst I have completed this edition, and has also agreed to continue as publisher for the foreseeable future.

Future editions of the JSM will be co-edited by myself and Susan Johnston Graf, of Penn State University, USA, and we hope that we can follow Dave's lead by further cementing the journal's reputation, promoting scholarly debate in the area of magic, and being a driving force in making magic, in all of its forms, an important and respectable field of academic endeavour. To this end we welcome articles of up to 8,000 words on any aspect of magic, from any academic discipline, concerning any geographical region, from any historical period. JSM 4 should appear towards the end of 2006. For further details and submissions please contact me at David2.Green@uwe.ac.uk

As outlined in the News section of this edition, we hope to drive forward the academic study of magic not only through the auspices of this journal but also by the recent re-establishment of the academic study of magic discussion e-list, and a planned revamping of the Society for the Academic Study of Magic (SASM) website. It is only through co-operation and participation in fora such as these that we can finally locate magic as an important destination on the academic map. I look forward to your contributions and company in what should be an interesting journey.

Dave Green

News

Floods

In August 2004 a major flash flood hit the village of Boscastle in Cornwall, home to the unique Museum of Witchcraft, who have been an important source for some articles in past editions of the JSM and who are a great support to academics studying in the field. Major damage was caused to the entire village, but thankfully no lives were lost. After a worldwide appeal to academics and museum conservation experts for advice much of the collection at Boscastle has survived (around 8-10% of the exhibited material being physically lost, or damaged so badly it could not be saved), and the library is completely intact. The JSM was delighted to give webspace to the appeal, and to use our mailing list to spread the word, and I know that many of our readers were incredibly generous to the museum in terms of expertise, time and-or money, for which they are hugely thanked. The museum re-opened in March 2005. The Asian Tsunami, which followed a few months later focused everyone's thoughts on just how fortunate Boscastle was, and the village raised around £10,000 for the Tsunami appeal. Since then there have been major floods in New Orleans but, thankfully, The Voodoo Museum has reportedly survived with little damage. Our best wishes to them all.

JSM Conference News !

As we go to press we are hoping to possibly organise a second JSM-related one-day conference in 2007, probably in the Greater London area, to continue the great work we started with our Bristol event in 2003. Due to the JSM being an annual publication we may be unable to give advance and specific notice of the conference details here, so for further details as soon as we know them please sign up to the mailing list on the website www.sasm.co.uk. (please note, the website is in the process of being updated to become a more interactive, accessible and extensive resource on the academic study of magic).

JSM E-list demise and rebirth

The JSM Online E-list, which had been a splendid venue for international multi-disciplinary debate and exchange of sources was closed earlier in 2005 due to the behaviour of a few people whose intransigent and unpleasant attitude on-list, and whose abusive and obnoxious behaviour to the moderators off-list has spoiled that resource for everyone. Nobody on the JSM board is paid for their work here, and even if they did I would not expect anyone to take the level of personal abuse that was directed at us; hence the list was closed for a time, despite fostering several research collaborations and possible joint-authored books with mainstream publishing contracts from contacts made on the list. The list has been re-started, now moderated by Amy Hale and Dave Green. Interested parties can join at:

http://www.jiscmail.ac.uk/lists/ACADEMIC-STUDY-MAGIC.html

Further details about the JSM, and extensive links and resources pages can be found on our website

www.sasm.co.uk/index.html and we can be contacted *via* email at **socacademicstudymagic@btopenworld.com**

We also maintain a mailing list for updates on the Journal (calls for papers, notification of publishing date etc) and a separate academic e-forum where researchers from any background can exchange ideas and generally 'network'. - Dave Evans

Obituaries

2004-5 was a tremendously saddening period for the number and variety of deaths in the areas of interest to readers of this journal, and as a mark of respect to those who have passed on we start the Journal with an obituaries section, rather than having it at the back of the publication as is more normal. Space precludes acknowledgement in greater depth of all of those who have passed on.

Dr Humphrey Osmond

The American Humphrey Osmond, M.D. was the inventor of the word "psychedelic". He died on February 6th, 2004 aged 86. He brought furore to the medical community in the early 1950s by drawing attention to the chemical similarity between mescaline and adrenaline molecules, and postulating his theory that the brain releasing a self-produced hallucinogen, possibly derived from adrenaline, might cause schizophrenia.

Osmond observed that mescaline 'trips' seemed to facilitate a mentally healthy person to have schizophrenic perceptions of the world, and he suggested that Mescaline be used therapeutically, and as a tool to allow medics to understand their patients better. This research attracted widespread attention, within both scientific and intellectual circles. When Aldous Huxley, the famous novelist heard of the research he wrote to Osmond to offer himself as a test subject. Despite Osmond's initial apprehension at the potential risk of harming the brain of such an eminent figure, the experience gave Huxley the inspiration for his famous philosophical study *The Doors of Perception* and the two men formed a lasting friendship, during which Osmond coined the term "psychedelic." In later years this term has been modified to 'entheogenic' and there is still much debate about the semantics, but Osmond's understanding of the mental states experienced under the use of such substances has been most influential in the academic study of such magical areas as the use of 'Shamanic' plants. Osmond wrote several books, ran a clinical practice and was a teaching professor of psychiatry until his retirement in 1990.

Humphrey Osmond, Psychiatrist and Psychedelic Researcher, 1918-2004

Soror Meral, aka Phyllis Seckler

The Canadian-born Thelemite magician Phyllis Seckler, who died aged 86 was one of the few surviving links to Aleister Crowley, and without her tireless work in America it is possible that the OTO would not have survived in that country. Seckler joined the OTO in 1939 and was the founder of the College of Thelema in California in the early 1970s, running her own lodge for over 20 years. One of her three husbands was Grady McMurty, a former direct pupil of Crowley, and the one-time head of the OTO in America. As well as being a talented magician Seckler was an artist, poet, writer and schoolteacher. In her last few months, Phyllis was apparently most excited about putting her writings upon the Internet, some of which can now be found on the Red Flame website.

Phyllis Secker, magician, poet, artist 1917-2004

Dennis Bardens

The journalist, writer and occultist Dennis Bardens, who died aged 92, was the founding editor of the British Broadcasting Corporation's *Panorama* current affairs TV programme, which is still being broadcast over 50 years later and is the template by which other, usually lesser, programmes are judged. He was also a great friend and admirer of the occult artist Austin Osman Spare, who is regularly mentioned here in the JSM. Bardens also met Aleister Crowley (once) and his one-time magickal disciple, the poet Victor Neuberg (who introduced Bardens to Dylan Thomas) many times. During World War 2 Bardens was a journalist, then served in the Royal Artillery, and was involved in secret service work in Czechoslovakia, later working for the Foreign Office. Several of Bardens' fascinating books concerned magical and paranormal subjects, on which he was an acknowledged expert, and he was still publishing on the subject in 2002.

Dennis Bardens, writer, broadcaster and occultist, July 19 1911- February 7 2004

Martin Booth

The writer and researcher Martin Booth, who has died at a sadly young age will be perhaps best known to JSM readers as the author of one of the better recent Crowley biographies, *A Magick Life*, and his editorship of a *Selected Works* of Crowley's poetry in the 1980s. Polite and most helpful in personal communication with academics, his research notes for the Crowley biography have been lodged with a University in Birmingham (UK) for the use of future scholars.

Martin Booth, writer, September 7 1944 - February 12 2004

Jhonn Balance

Jhonn Balance (aka Geoff Rushton) was firstly a musician and lyricists, but took much of his vision and inspiration from occult topics, notably Austin Spare and Crowley. Balance was a champion of Spare's work for 2 decades, as well as being a notable collector of occult materials. He was horrified by the flood at Boscastle (see News section) and was preparing to loan or donate materials to the Museum from his extensive and unique collection, but his subsequent sudden death in a fall prevented that, and much else besides happening. His band Coil have now ceased to be. Further details can be found at the Threshold House website.

Jhonn Balance, musician February 16 1962 –November 13 2004

Andrew Chumbley

Andrew was one of those among us who strode the liminal area between pure scholarship and pure magicianship, in that as well as being a gifted researcher, at the latter stages of writing his PhD on Dream Incubation in Greek Magic; he was also the Magister of the Cultus Sabbatai, a collaboration of traditional witch groups. He had also been a member of the Illuminates of Thanateros and the Typhonian Ordo Templi Orientis and was a gifted writer and artist. His death at the tragically young age of 37, along with that of his friend Jhonn Balance (see above) has precluded the intriguing prospect of a performance/spoken word magical piece that the two had been planning.

Dave Evans

Book Review Policy:

Following debate within the editorial panel about exactly what kind of books we should be reviewing (inspired by an unsolicited review copy of a very good practical magic book that we were sent by a publisher, and which is reviewed herein) we have reached the view that we would not be doing our job properly if we ignored what occultists are writing - this would be akin to producing a Journal about French culture yet reading nothing written in French or by a French person. This does not mean that we will be reviewing every last 'how to do spells' book, occult novel or collection of magical verse that is published, but we shall endeavour to cover some of the more significant books by practitioners in this and future issues, in a proportion of perhaps 1 practitioner titles to 4-5 academic titles. Would publishers and authors who wish to submit practical occultism books for review please contact us *first*, to discuss their potential review copies and whether we are able to review them. Thankyou.

Responses:

We welcome responses to articles, written in a reasoned, academic style and of less than 1000 words. If suitable these will be included in a future edition of the JSM, with a reply from the author of the original article. Responses of a longer nature will possibly warrant the respondent writing a full article for us.

A Technical Note for Prospective Authors:

As a multidisciplinary journal receiving articles from disparate scholars trained in multitudinous methods of citation we have decided that from JSM 3 onwards we will be moving to the somewhat more straightforward

Harvard academic referencing system; since this seems to suit the majority of our submitting authors. Please see the website **www.sasm.co.uk/index.html** for further details on the implementation of this process. Full details of how to submit an article to the JSM can also be found there.

Editorial Board

General Editor: Dave Evans

Peer Review Editorial Board:

Prof Ronald Hutton (University of Bristol, UK), Prof Geoffrey Samuel (Cardiff, UK), Prof Sabina Magliocco (California State University, Northridge, USA), Dr Owen Davies (University of Hertfordshire, UK), Dr Robert J Wallis (Richmond College, The American University in London, UK) , Dr Matt Lee (University of Sussex, UK), Dr Sarah Pike (California State University, Chico, USA) , Dr Jenny Blain (Sheffield Hallam University, UK), Dr Susan Johnston Graf (Penn State University, Mont Alto, USA), Dr Alison Butler (formerly University of Bristol UK), Dr Dave Green (University of the West of England, UK), Dr Justin Woodman (University of London, UK), Dr William Redwood (University of London, UK).

Book Review Panellists:
Bradley Skene (independent scholar),
Neil Inglis (independent scholar)

JSM2 Contributors list, in Alphabetical Order:

Alison Butler is a Peer Review Editor of this Journal

Owen Davies is a Peer Review Editor of this Journal

Dave Evans has recently submitted his PhD on *Themes in the History of British Occultism since 1947* to Bristol University, is a freelance researcher and General Editor of this Journal.

David Geall teaches English language and linguistics at the University of Westminster, and researches English literature as an independent scholar.

Dave Green is a Peer Review Editor of this Journal

Susan Gorman has a doctorate in comparative literature from The University of Michigan, Ann Arbor, and teaches on the writing programme at Boston University.

Amy Hale is Adjunct Professor in Humanities and Anthropology at the E-Campus of St. Petersburg College, St. Petersburg, Florida, USA.

Johann Hasler is a doctoral student at the University of Newcastle-Upon-Tyne, UK, exploring the relationships between music, composition and Western esoteric traditions.

Mary Hayes teaches in the English department of the University of Kentucky, USA.

Neil Inglis is an independent scholar and author.

Kate Laity is Assistant Professor of English, with a specialism in Medieval English, in the English Department at the University of Houston – Downtown, USA.

Amy Lee is Assistant Professor on the Humanities Programme in the Department of English Language and Literature, Hong Kong Baptist University, Hong Kong.

Penny Lowery is currently a research student and teaching assistant at Exeter University, UK.

Jonathan Paul Marshall works at The University of Technology, Sydney, Australia. His research interests include online communities, Jungian psychology, theories of the imagination and Social Category Theory.

Bradley Skene is an independent Classics scholar and writer.

Sabina Magliocco is a Peer Review Editor of this Journal

Francesca Matteoni is a PhD student at the University of Hertfordshire studying Blood Beliefs in early modern Europe.

William Redwood is a Peer Review Editor of this Journal

Hannah E. Sanders gained her doctorate in Cultural Studies from Norwich School of Art and Design entitled, *New Generation Witches: The Teenage Witch as Cultural Icon and Lived Identity*. She has since emigrated to Boston, where she lectures in Visual and Media Arts at Emerson College, Boston, USA.

Robert J Wallis is a Peer Review Editor of this Journal

Justin Woodman is a Peer Review Editor of this Journal

Buffy and Beyond: Language and Resistance in Contemporary Teenage Witchcraft

Hannah E. Sanders

The relationship between female corporeality and the uncanny, the mysterious and the magical can be traced across cultures and throughout the development of modern Western history. Representations of mysterious women as witches have recently developed in the contemporary media environment to incorporate a vision of femaleness and femininity that includes the teenager, the space between child and adult, where identity and subjectivity are in the process of formation. The mid 1990s was a time at which various cinematic, literary and television forms began to rearticulate magic, repackaging it to both male and female audiences, adult and child alike. In the centre of these new revisions came *Buffy the Vampire Slayer*, alongside the *Harry Potter* phenomenon, *Sabrina the Teenage Witch* and films such as *The Craft* (Andrew Flemming, 1996). Teenagers accessing traditional and forgotten forms of power or magical technologies, are increasingly represented in these mainstream shows. Subsequently, these predominantly American media reconfigurations have inspired a generation of young British men and women to investigate the spectacular powers such characterisations embody. Through a complex engagement with these mainstream images, girls particularly, although not exclusively, have established a new counter culture - the 'teen witch' phenomenon.[1]

This article examines the specificity of language as both a form and channel of magical power in the representations of teenage witchcraft and the ways in which this magical language is reflected in the dialogues of online teen witches. To demonstrate the relationship between shows such as *Buffy*... and British teen girls identifying themselves as practitioners of witchcraft, I refer to ethnographic audience reception data gathered from my research web site, www.witchwords.net, launched in November 2001.

Despite the difficulties associated with data gathered through the internet for cultural studies research, the website provided several fertile spaces for open discussion between self-identified teenage witches, and between myself and the growing online community. Due to the sensitive nature of the research area, and the belief that teen witches may be at odds with familial religious / ideological values, or that their family may not be aware of their witchcraft interest / practice, the internet supplied a means of gathering data that in certain ways circumvented issues of parental consent due to the implicit confidentiality enabled by internet usage. To ensure participants' safety, personal details such as e-mail addresses and telephone numbers were blocked from the site and I facilitated discussions and policed where behaviour became hostile towards and between participants. The respondent sample was self chosen and self monitoring. Therefore, at any point respondents could remove themselves from the dialogues. Despite the initial difficulties with negotiating my involvement with the respondents, as researcher and site facilitator, one of the central benefits of using the internet as a means of data collection is that internet research cuts down reactivity bias, detailed by Raymond Lee (2000, pp 115-6). The levels of intervention on the part of the researcher found in face to face interview techniques and other ethnographic / sociological data gathering methods are negotiated by the mediated nature of the research relationship. Yet like these older methods, the internet provides in-depth qualitative data and in my research, enabled a researcher-participant relationship to build over a period of time. Further, as a feminist researcher interested in the development of a teen girl culture, a self-reflexive approach to respondents meant that communicating my personal involvement with Neo-Pagan Witchcraft and my position as a researcher sympathetic to their lifestyle choices and practices was crucial to creating a research space that respondents could speak within without fear of persecution or humiliation.

A further advantage to using the internet as a data collection tool, is that it is ideal for capturing both qualitative and quantitative data. Questionnaires, polls and spaces for open discussion such as message boards and live chat rooms are available to the researcher. The discussions and analysis of message board postings in my research were partly shaped and informed by initial questionnaire data.

The greatest problems with gathering both qualitative and quantitative data via the internet are those Tim Jordan identifies in his writing on identity within the cultures of cyberspace: Identity fluidity is the process by which online identities are constructed and these are identities not necessarily close to off-line identities (1999, p 62). Put plainly, how can

I suggest that the teenagers responding to the online dialogue are authentic teenagers? Jordan outlines various means through which online and off-line identities are connected and offers models that can be used by the ethnographical researcher to help validate the online-offline identity connection. Criticisms of using internet data as a resource for analysing lived experiences of individuals are centred on the assumption that subjects encountered through analysis are stable and fixed subjects, and are able to mask their true nature through various fantasy / fictional identities enabled by the internet. What this position fails to recognise is in some way addressed by post-structuralist and post-modernist discourses surrounding the fragmented and performative creation of subjectivity and identity. This is not to suggest that the research states that there is no such thing as a teenager. Rather than discrediting the entirety of data on the basis that the responses may be adults posing as teenagers, teenage boys posing as teenage girls through the use of an avatar, etc., these considerations have become an integral part of the data analysis, through focusing on points of continuity and disparity between respondents. I found that in studying a subculture group that felt they didn't have a social voice, that they were doubly marginalised, both from dominant culture and the adult Neo-Pagan/Witchcraft subculture, they were very keen to be heard and to be represented.

The number of girls online is growing in the UK and across the globe. With the internet's increasing ability to target youth audiences, increased online shopping facilities, along with marketing strategies such as peer-to-peer marketing, personal web pages, teenagers have become more net savvy. Subsequently, the gender imbalances that were first recognised in teenage internet users during the early to mid 1990s have shifted to accommodate girl cultures and actively target this audience. Throughout the duration of the site's activity the majority of postings were from those identifying as female, who used the internet on a daily basis. Although the sample is relatively small, as these mainstream texts encode teenage girls as central characters it is perhaps unsurprising that the responses to the web site have been primarily, if not exclusively, from those identifying as young women and girls. The data discussed in this article is drawn from questionnaire responses, direct e-mails, poll reviews and discussions on the sites message boards. I have narrowed the relevant data to a total of 72 female respondents, all British residents aged between 11 and 18.

In looking specifically at the British teenage audience, 69% of total respondents state that they have been practicing witchcraft for under two years which places the establishment of their interest between 1999 and 2003. 67% of the samples questionnaire respondents answered that they regularly enjoyed watching *Buffy*... (closely followed by *Charmed* and *The Craft*). Willow (Alyson Hannigan) was voted the most popular screen witch in a site poll, receiving 43% of total votes. Interest in this text is further substantiated by the fact that all of the teen magazine articles and teen witch manuals on the rise of the witchcraft phenomenon since 1997 have referenced *Buffy*... as a central motivation for teenagers interest in witchcraft. This implies a perceived relationship between *Buffy*... and the development of a female centred subculture. The majority of respondents place their initial interest in witchcraft as post 1998, the mean grade states their initial witchcraft practice between 1999 and 2002 (irrespective of age, or point of arrival into the online community), a time when both *Buffy*... and *Charmed* were visibly marketed on UK television and when teen witch literature began appearing on the shelves of mainstream book sellers. Such a simplistic and rather deterministic relationship between these media representations and subculture development is limited, yet points to the crucial relationship between mainstream encodings of magical girls and the possibilities which such texts open up for a spiritual dimension of teen girl lifestyle choices.

When the online respondents were asked in the questionnaire what first inspired them to become interested in witchcraft, a range of responses were given, from internet information, books, television programmes and friends. Yet in their message board discussions, the centrality of these shows tells another story, suggesting that televisual images inspired and helped maintain an interest in the practice of witchcraft. Descriptions of their initial interest also reflect discourses found in adult Witches' 'coming out' narratives. Several answers included some reference to an urge, a feeling and a desire to do 'something different'. The language of the slippery and bricolaged screen witch, transposed into the language of these online teen witches in many ways, articulates a series of encounters which words cannot adequately express yet facilitates the creation of a distinct spiritual community in their descriptions of their practice and its inspiration. Language, from the generation familiar with 'text speak' is fragmented; full of abbreviations, without sentence structure, grammar or spelling conventions. This idiom is found in all interactive components of the web site. It is clear from this initial internet research that teenagers interested in witchcraft are actively using and reinterpreting linguistic codes, entering into a language they are creating, partially inspired by representations of screen witches.[2]

Within *Buffy*... there have been many diverse representations of magic, but for the female teenage audience in Britain, aside from Buffy (Sarah Michelle-Geller), whose supernatural vampire fighting abilities are part of a divine birthright, there are two other central female characters whose magical prowess is less determined by mystical genealogy and more explicitly connected to discourses of the female body in transition. Willow (Alyson Hannigan) and Tara's (Amber Benson) access to magic, its modus operandi, is markedly distinct from the other range of magical practitioners in the show.[5] A central part of this magic, constructed in the show's universe as a form of feminine power, and these characters access to it, operates through their structured corporeal identity and their access to a range of knowledges, through language. Within the context of the show, magic operates as a series of languages which act as points of cultural resistance, not simply as an exotic vision of teenage rebellion or a resolution to teenage anxieties. In this way, by employing the writings of post-structuralist Michel Foucault, I describe the ways in which those subjects frequently marginalised by dominant culture or simply constructed as the consumer dupes of this culture (teenage girls for example), create spaces of cultural resistance and voice through the embodiment of a once renegade feminine icon and engagements with derided forms of knowledge. The relationship between the screen teen witch and contemporary British teen witches practice of magic is one which contains a series of discourses described as practises or techniques of the self. Michel Foucault explains techniques of the self as a means of establishing:

> [T]he procedures,...suggested or prescribed to individuals in order to determine their identity, maintain it or transform it in

terms of a certain number of ends, through relations of self mastery or self knowledge. (Foucault in Rabinow, 2000, p 87)

If the teenage witches magic is constructed in *Buffy*... as a discourse of self knowledge and / or self mastery, then this has to be considered when understanding the impact of this cultural icon upon teenage lifestyle choices. Through claiming Foucault's discussion of how individuals have degrees of autonomy within culture through choosing how to interpret and embody discourses of identity construction, I suggest that the teen witch embodies a set of discourses which exemplify a process of 'double conditioning'. This is, by appropriating alternative values from within mainstream representations, contemporary teenage girls are interpreting their experiences of the world and self. It is the celluloid teen witches' access to knowledge, their desire for power and her ability to transform her surroundings through relationship with various modes of language, that has influenced a generation of young women searching for empowering models of identity construction.

In assessing the teen witches' magical abilities in *Buffy*..., it is key to begin by looking at the range of knowledges attributed to them, and the means through which the show signifies the basis and source of their difference. For the teenage witch characters in *Buffy*..., the structure of language is particularly important. The language that the teenagers in the show are given is typical of teen speak, often used to interpellate a teenage audience. This is exemplified by the character Willow, as throughout the series her access to language is displayed as different from the other teen character's language usage, although all could be said to be idiosyncratic, used as a weapon against the forces of darkness (see Overbey and Preston-Matto in Wilcox and Lavery 2002, pp 73-

84). Willow's alternative use of syntax and language, her incomprehensible humour, which is childlike in its intent and content throughout the series, points to her identity as other, as unfixed, at the point between child and adult. The mix and match of verbs and nouns, and the generative use of the English language displays an uncertainty, suggesting that these characters find it difficult to adequately express themselves. Before her involvement with witchcraft, Willow is often apologetic, her speech full of long and rambling sentences interjected with drawn breaths, leaving her often literally lost for words. Similarly, Tara, introduced during the latter part of Season Four, has a slight stutter and a bizarre sense of humour often misread by the other characters, which interrupts the coherence of her speech (*Family*, 5:06). As the series develops, we find that the inverted use of language is given a particular force through the practice of witchcraft; that the language of witchcraft itself is constructed as a language of interruptions, of irrationality, a language that has a unique form linked to the female body in transition. It has been argued, (Krzywinska, 2000) that witches' use of language is that ascribed to the hysteric, an incoherent world of broken signifiers and signs which has its roots in women's biological difference. Yet, as Tanya Krzywinska argues:

> The monstrous desires of the witch may well help provide a symbolic language through which women can articulate the hidden and the unspoken, as well as the contradictions that life throws up. Witchcraft therefore provides a language that moves beyond the inchoate world of hysteria. (2000, p 153)

I would go further to suggest that the construction of the teen witches' language contains an element of mistake which, in Foucauldian terms implicitly suggests a discourse of risk taking, a playing of codes and conventions which leaves room for chance but which resembles a break in coherent communication (Foucault in Pearson, 2001). Focussing on the loss of a structured language implies a reduction of meaning. Instead, it is Willow's ability to convey *appropriate* meanings and solutions to the problems encountered by the 'scooby-gang' that gives her an elevated status. The construction of the teen witches' verbal mistakes contains the possibility of being misunderstood, but acts as a resistance to the normal discourse of structured language and speaks an alternative truth. Another truth is offered through the screen witches' use of language, the truth of the mistake, the truth of stories and powers that exist outside the normalising discourse of teenage power, one that shares a belief in a supernatural power other than God and includes a multiplicity of micro narratives about the nature of these powers, drawn from a variety of sources. The possibility of changing the status quo through enacting magic is enabled through this grammatical or syntactical mistake. This is exemplified in the construction of the teen witches' magical operation, the spell or ritual, where language is used in a fluid, often bricolaged fashion, breaking down the codes of normal speech in order to channel universal forces and cause some form of transformation. The performance of magic, encoded through the saying of spells and charms, threatens to fall into incoherence and it is through the enactment or speech act that magic transforms the linguistic mistake into a discourse of empowerment and power. There is a changing discourse of power relations here, where the use of mistake, and the teen girls' appropriation of language is signified as empowering and transformative, enabling another form of knowledge to come to power. An example can be found in *Something Blue* (4:9) where Willow, recovering from a break up with

Oz (Seth Green), performs a spell to rid herself of her grief and frustration:

> Willow: Hearken ye elements I summon you now, from this eve forth my will be done - so mote it be.
>
> [Looks into a mirror]: My heart be healed.
>
> [Picks up a book]: This book speaks to me.
>
> [Holds up a bent cuticle tip]: This cuticle tip... becomes unbendy?

Although the above spell doesn't work according to plan, the power it invokes transforms Willow's words into literal truths which impact upon her friends. When she speaks, Giles (Anthony Stewart Head) becomes temporarily blind, Buffy arranges to marry Spike (James Marsters) and Xander (Nicholas Brendon) becomes a demon magnet. These magical accidents can be read as part of Willow's entrance into a new mode of being, one which is as yet beyond her total control. It is only in Season six that the teen witches magic is no longer prone to misfiring and their access to magical language is more controlled, deliberate, filled with confidence and enormous power.[4]

The play between the established use of words, the incongruity between the magicalised language (referencing seventeenth century English) and the mundane objects and the colloquial ending of the spell, demonstrates a childlike belief in the power of words and tells a particular truth about the nature of the world. By positioning themselves as active agents of language through magic, they can manipulate words and linguistic conventions in order to demonstrate the truth of this alternative vision of power relations.

For contemporary British teen witches, spell casting is the most cited form of magic sought after and used. The majority of teen witch respondents stated that they practised magic alone (not in a group / coven) and spells accounted for 61% of the primary interest in witchcraft, spells which can effect some form of change both externally and within the self:

> **sarah**
> posted 7/8/03 11:38 AM
>
> im 15 iav bin practisung for 2yrs it runs in my family! witch craft is such an amazing thing the feeling you get wen u cast a spell the warth sumtimes i fell my whole body burning i beliv da wider u spread ur magik da mor powerful u becom

For these online teen witches, the internet facilitates a particular vernacular, as seen above, which breaks with the coherence of traditional communications, and allows them to express themselves in a way that 'speaks' their sense of being a teen witch. The teen witch describes a knowledge that will, exercised through words, can shape their experience of the world:

> **sarah**
> posted 11/8/03 2:08 PM
>
> hi every1 does any1 knw a good free website for spells bcoz every time i type in spells they always charge u money n i beliv

its a gift and shoulnd charge money so if u culd plz let me knw asap!

The initial postings that came onto witchwords.net from new respondents, were predominantly requests for information or forms of 'coming out stories', describing the trepidation surrounding the new witch attempting to come to terms with her desire for this identity. In this way, the respondent sought approval from the online community and frequently ascribed some form of danger to the description of her early experiences with witchcraft, or the possibilities of being a witch. Much like the screen teen witch, the power of speaking the truth of her experiences comes at a price, and this is perceived as a risk of being outcast from or victimised within a social group.

Lianne posted 6/1/03 12:28 AM

hello! i don't really know where to start, its kinda hard sitting down at my computer and writing my feelings to anyone who may read this. I just want to talk to people, if you know what i mean. All my life ive been a bit different to everyone, you know, 'strange' things happening that no one would believe were true, ive never had any friends that really believed me when i said i saw people in my room, or done something 'magical' and kept it to my self for a long time. Then a couple of years ago i met a girl in class and i felt like we clicked, you know? We wernt close but got on. Then about a month ago we sat together for a whole evening and talked about our feelings, it turns out she has had 'strange' experiences and thinks just like me, bout the world, people, it was like i finally found the person id waited for so long to talk to and now i feel we have a connection. I know when shes going to phone before she does, things like that. I just feel this is such a big step for me and really wanted to tell people, i know im probably rattling on! I just felt like i wanted to talk to more people now, i love reading what people have written in here and hopefully i can talk to some of you(type!)xxit makes me feel so happy that there are so many people willing to share their experiences here, anyway, i had better let you go now.bye. x

sarah posted 8/7/03 11:53 AM

wen i tell pepl im a witch and practise the craft thy think id hav a wart and fly a broomstik on weekdays! alkso do find pepl fink ur a satanist an worship the devil its crazy iknw al chritians go 2 church does any1 get that

sam posted 9/7/03 6:02 PM

I totally know wat u mean, every1 asks me if I am a black witch (am Goth, always wear black) Ha ha ha, very bloody funny. It's because pepl don't no about wicca an stuff. if u wer budist they would ask you if you wore orange bedsheets at home.

In this sense the teen witch could be described in part as a parrhesiastes, a teller of truth. In *Fearless Speech* Foucault describes the parrhesiastes thus:

> Someone is said to use *parrhesia* and merits consideration as a *parrhesiastes* only if there is a risk or danger for him in telling the truth (in Pearson 2001, pp 15-16).

The two forms of parrhesia he defines are those taken from Greek literature from the Fifth century B.C.E. to the Fifth century C.E. The first is the parrehsiastes who 'chatters', a pejorative meaning of the term, someone who speaks their mind continually 'without qualification' (*Ibid.*: 13). The second is embodied in Plato's writings by Socrates as the man who confronts the Athenians and Alcibiades with the truth, however dangerous this activity might be, in the hope of bringing their attention to those elements considered of import if the subject is to care for him / herself: wisdom and truth.

For both the television characters and real teen witches, language is presented as a discourse of risk, as it places the body of the witch as a site for empowerment beyond the reach of normalising discourses, using, as a form of reverse discourse, the dominant image and power relations constructing femininity as mad, inchoate and irrational. The risk of danger that perhaps entitles the teen witch to the term parrhesiastes is that of being labelled mad and cast out from the safety of the norm. Foucault's discussion of the role of the truth speaker, the parrhesiastes, cannot be covered at length here but is important in understanding the element of risk taken and the display of truths from below in the teen witches appropriation of magical language as a conduit of change. All of the screen teen witches contain elements of this role, as through the act of magical speech they demonstrate the multiplicity of truths found in subjugated knowledges; forms of knowledge that are not privileged by dominant culture but remain marginal, hidden, despised or mocked.

These are esteemed in the context of *Buffy*..., detailed as the languages of myth, fairy tale and magical stories, whether drawn from fiction or ethnographical accounts. The appropriation of multiple foreign and ancient languages (Latin, Hebrew etc.) contains traces of alternative truths, as their enactment through speech can bring about change from a position of social inferiority. For the witches, this call to change is seen as a duty: 'no one forces him to speak, but he feels that it is his duty to do so' (Foucault in Pearson, 2001, p 19). This can be seen in their continual use of magic to solve group problems, or for example, when Tara and Willow confront each other on the use of their magic in *Tough Love* (5:19) and discuss the dangerous dynamics of their relationship when Willow becomes over dependant upon magic in *All the Way* (6:06). The use of magical is a way of regenerating subjugated, hidden truths. This act of magical speech is used as a practice of the self, a way in which the teenage witch utilises an existing character trait, the peculiar use of language for example, and a 'lesser' form of knowledge as a means of entering into a new and empowering sense of self. This is expressed through the act of magic, which does not exist in the show without words.

It is not only this use of language which demonstrates how the teen witch challenges rational and adult modes of communicating, developing a form of speech which celebrates the irrational and the playful, creating new configurations of truths. It is the teen witches' love of accumulating knowledge which suggests that their access to power is not simply constructed as playful, fictional and mistaken. Within *Buffy*... Willow is the genius child. Valerie Walkerdine (1990) argues that adolescent heroines, in teen magazine texts particularly, are often portrayed as clever.

Walkerdine proposes that the accumulation of knowledge is rarely portrayed as a desire emanating solely from subjective motivation, but through parental obligation or appeasement. The teen witches' drive and desire for both subjugated and culturally endorsed knowledge questions this notion.[5] For Willow, the range of knowledges, from academic work in which she excels, to knowledge of the technologies of magic and her uncanny ability with computers, are acquired and actively used for both personal and group achievements. In this respect, the show details a development of feminine heroine representations. Rather than rebelliousness being demonstrated through a denial of intellectual knowledge in place of an investment in sexual knowledge, Willow's identity is centred around her intellect, and by extension, her eccentricity.[6] It is Willow's intellectual ability that often enables the group to find the right answers to their demon-hunting dilemmas.

The two central ways in which the teen witches accumulate knowledge are books, and for Willow, computers. Within *Buffy*... books are the primary means through which magical knowledge is gained. The book allows the witch characters (along with the other members of the 'scooby-gang') to research, find information, and develop their knowledge of magic. Books are similarly central to the online community of teen witches, as sources of knowledge, and as a signifier of status within the community. Within *Buffy*..., it is the combination of the witches' book knowledge and their receptivity to this knowledge, an ability that is represented as innate to their corporeality that signifies their special relationship to knowledge and language. Willow and Tara are frequently shown studiously devouring books, inquisitive and curious, demonstrating their particular expertise with othered forms of knowledge.

Book knowledge is portrayed in two separate ways. Books enable the witches to uncover, or discover a solution to a problem, but they also give directions, much like a cookery book, on how to enact the knowledge through the use of words and physical gestures. Books are constructed within *Buffy*... as a product of alternative authority - a repository of power. There are books which are locked or hidden in *The Magic Box*, the show's resident magic shop, and the majority of the books used by the witches are owned or monitored by Giles. That the show details Willow and Tara as characters who have an innate love of study and books of all kind, and are able to read and retain their information with ease, suggests that the teen witch is an open body and mind (as specific from Giles' and Jenny Calendars [Robia LaMorte] adult bodies), a receptacle for knowledge that is both corporeal and intellectual. Thus, the accumulation of these knowledges articulates a practice of the self, a way in which the witches' actively use knowledge sanctioned for certain adults, yet outside mainstream knowledges, as a part of their search for new modes of being powerful. They understand that these texts are keys to becoming an empowered being, one that challenges the confines attributed to dominant notions of clever girls. Cleverness becomes a heightened desire to accumulate a knowledge otherwise deemed inappropriate for young eyes, and in turn becomes one of the key components of the witches' search for identity.

For the witches in my study, books are pivotal in constructing an identity as a witch.[7] Despite the centrality of the internet as a means of communicating with other teen witches and finding information, much of their knowledge regarding magic, spells and the philosophy and practice of witchcraft comes from the growing number of teen witch text books aimed at this market. On a site poll entitled 'What is the best way to learn about Witchcraft?', 56% of respondents stated that books were the most effective way, and this is corroborated by the continued appearance of books and knowledge of authors in their message board discussions, seen in the thread below:

> **Hannah**   posted 10/4/02 3:33 PM
> theres a new teen witch spell book out called ' Spellcraft for teens: A magickal guide to writing and casting spells' by gwinevere rain. have just got a copy so will tell all, unless someone else has already read it...
>
> **Lucy**   posted 11/12/02 8:19 PM
> i have read it!. i found it very useful as to writting spells. it made it a bit more clear and showed that its not as complicated as some books made it out to be. it also helps in how 2 write chants and incantations. its a good resorce book to have as its not alot of writting and easy to read. so if your having trouble then this is a good book. its also a great resorce book to have!! i recomend it but thats just me. Blessed Be.
>
> **Lucy**   posted 12/2/02 8:03 PM
> its a kool book to use as a referance! i must remember to get it back off my friend cause i think shes fallen for it to haha Blessed Be Lucy XxX

hollydaivy posted 12/12/02 11:32 PM

hay i've just joined have you reada book called "The real witches kitchen" by kate west it's a goody for incence and matching it with your star sign etc. I recommend it :-) Blessed be xx Holz

Sage Fire posted 4/2/03 4:02 PM

Yeah I've just finished reading it. It's quite good and I learnt how to make my own spells. I made my 1st a few days ago. A love spell to put into my book of shadows.

Knowledge of books becomes an indicator of seriousness, of status and a means through which knowledge is transferable for their own resources. Further, as seen above in Sage Fire's response, the role of the Book of Shadows becomes an extension of this love of books. The Book of Shadows, containing rituals and spells favoured by many Neo-Pagan Wiccan practitioners, is described by modern Witchcraft author Doreen Valiente thus:

> This is the name given by modern witches to the book in which they write their rituals, invocations and charms. Witches copy from each other's books that which appeals to them, and things which have been learnt from experience; so that in practice no two books are exactly alike.[...] Such a writing is called a Book of Shadows, because its contents can only be this world's shadow of the realties of the Other World; the

world of magic and the Beyond, the world of gods and spirits (Valiente, 1973:47).

Contemporary teen witches discuss the Book of Shadows importance as a record / diary, where they become authors of their own magical texts, combining autobiographical dairy entries and their magical experiences.

Unlike the discussions above, book knowledge for the screen witch is linked to the physical enactment of magic; the effect of magic lies within the utterance and the action or gesture directed by the text. Therefore the screen teen witch develops knowledge from experience and through hard research, resisting the idea that one form of knowledge has dominance over another. Although contemporary teen witches discuss the importance of magic and information gathering they rarely discuss spells performed, their efficacy or outcome.[8] Yet to both the screen and the contemporary teen witch, knowledge is portrayed as essentially powerful and potentially dangerous. For witch characters Willow, Sabrina, the Halliwell sisters in *Charmed* and even Hermione in the *Harry Potter* franchise, it is the correct and morally guided use of this knowledge that enables the witch to work magic successfully. Knowing the moralities of magic for the witchwords.net teen witch is of similar importance and marks their status as a knowledgeable witch within the community, seen in the thread below:

> **Heather**   posted 15/3/03 8:15 PM
> hi, for mothers day i am going to make my step mum a magical pouch, with crystals and herbs etc. She asked me if i could put

a love spell or a love charm in it. Doe's any one have any sugestions? Many thanx, blessed be.

Lucy posted 16/3/03 12:09 AM
Hi Heather! , theres a kool book called 'spellcraft for teens' and its got loads of charm ideas 4 love. they have... pennies,copper,rings,acorns,pinecones,rice,feathers,heart symbols,seashells,shells with holes,sea salt,regular salt,morning dew. rose quartz is a good one 2! if you want i can bring the book in for you on thurs! hope that helps
blessed be Lucy x

rox posted 3/6/03 10:51 PM
i read somewhere that love spells are not good to do cuz the manipulate people. is this true?

crystalmoon posted 4/6/03 2:47 AM
it is true that you cant do lovespells to make a specific personfall in love with you but you can dospells to attract love. a goodcrsytal to use in a charm would berose quartz. bright blessings xxx

amber posted 14/6/03 4:50 AM
not to be rude or anything but i don't think that a love charm/potion is a good idea because ive herd, many times, that it is never good to manipulate ANYONE into doing something that they don't want to. true love should..(in my opinnion) come from the heart and if the person truly loves u then u wont need magick!~*amber*~

Morality and magic are sites of contestation within both *Buffy*... and the teen witch dialogues seen above. In both, the moral dictates of magic use are learnt rather than seen as 'common sense' or innate within the body of the witch and it is this knowledge that marks the witch as 'good'. It is the truth telling regarding the moral use of power, the teaching from one teen witch to another than demonstrates the centrality of language in communicating discourses of status, learning and power between teen witches.

Both corporeal experience and book learning are discussed as interconnected forms of knowledge and power in representations and realities of teenage witchcraft. Yet there is a third component which is central to the composition of the contemporary teen witches' knowledge: the computer. Willow's individualistic ability with computers in *Buffy*... is constructed much in the same way as she accesses the knowledge in books, as a type of hacker magic. From her relationship with computers, Willow could be described in Donna Haraway's terms (1985, p 1991) as a cyborg, a body which redefines the boundaries between human and machine.[9] What is interesting to my argument here is how the vision of the teen witch encodes a teenage girl (albeit a white, American, middle class girl) as an active agent of subversion. Frequently the knowledge Willow accesses is prohibited in some form. Through the computer she enters government agencies, decrypts mystical codes (*Primeval*, 4:21) and spies on other characters. Willow's ability to use information kept locked away from the general public through the computer (notably accessed through the internet), demonstrates how she weaves dominant forms of information into the range of subjugated knowledges, using them without distinction to solve the strangest problems.

The truths, (which as Foucault understands are linked to the production of knowledge and therefore dominant power relations) found on the internet are not questioned for their factual validity, but considered as one source of information amongst many regimes of truth used for her advantage. The screen witch becomes a resistant figure through her refusal to acknowledge the distinction between the authority of books, her personal experience of magic and the information found via cyberspace. Although it could be suggested that consequently the teen witch becomes a rag bag for subjugated knowledges (magic and cyberspace as fragmented lesser sources of authority to expert / authority validated truths), that she is shown interacting with a wide range of knowledges from both sides of the binary implies that she embodies, through the practice of these knowledges, an autonomous status.

The computer is central to my research method, and therefore it is difficult to establish a difference between the practices of teen witches online and those without internet access. However, as the online respondents referenced other internet sites as points of inspiration, if not with the same tendencious attitude given to books, the internet is seen as a resource for meeting with others if not for information gathering. Further, since 2004 the rise of online covens established by teen witches suggests that there is a growing interest in using the internet as a new magical / social space (see Nightmare, 2001, pp 209-210).[10]

With her emphasis on connectivity, *Buffy*... details Willow's ability with computers as a kind of magic. In *Smashed* (6:09) Willow does not access the internet through the keyboard and screen but instead searches the web by connecting to the internet via magic using her mind as the screen, unnerving Buffy and Xander. Willow is able to make these connections with supreme ease, finding the right information because hers is a body constructed as open, connected with other bodies (portrayed by her intimacy with the 'scooby-gang' and Tara) and bodies of knowledge. Having a body which is intensely fluid and open to a range of knowledges conveys an essentialist vision of what woman or girl could be. However, by utilising knowledge of both the corporeal and hyper real, the teen witch becomes a wonderful invention, 'a kind of disassembled and reassembled, postmodern collective and personal self' (Haraway in Nicholson, 1990, p 205). She is connected to discourses of knowledge associated with the masculine, feminine and the in-between other. Thus, the teen witch is a receptacle for a range of knowledges which, as practices of the self, transform her into a powerful figure of adolescent femininity.

Through the use of words and access to a range of knowledges which are not hierarchically divided in a particular configuration, the teen witch is able to cause change in order to interrupt the flow of events. Through the use of magical language the teen witch's body is open to supernatural powers which enter into the teen witch in order to aid her work. In *Buffy...* this can be seen in episodes such as *Family* (5:6), *Triangle* (5:11), and *Smashed* (6:9). Language is the medium which both actively renders the teen witch body as powerful whilst constructing it as a receptive body open to other powers - powers of demons, gods and spirits. The magic performed by the teen witches in *Buffy...* is generated through their bodies (and the forms of knowledge discussed earlier; books and computers which are inextricably linked to the witch's body) but is not primarily projected into conventional areas of teenage femininity.[11]

For the contemporary British teen witch however, magic is used to transform the body and the subject's relationship to herself and others, primarily projected into areas traditionally associated with teen girl desire, discussed by both Angela McRobbie (2000) and Valerie Walkerdine (1990). Yet, in keeping with the changes in girl culture since their seminal writings, teenage witchcraft is constituent of current 'girl power' discourses in popular culture, described by Anita Harris as, 'a unique category of girls who are self-assured, living lives lightly infected but by no means driven by feminism, influenced by the philosophy of DIY, and assuming they can have (or at least buy) it all' (2004, p 17). For all the possibilities the representations of teenage witchcraft may offer, teen witch respondents described the possibilities of magical practice as focussed into arenas where girls feel disempowered or lacking in the face of provocative new images of feminine empowerment: romantic love, helping others, and countering bullying or other forms of victimisation.[12] The teenage witch in *Buffy*... cannot be read as entirely liberational in relation to previous models of teen girl empowerment. Eventually these practises of the self have to negotiate with regulated forms of identity and subjectivity. Teen witches are shown having to adhere to universalised moral constraints on the nature of right and wrong practice of power, and their magic in effect always contains a conditional actualisation of resistive power. When Willow misuses her power for personal gain in Season six of *Buffy*..., it takes the form of addiction and requires rehabilitation, complete with moral lessons and magical training from witches in England.

The discourses of teenage femininity found in these representations of power may challenge traditional embodiments of feminine knowledge, through the signified combination of both masculine and feminine epistemologies, yet are only effectively used and valued when in service to the greater good. This encourages a view of the self and of teenage feminine power that exists only as far as it is useful to a higher purpose, and where it is most challenging, it is only temporary, eventually negotiated back into culturally endorsed modes of feminine teen behaviour and subjectivity.

Contemporary teen witches are teenagers, who, like Tara and Willow in *Buffy*..., are hungry for knowledge and empowerment. As highlighted earlier, the majority of first time correspondence that came to the web site message board, or to me personally via e-mail were urgent requests for information. These reflect the construction of the teen witches desire for knowledge in *Buffy*..., the desire to accumulate information, whether asking for spells, as seen in earlier threads or information on how to become a witch.[13]

To return briefly to the questionnaire data, when respondents were asked what their main interest was within the field of witchcraft all 11 and 12 year old respondents answered that it was spell working, and across all age groups, spell working accounted for over 50% of their primary interest. One 18 year old respondent succinctly stated that her interest in spell working stemmed from a desire to make things happen. The effect of making things happen and accumulating the right knowledge about witchcraft is exemplified in the answers to the final open ended question. I asked respondents how they felt the practice of witchcraft had changed their lives. From the responses received only two respondents answered that it hadn't made a difference or that they felt no difference yet. Of the others, certain themes arose, and to demonstrate this I quote a representative sample with the respondent's age:

> i feel more confidant (18)
>
> made me more confidant in myself (18)
>
> more aware of our lives and our ways (17)
>
> more positive on life (16)
>
> made me more myself (15)
>
> made me more confident about myself (15)
>
> Its made me confidant and makes me feel whole (14)
>
> It has made me a lot happier (13)
>
> i feel more spiritual and aware (12)

From an initial reading of these answers it would seem that witchcraft has become a practice of the self, a set of tools, a lifestyle that gives these teenagers the sense that they are able to alter their relationship with themselves and the world. The repeated use of the word 'more' and the term 'made me' indicates that witchcraft has been appropriated as a set of philosophical and practical tools. These teenagers are actively using the powers displayed through these images to construct a lifestyle that, as the use of adjectives such as confident, aware, happy and secure detail, leads to a similar result to that found in *Buffy*... . A sense of personal power, and the facility to articulate their own desires and wishes through the practice of magic has enabled these young women to *feel* more confident and autonomous.

Returning momentarily to Foucault, the ability to describe magic as a practice of self-mastery and self-transformation seen in *Buffy*... is plainly expressed in the dialogue on the message boards and the questionnaire responses - these girls want to transform others, the world around them, and themselves. All of this is made possible through certain engagements with language. Personal issues regarding family disruption, illness and romantic trouble are discussed and sources of strength are described in terms of communication strategies and magic, as seen below:[14]

> **Giaka** posted 26/11/02 7:49 PM
> hey, i seem to have this really confident front like i'm this really powerful person. But it's just a mask and i just thought i aught to tell you all why i act like such an arrogant person. It's because recently i was told that i may have a Brain Tumor, and after two weeks i haven't got my appointment for a brain scan yet. I am petrified as i am only 13. I don't want to die and i don't want to put my family in that position. I know not many people would miss me but i care alot about those that would. I don't want to be selfish and try to help myself as i don't plan on spending my last few months being a satanist. Is there anything i can do or make my coven aware of that may help. Please help me, i am paranoid i am dying. Blessed Be One and All. Giaka

Lucy   posted 27/11/02 1:10 PM

oh sweetie you sound like your having a rough ride at the moment and i kind of know what your going through. See i have a serious heart condition and have had some near death experiance and im only 16!! Im sure alot more people will miss you than what you expect!! Know one wants to die especially at a young age! Talk to your parents n tell htem how you feel and also have your friends real close because you will need them the most at the moment!! i Know its Scary but im sure everything will be ok!! I would talk to your coven and tell them how you feel they might help and you are not being selfish is you want to help yourself!! I hope everything goes well * Blessed Be* and i hope everything goes well for you
Lucy

The validity and truth of a magical universe and power is never questioned by contemporary teenage witches. Instead, as seen above, what is sought after is how to accumulate the right knowledge, and whether it is morally right to use it for 'selfish' reasons. The personal confessional here becomes a form of disclosure that asks for communal validation and seeks comfort and support. Although these teenagers are not fighting the forces seen in *Buffy*... in glorious technicolor, their demons are inescapably poignant. The practice of witchcraft leads to a *belief* in self mastery and autonomy, of acting in a subversive fashion, causing change through the articulation of these desires though spells. Yet the belief in and the actualisation of these powers for screen and contemporary teen witches are still hampered by certain codes that confine the possibilities of magical power within gendered and mainstream moral frameworks.

What, we have to ask, is the result of this new found confidence that teen witches speak of? Will this access to a revised form of power create speech acts outside cyberspace and the private spaces within which most of this dialogue takes place? At the point of writing, the teen witch community in Britain has fragmented, split between those older practitioners who have been involved since the late 1990s, and younger teenagers (or tween-agers), less inspired by *Buffy*..., instead interpellated by the vast range of teen witch literature now available. As such, it is tempting to suggest that the resistive potential for teenage witch-dom has finally waned, entering into mainstream DIY spiritual self-help discourse, and fuelled by commercial drives for profit. It could be assumed that the emergence of this youth culture at the turn of the millennium is simply a phase, reflecting the dynamic so frequently witnessed in analysing alternative youth groups as they are hegemonically renegotiated into mainstream culture. Despite these observations, the teenagers at the outset of my research in 2000 are now entering adult life and potentially entering adult Witchcraft communities.[15] Perhaps it is there, with the changing status of Neo-Pagan Witchcraft as a belief system and practice in contemporary culture that we can assess the impact of this subculture. These new voices, initially fuelled by media representations and a desire for 'girl power', educated in both old and new technologies of magic, communication and community have the potential to open up new dialogues within adult Witchcraft communities and mainstream spiritual cultures.

Notes

1. In keeping with contemporary scholarship, throughout this article I refer to Neo-Pagan Witchcraft and Wicca as a magico-religious practice and philosophy. Thus, these terms are capitalised. When referring to historical descriptions of witchcraft, celluloid depictions of witchcraft, and teenage witchcraft I use the lower case. This is a distinguishing classfication tool used for clarity and does not intend to describe teenage witchcraft as a lesser form of magico-religious practise

2. This vernacular is particular to the female identified teenage respondents. Although a comprehensive discussion is outside the scope of this paper, adult and adolescent male identified voices are distinctive, as their adherence to formal structures of language is greater and their mode of information sharing frequently less discursive. A more detailed analysis of this can be found in my doctral thesis 'New Generation Witches: The Teenage Witch as Cultural Icon and Lived Identity' (Sanders, 2004).

3. I do not discuss Amy's (Elizabeth Anne Allen) construction as a witch, as her character is peripheral, appearing briefly during the first three seasons to return during Season six. The discussion of the teen witches access to language can be applied although tropes of Amy's characterisation could be said to conform to more obvious stereotypes of fairy tale witches and rebellious teenagers, seen during Season six where she introduces Willow to the darker side of magical addiction.

4. In *Bargaining: Part 1* (6:1) Willow, is able to communicate telepathically to the other members of the 'scooby-gang', and it is from this point that we are shown that she has become more powerful since Buffy's death at the end of Season five, with her plan and execution of Buffy's magical resurrection. It is also at this point that she is shown beginning to use magic indiscriminately for frivolous purposes alongside her ability to aid the group in fighting evil.

5. The representation of the clever, socially outcast girl is not new to representations of teen witches. Hermione in the *Harry Potter* franchise is constructed in this way. However, what makes Willow unique is that the show's premise rests on the notion that it takes place in the real world, as opposed to the fantasy school for magic found in *The Worst Witch* series and the *Harry Potter* texts. In *Buffy...* (and similarly in *Sabrina the Teenage Witch*) there is a clear distinction between the two forms of knowledge, one culturally acceptable and the other for the talented few.

6   The accumulation of knowledge for Willow is likened to a heightened sexual experience, as in *The Freshman* (4:01) when she enters into the library and is awe struck at having access to such a wealth of information, exclaiming her excitement with terms such as penetrating, thrust into etc.

7   Current teen witch how-to manuals, distinct from the anti-commercial magical texts found in *Buffy*... interpellate a populist consumer audience familiar with self-help and therapeutic discourse. However, these new magical manuals frequently invoke the appearance of these fictional magic books in their visual design alongside established modes of design employed in teen girl magazines.

8   During Season five in particular, episodes often detail the way in which the teen witches spells backfire, that it is not simply their ability to read text accurately that enables their magic to work correctly. This can be seen in *Family* (5:06), when Tara's spell has life threatening results, *Something Blue* (4:09), when Willow's desire to be rid of grief through magic leads to her unknowingly harming her friends, and *Triangle* (5:11) where the fight between Willow and Anya (Emma Caulfield) causes a witch and demon hating troll to appear. Later in Season six it is not the witches' inexperience with the technologies of magic that cause the spells to go awry but their intent. However, at this juncture in the series it can be said that although initially the witches' magic is less than efficacious, it does not stop her from continuing to gather and practice - she retains the belief that it can and will work.

9   This is not to suggest that the teen witch characters are part machine as in Haraway's original conception of the term, but that the body of the teen witch is technologised. Through its liminal status it has intimate connectivity with this discourse of power. Thus, although the teen witch is not made of or part machine, her uncanny ability with computers renders her body open to discourses of cyborg-ness.

10 Teenage covens have grown since the completion of this research and suggest avenues for further study. It is difficult at present to assess the number of active online teen covens in the UK, but any internet search will reveal and increasing number of teenagers using home pages and other web hosting facilities as a means of meeting and magically 'working' with other teens. The Witches' Voice, one of the first and largest online American Neo-Pagan Witchcraft organisations lists eighty

operational teen groups and covens, both on and offline in January 2005.

11 Magic within the show is utilised for a variety of purposes which go beyond the stereotypical representations of witchcraft. Tanya Krzywinska (2002) draws upon psychoanalytical models to suggest that teen witch narratives and the magic employed within them centre around the dyadic relationship between mother and daughter. Robin Briggs (1996), Krzywinska (2002) and Diane Purkiss (1996) amongst others suggest that the focus of witchcraft practices (historically and in contemporary representations) are the renegotiation of household, community and conjugal duties and the ensnarement of men. The practice of teenage witchcraft in *Buffy*... does not wholly conform to these essentialist and body-oriented tropes but does incorporate them at various narrative points.

12 Here I refer to my findings regarding teenage witches' use of magical power, which is predominantly directed into well established areas of feminine desire: romantic and heterosexual love, personal happiness, peer group acceptance, familial well-being and anti-discrimination.

13 The Pagan Federation's figures from 2000 state that 80% of their enquiries (of which there are hundreds every month) are from girls aged between 14 and 18 asking when they'll come into their powers or how should they become a witch. This information is gathered from private correspondence with Jess Wynne, The Pagan Federation's appointed Youth Officer for 2000.

14 There was continual dialogue between Giaka and Lucy and other witchwords.net community members. Giaka's tumor was fortunately found to be benign, but Lucy unfortunately passed away in January 2004. Her dialogues are reproduced here with the kind permission of her family.

15 There is currently no comprehensive research on whether teen witches entering adulthood are pursuing their practice of Neo-Pagan Witchcraft. Doug Ezzy and Helen Berger are currently compiling research on this subject with post-teen witches from Britain, America and Australia. See Berger, H. and Ezzy, D. (Forthcoming) *Teenage Witchcraft*, Rutgers University Press.

References

Briggs, R., 1996, *Witches and Neighbours*, Fontana Press, London

Foucault, M., 1982a, 'Technologies of the Self', in P. Rabinow, ed., 2000, *Michel Foucault: Essential Works of Foucault 1954-1984, Volume 1: Ethics*, Penguin Books, London

Haraway, D., 1985, 'A Manifesto for Cyborgs: Science, Technology and Socialist Feminism in the 1980s', in L.J. Nicholson, ed., 1990, *Feminism / Postmodernism*, Routledge, London

Haraway, D., 1991, *Simians, Cyborgs and Women*, Routledge, London

Harris, A., 2004, *Future Girl: Young Women in the Twenty-First Century*, Routledge, New York

Jordan, T., 1999, *Cyberpower: The Culture and Politics of Cyberspace and the Internet*, Routledge, London

Krzywinska, T., 2000, *A Skin for Dancing In: Possession, Witchcraft and Voodoo in Film*, Flicks Books, Wiltshire

Lee, R. M., 2000, *Unobtrusive Methods in Social Research*, Open University Press, Buckingham

McRobbie, A., 2000, *Feminism and Youth Culture, 2nd ed*, Macmillan Press, London

Nightmare, M. M., 2001, *Witchcraft and the Web: Weaving Pagan Traditions Online*, ECW Press, Toronto

Overbey, K. E. and Preston-Matto, L., 2002, 'Staking in Tongues: Speech Act as Weapon in *Buffy*', in R. V. Wilcox and D. Lavery, eds., *Fighting the Forces: What's at Stake in Buffy the Vampire Slayer*, Rowman and Littlefield Publishers Inc., Oxford

Pearson, J., ed., 2001, *Michel Foucault: Fear-Less Speech*, Semiotext(e), Los Angeles

Purkiss, D., 1996, *The Witch in History: Early Modern and Twentieth-Century Representations*, Routledge, London

Sanders, H., 2004, *New Generation Witches: The Teenage Witch as Cultural Icon and Lived Identity*, [Thesis Monograph], Norwich School of Art and Design, Anglia Polytechnic University, Cambridge

Valiente, D., 1973, *An ABC of Witchcraft Past and Present*, Robert Hale, London

Walkerdine, V., 1990, *School Girl Fictions*, Verso, London

A Language of Her Own: Witchery as a New Language of Female Identity

Amy Lee

The magical figure of the witch has occupied both the professional and lay imagination for centuries. One conjures up shapes and sizes of all sorts when the image of a witch is called forth to the consciousness. Shakespeare's *The Tempest* and *Macbeth* are probably among the best known texts featuring a witch in early modern western literary history, though the image and power of the witches are very differently depicted and interpreted. *Macbeth*'s three weird women fascinate and confuse the powerful individuals by their awesome cooking cauldrons and their prophetic words of multiple meanings. The way they are attired, their actions and most of all, their narratives exert absolute control over the willing preys of ambitious hearts. Macbeth is trapped because he chooses to elicit wonderful promises from the stories told by these three weird women. The witches have the last words in the story of the noble and the powerful because they fashion their narratives to be polyvalent, thus hiding the true meaning up their sleeves until the last moment.

Interestingly, the witch Sycorax in *The Tempest* is represented in her absence. While the witches in *Macbeth* punctuate the play at critical moments, Sycorax never for once appears personally in the play. As Diane Purkiss (2001) mentions in *The Witch in History*, all that the readers know about Sycorax, namely that she is Caliban's mother, and that she practices dark magic, is related to us through the voice of one of her victims, Ariel the spirit. To make matters worse, even Ariel itself is not sure of the reliability of its own memory. The story of Sycorax is therefore a highly unstable narrative, a site of even more interpretations than perhaps the polyvalent narratives of the three witches in *Macbeth*. Conventional reading has put Sycorax opposite Prospero, the great learned man who is too devoted to his study and too naïve to notice his own brother's worldly ambition.

In this binary positioning of the absent Sycorax against the very much present Prospero, *The Tempest* has not only reinforced the stereotype of a witch who is an old, unattractive 'hag' who imposes curses on her victims, but also laid down criteria to distinguish among various types of magic, performed by different wonder workers. Prospero the scholarly administrator lands on the remote island as a victim of a plot against him, and transforms the island into his refuge for recuperation. He frees Ariel from Sycorax's curses, and goes on to instill some notion of human dignity in Caliban through education. Prospero, thus portrayed as one who uses magic to bring order, stability, and freedom to the island, puts the previous master, Sycorax, in perspective as the power of darkness, confusion, and bondage. These two consecutive masters of the out-of-the-way island demonstrate what may perhaps be the Elizabethan society's idea of good magic and bad magic.

Good magic or bad magic, these early modern figures of wonder workers represented in fictions are human, although they inhabit a strangely liminal position between mere mortals and the invincible gods. Their ability to perform super-human acts puts them in a special category of existence on the margin of normal human society, and narratives about their success or failure to merge into mankind's daily activities may become a reflection on cultural attitudes towards some of their attributes. Hugh Parry's (2001) *Visions of Enchantment*, a study of the representation of magic in fiction, starts with the note that magical power, or the power to perform super-natural acts, lies only with the gods in pagan literature. Magic used to be the exclusive domain of the gods, each yielding different power corresponding to their assigned duties in the hierarchy of the god's power structure.[1]

Thus in pagan literature, magic is a highly hierarchical element. The potency of both the male and female gods' magic is directly related to how important they are in the godly ranks. Gods and goddesses can use their power to further their ambitions and there is no distinction between good magic and bad magic. There is no human sense of fairness or justice in the way things turn out: the 'good' gods may not always triumph over the 'bad' gods simply by force of their morality righteousness. Instead, very often the outcomes of celestial confrontations are determined by the intervention of Fate, who is sometimes personified as female in the literary space of pagan gods. The indeterminable interference of Fate which can turn the table around what apparently is a straightforward combat of power creates in the pagan literature a space of indefinite possibility which is gendered.

From the site of exclusive pagan origin of magical power, Parry's observation in the opening chapter of his book provides a useful background to see the changes in representations and perceptions of these wonder workers in later literary works, and what might have constituted these changes. Female enchanters, or witches, in particular, become a major literary interest starting from Greco-Roman fiction.[2] These female enchanters are basically human and mortal, though they have various abilities to perform acts beyond the comprehension of other mortal beings. Their appearance, power, status, and identities are very often dressings dipped in cultural and ideological flavorings of their times. As Parry has summarily demonstrated in his book, the constitution of each prototype of these witches has a direct link to the political and ideological atmosphere of a particular society.

Erichtho, for example, is constructed as a typical ugly hag probably because of the fear and disgust felt about certain powerful and ruthless female figure during its time of composition.[3] The creation of other prototypes, such as the sensuous and seductive younger witches, as well as the witch as an unstable woman who is not in full control of her passions have also been shown to have their origins in contemporary society and current thoughts. Medea, possibly one of the most memorable female wonder workers of all ages, is a good example of how the same figure acquires different identities and subjectivities in different ages.[4] She has been variously read as the primary outsider, cut off from a people because of cultural, linguistic and moral difference; or the ultimate mad woman who cannot control herself once her vengeance is unleashed. Rebellious daughter, ruthless lover, obsessive mother, and intelligent trickster are just some of the numerous identities attributed to her in different literary readings.

The potency of these figures of witches from early literature comes from their inherent instability due to their state of in-between-ness. Witches, at least those appearing in Greco-Roman literature onwards, are by nature figures of liminality. They are mortal and yet they have power to intervene with the natural order of things; they possess supernatural abilities and yet they are within the bounds of fate. The portrayal of their association with animals (especially cats) even relegates them to the shadowlands between human beings and animals. Narratives about their connections to what are regarded as their "familiars" seems to be the last straw in creating a class of female beings who are marginal to their conventional counterparts in every aspects of their identity. Their attribute, namely the ability to perform magic, isolates them to the extent of querying their fundamental identity.

This element of being marginal to the common perception of what is the normal female and human identity persists in the narrative space of early modern literature. Purkiss in *The Witch in History* traces the appearances and transformation of the witch figure in early modern narratives, including both fictional characters and witnesses' stories in trial records, and discovers in the depiction of the witches a response to the prevailing image of a proper female citizen of the time. The trial records reveal numerous stories told by supposed victims of the witch, relating occurrences which are a challenge to the traditional role of a food provider in the household and a care provider to children. The first signs of some failure in the domestic process of food-making, or children falling sick incomprehensively, are very often taken as proof of the work of witchcraft. The witch, at least from these victims' stories, is the anti-housewife or the anti-mother because of her interference with these primary duties of the woman in the house.

From goddesses to anti-housewife and anti-mother, the femininity of wonder workers has stood out and persisted in historical records as well as in literary imagination. Purkiss has pointed out an interesting correlation between the visibility of witches in the legal records and the literary imagination in early modern period. It seems that the more visible the witch figure is in the everyday life, the more invisible and voiceless she becomes in fiction and cultural representation.[5] Yet no matter whether in the trial records or in the literary imaginative space, the witch in her various guises is not given a rightful space to speak for herself. The trial records note the supposed victims' stories, while the fictional representations focus on the appearance and fearful deeds supposedly committed by the witches, culminating in the silent and moreover absent Sycorax whose legacy is the barbarous Caliban who is hardly teachable.

The silence and absence of the witch as a subject could be seen as one of the issues taken up in Maryse Condé's 1986 novel, *I, Tituba, Black Witch of* Salem. True to the history of the witch, the heroine of the novel inhabits the lands of the in-between, conceived at the sea, born in a foreign land, adopted by witches, transgressing between the land of the real and the space of the dead, and finally dying and coming back to life in an alternative form. Tituba's story conforms to many of the events and features assigned to stories of witches, but with an essential difference. This time the witch is taking centre stage and telling her own story from her own perspective through the writer whose name appears on the cover of the book. It is an autobiography commissioned by a witch materialized by the hand of a female African diasporic writer, a dual-voiced autobiography of a historical witch.

This discussion does not aim to unravel the 'truth' about witches. There have been historical researches into the content of the trials, examinations of the written records penned by the judges and other medical doctors concerned. And scientists of the modern age have also put forward theories as to the possibility of an outbreak of a plague which was not recognized at that time, and thus wrongly attributed to be signs of evil spirits.[6] This discussion looks at the novel as a deliberate narrative act performed at the end of the twentieth century, by a female African diasporic writer who uses the colonial language of French.[7] The dual identity of the subject of the narrative, the interesting relationship between the content and the way these details are related to us, as well as the way conventional features about the witch is treated in this 'insider's story' will be examined.

Jeannie Suk (2001) looks at the development of some modern French Caribbean writing to explore the language of magic for marginalized female identities such as that created by the postcolonial context. She puts Maryse Condé's novel as a parallel to other French Caribbean writing in its elucidation of a postcolonial identity, and suggests that sorcery offers a new kind of subject which creates a text to fill in the gaps and holes of the mainstream narrative, especially in the case of the grand narrative of colonial masters. Building on Suk's suggestion, this discussion explores the concept of sorcery as a site of possible rewriting and rereading of existing texts which seems to be unmarked and offering a neutral picture of the world. In particular, the picture of the witch who has always been represented by the voice of the other is here being unpacked and re-interpreted for possible alternative identities.

This narrative intention of recovering a possible alternative identity is obvious in the novel even before the beginning of the story-telling. Maryse Condé the author remarks: 'Tituba and I lived for a year on the closest of terms. During our endless conversations she told me things she had confided to nobody else.' Here the author, a real living being in the contemporary society, claims to have absolute confidence from Tituba, a historical witch, and is uniquely capable of relating to us the most secret things of Tituba this woman. To enter the narrative from this point requires one to put one's rationality in suspense, and to understand the story in its symbolic significance rather than a literal belief of its facts.

Thus this contemporary version of Tituba's autobiography once again demonstrates what Purkiss has noted in her book as the usability of myths concerning witches. From the early modern period up to the twentieth century, stories about witches have been incorporated into different discourses by different groups for quite diversified purposes. The witch may be sexually aggressive or attractive, or she can be the most sinister and grotesque female figure. She can be the wise woman who knows about herbs and helps her neighbors, or she can also be the ally of the devil to jeopardize decent village life. But whatever the nature of this figure of the witch, portrayal of her doings can be read as a return of the repressed desires and fears in a given society. Her status of being the repressed, the voiceless, and the unconscious makes her emergence in a literary work all the more fertile with meaning.

And what has this voice to say to her readers in the late-twentieth century? The autobiographical subject, Tituba Indian the accused witch, refers directly to the official records of the 17^h century Salem witch trials, and says: 'There would be mention here and there of 'a slave originating from the West Indies and probably practicing "hoodoo".' (Condé, 1992, p 110). Although the Salem witch trials are famous for a number of different reasons, Tituba, being one of the surviving victims in this mad vengeance, gets mentioned only in the most oblique and impersonal way. The reference to 'slave', 'West Indies' and 'hoodoo' here immediately relates the cause of her voicelessness to factors of race, culture and gender, which interestingly are the very same reasons for Sycorax's silence/absence in Purkiss's rereading of her story in *The Tempest*. The recreated subject of Tituba is thus speaking with a postcolonial voice when she situates herself as the other in relation to the grand narrative of the colonizers.

The polyvalent discourse of identity embodied in a site of postcolonial interpretation is raised by Purkiss in relation to the character of Sycorax. Physically absent in the play, Sycorax is a legacy made of words transmitted from Ariel to Prospero, making everything about Sycorax merely hear-say from the unreliable mouth of Ariel. Not having a definitive Sycorax, she can be anything. Purkiss chooses as an example the issue of Sycorax's blue eyes. While Shakespeare's text is heavily annotated with the contemporary idea that a pregnant woman has blue eyelids, it is also possible to locate the blueness in the eyes rather than the eyelids of the witch. Having the witch in *The Tempest* as a blue-eye Caucasian will overthrow the reading which takes Sycorax and Caliban as the barbarous figures of the native and the white Prospero as the civilized colonizer. The absence of Sycorax's physical voice, therefore, may be turned into a powerful endowment due to the possible heterogeneity of her identity.

Heterogeneity as a possible source of subversive power is an important concept put forward by postcolonial theorists such as Bhabha. Colonization is not a clear-cut process of one culture 'covering' another, in which the individual cultures can simply resume their 'original' state after the experience. Even for the ex-colonizers, the colonial experience is nothing like a one-way transmission of culture and beliefs to the native people of the colony. What actually happens is a mutual fertilization of culture between the colonized and the colonizer, resulting in a new heterogeneous culture for both parties. The site of postcolonial cultural products is thus a field of ingenious creation both consciously and unconsciously by the ex-colonizer or the post-colonized. Bhabha, and other postcolonial theorists, have drawn attention to the immense possibilities inherent in texts which can lend themselves to a postcolonial heterogeneous reading concerning identity formation.

In this sense, Condé's novel, which draws attention to its own status as a response to mainstream colonial history, is at the same time questioning the seemingly seamless narrative of the main historical consciousness, not just about the colonial subjects, but the subjection of other identities under various ideological suppressions. Tituba the witch is burdened not only with the baggage of the super-human deeds, but also the violation of conventional protocols of behaviour in various aspects. By embodying Tituba's voice from beyond, across the boundaries of life and death, trajecting through the languages of different cultures, the narrative is made into a site of multi-discourses. Just as contemporary feminists embrace the timeless and indefinite narrative of the witch for their own purposes, Condé's choice of a witch as the protagonist of her novel paths the way for a contest between different identifying stories:

'Abena, my mother, was raped by an English sailor on the deck of *Christ the King* one day in the year 16** while the ship for sailing for Barbados.' (Condé, 1992, p 3). In many ways this is the genesis of the story. On the one hand, the first person narrator Tituba is talking about her own birth in the manner of a typical autobiography; but on the other hand, reference to the personalities involved in this act of 'creation' is too obvious to miss. The woman setting forth to Barbados is obviously a slave, the typical Other to the English sailor who is in charge of such a ship bearing the name of male supremacy. The setting of the scene immediately highlights the main issues of identity to appear in the following narrative. Out of the primal act of oppression on the ship, the readers are to witness a shift of power from the colonizer to the colonized, not just at the textual level when Tituba's triumph is to be told, but also at the extra-textual level through the postcolonial writer's intervention.

The transgressive quality of Tituba's voice is shown not only through the details she unveils to readers for the first time, but is also visible in her claim that her story extends beyond the boundary of death. She says in the Epilogue:

I am hardening men's hearts to fight. I am nourishing them with dreams of liberty. Of victory. I have been behind very revolt. Every insurrection. Every act of disobedience. (Condé, 1992, p 175)

Her afterlife presence has a specific orientation: She encourages the oppressed people to fight back in the name of freedom, almost like a continuation of what she has done in her lifetime. Tituba introduces the epilogue of the novel by saying that 'my real story starts where this one leaves off and it has no end'. (*Ibid.*) Her physical elimination from the world does not remove her presence or her influence to those who are living. This ability to assert herself over conventional barrier is a repetition of what we have seen in her mother and her mother-surrogates.

In fact, in Tituba's narrative, the maternal figure is the power source of all her experiences. Although Abena, Tituba's biological mother, was raped by an English sailor and accused of murder, her example has taught Tituba not to be subjected to sexual humiliation again. Mama Yaya, who adopts Tituba and teaches her the magical language of nature, has helped Tituba developed her potential as a healer. Even chance encounters such as Hester Prynne,[8] gives Tituba new insights into her own identity and her power. Tituba herself continues what she sees as her responsibility towards her child even after her own physical death. Together these female characters demonstrate the maternal power of nurturing and sustenance. True to the nature of the Moon Goddess who is traditionally venerated as the origin of witchcraft,[9] these maternal figures embody the qualities of the goddess' triple manifestation. Their life-giving and life-sustaining capabilities, as well as their feminine sexuality, create a legacy of continuation which goes beyond ordinary barriers of mortality.

This group of women who create, bring forth, and transcend boundaries, have not only demonstrated the inherent maternal power, but have also collectively woven a special space of fluid identity, where a new language and new definitions are required. The art of sorcery, or witchcraft as the judges at the Salem trials would like to call it, can be seen as an alternative way of encoding and decoding the signs of the world. Tituba's own sexual experience causes her to rethink her mother's moaning when raped by the sailor; Mama Yaya's knowledge of the herbs forms a different symbolic system in which the natural world and human life are linked; and Hester's thoughts and actions may well be examples of pioneer feminism. The important women in Tituba's physical life serve as advisers to her in the sense of giving her a different language to think, to feel and to interpret her surrounding world. If this 'language' is labeled as sorcery, or witchcraft, there is no doubt that witchcraft is meant to be an inherent quality of the maternal figure.

This new language is most clearly described by Hester when she encourages Tituba to confess:

> [Give] them an element of doubt and, believe me, they'll know how to fill in the blanks! At the right moment shout: 'Oh, I can't see any more! I've gone blind!' And you'll have pulled the trick off. (Condé, 1992, p 100)

Confession is a 'trick' because it is understanding what one's oppressors want and tailor-make something to humor them in order to make life easy for oneself. Tituba's confession here is an ingenious discourse to free herself from the naming system of the patriarchal religious authority. By fashioning herself through double-talk, Tituba draws energy from alternative representation of identities, and regains personal autonomy. In fact, the power politics involved in a confession in witch trials is an interesting issue. While the majority of fictional depictions of witch confessions describe it graphically as a torturer-victim interaction between the authority and the witch, Purkiss points out that in England during the peak period of witch trial, the use of physical torture in real trials is rare. Rather the stories recorded are agreed between the authority and the witch.

Seen in this way, Tituba's 'confession' of her confession in *I, Tituba, the Black Witch of Salem* forms a fine rapport with Purkiss's book of early modern witches. While Tituba's skillful manipulation of the rules of the witch hunt and trials shows up the inherent anxiety and fears in the patriarchal puritanical authority, Purkiss's research document highlights the numerous uses the myth of the witch has been made. Tituba's recalling of her life and her mother-surrogates' participation demonstrates the vastness of the female identity, which interestingly finds confirmation in the potential uses of the timeless myth of the witch as recorded in Purkiss's book. It is an acknowledgement of the depth and substance of the Witch figure that even contemporary feminist organizations are still capitalizing on the content of its image.[10]

Whether her knowledge of the herbs makes her a witch is beside the point, but Tituba's embracing that identity ironically gives her freedom. Witchcraft (or sorcery) grants her the ability to transcend existing boundaries of fixity, definity, and homogeneity. Seen in this way, Condé's creation of the story of a witch Tituba is not only a positive response to the historical anonymity. The story of a witch is rather an imaginative space for performing identity transcendence beyond the restrictions of historical realism. Condé as a postcolonial female writer performing in the language of the ex-colonizer is very much aware of the need of a new "language". The language of witchcraft makes it possible to question the rigidity of the apparent reality and to facilitate a crossing over, a mutual fertilization of the cultures involved in the postcolonial.

Notes

1. For details of how magical powers is restricted to the godly figures, please refer to chapter one "Enchanting Gods" in Hugh Parry, *Visions of Enchantment*, 1-24.

2. In Greek and Roman fictions, those with magic powers are mainly male characters, usually cultic priests. Female enchanters or wonder workers do not become a major image until Greco-Roman times. This phenomenon also runs parallel in European folklore. For the representation of magic and magic performers in the European folklore, please refer to chapter two of Parry's book, "Magic in Folktale".

3. Hugh Parry suggests that the image of Erichtho comes possibly from a fear of the powerful figure of Nero's mother, whose intervention in politics indeed could change the future of many people's life; just as Erichtho is reputed to have the power of revealing what the future has in store for human beings.

4. Hugh Parry has explored the different transformations of the Medea character in her various incarnations. From Euripides to Seneca, up to the 20th century drama written by Maxwell Anderson, Parry has demonstrated the shifting focus in these literary texts and how they recreate Medea once again for their audience in the light of their social and political concerns.

5. Purkiss points out the negative correlation between the visibility of witches in real life and in fictional and dramatic depiction. She notes that while the number of witch trials in England peaked in 1580-1590, the theatre, the most popular mass entertainment at the time, did not show any particular interest in the subject of witches and witchery. Also because of political factional conflicts, people were afraid to be thought of using the witch figure as a queen-associated image. For details of this phenomenon, please refer to chapter 7 of her *The Witch in History*.

6. Bernard Rosenthal (1993) has presented the whole event of the Salem witch hunt and trials from its beginning to the end in his book, *Salem*

Story: Reading the Witch Trials of 1692. He concludes that possibly the dramatic fits and trances so spectacularly exhibited by the victims may be a form of an allergy. Other theories interprets the behaviour of the individual as a kind of mass hysteria where the individual believes that he or she is undergoing real physical suffering when the only affliction is of a psychological nature.

7   In Jeannie Suk's (2001) discussion of the book, she also refers to the cover design of the first English edition of the novel, when the title of the book and the name of the author is presented in such a way that the two names Tituba and Maryse Condé appear as parallels. Suk remarks that instead of writing the story of Tituba, it can be seen that Maryse Condé is possibly using Tituba as an excuse to write her own story.

8   Hester Prynne is of course the famous bearer of the scarlet letter of adultery in Nathaniel Hawthorne's novel. Maryse Condé refers to her appearance in this novel as a personal touch. While Hester bears a daughter and quietly tolerates humiliation from her society because of this daughter, here in Condé's novel the Hester is a very different character. She is portrayed as a frank woman who is open about her sexuality, and who commits suicide in the prison before she gives birth to her daughter, read by some people as an act of protest. Both in the opening remarks by the author and throughout the narrative, the relationship between Tituba and Hester is ambiguous in its nature. It is even possible to read them as enjoying an erotic relationship with one another when Tituba mentions the spirit of Hester coming to visit and lie with her.

9   See Zell and Zell (2003)

10 Here it is referring to the fact that contemporary feminist organizations use the acronym of W.I.T.C.H. to represent different issues they are addressing. Purkiss points out in her book that while the actual content of that which they are addressing is different, the staying power of the name reflects a deep-seated fascination with the potential of this cultural icon.

References

Barnes, Paula, 1999, 'Meditations on Her/Story: Maryse Condé's *I, Tituba, Black Witch of Salem* and the Slave Narrative Tradition.' in Janice Lee Liddell and Yakini Belinda Kemp (eds.), *Arms Akimbo: Africana Women in Contemporary Literature*, University Press of Florida, Gainesville, 193-204.

Condé, Maryse, 1992, *I, Tituba, Black Witch of Salem*, Trans. Richard Philcox, University Press of Virginia, Charlottesville.

Cox, Timothy, 2001, *Postmodern Tales of Slavery in the Americas: From Alejo Carpentier to Charles Johnson*, Garland Publishing Inc, New York.

Donadey, Anne, 2001, *Recasting Postcolonialism: Women Writing Between Worlds*, Heinemann, Portsmouth.

Dukats, Mara, 1998, 'The Hybrid Terrain of Literary imagination: Maryse Condé's Black Witch of Salem, Nathaniel Hawthorne's Hester Prynne, and Aime Cesaire's Heroic Poetic Voice', in Kostas Myrsiades and Linda Myrsiades (eds.), *Race-ing Representation: Voice, History, and Sexuality*, Rowman and Littlefield Publishers Inc, Lanham, 141-154.

Parry, Hugh, 2001 *Visions of Enchantment: Essays on Magic in Fiction*, University Press of America Inc, Lanham.

Pfaff, Françoise, 1996, *Conversations with Maryse Condé*, University of Nebraska Press, Lincoln.

Purkiss, Diane, 2001, *The Witch in History: Early Modern and Twentieth-Century Representations*, Routledge, New York and London.

Rosenthal, Bernard 1993, *Salem Story: Reading the Witch Trials of 1692*. Cambridge University Press, Cambridge.

Suk, Jeannie, 2001, *Postcolonial Paradoxes in French Caribbean Writing: Cesaire, Glissant,*

Zell, Otter, and Zell, Morning Glory, 13-12-2003, 'Satanism vs. Neo-Pagan Witchcraft: Confusions and Distinctions' *Green Egg, [on-line]*, http://www.holysmoke.org/wicca/satvnp.htm.

Discovering the Witch's Teat: Magical Practices, Medical Superstitions in The Witch of Edmonton

Mary Hayes

Introduction

The suspicion among the townspeople of Edmonton that Elizabeth Sawyer was a witch culminated in her trial and execution on April 19, 1621. In the record of Sawyer's trial, The Wonderful Discoverie of Elizabeth Sawyer, a Witch, Late of Edmonton, her conviction and condemnation and Death, Henry Goodcole notes that Sawyer's estrangement from her neighbours began when 'they would not buy brooms of her' (B1v). Given how strongly the scene of the witches' magical night flights to their demonic sabbats had captured the early modern imagination, broom making could not but have been an unfortunate occupation for an accused witch. Albeit curious, this and other incidental details about Sawyer were confirmed by a search of her body that uncovered a 'private mark' located 'a little above the fundament.' In a different context, it might seem strange that this unobtrusive mark would look 'as though one had sucked it.' The inquisitors in the Sawyer case, however, knew what odd discoveries the search of a witch's body might yield. They were able to discern that this private mark was in fact a thing like a Teate' by which Sawyer would nurse her demonic familiar, a dog named Tom (B3v). This teat-like mark thus supported the townspeople's theories about Sawyer's occult traffic with the devil and proved her guilt as it did many other accused witches in 16th-17th century England.

Unique to English witchcraft trials, the witch's teat may strike modern-day readers as evidence of nothing but pre-modern superstitious tendencies. I contend, however, that the teat evinces the influence of Renaissance anatomical science on witchcraft proceedings. Although England lagged behind the continental anatomical tradition inspired by the work of Andreas Vesalius (1514-54), dissections in England became more frequent and visible during the reigns of Edward VI (1547-53) through James (1603-25), years that, interestingly, also saw the peak number of trials and executions for witchcraft in England. We can see a connection between these contemporary magical and medical phenomena if we recognize that, like anatomical dissections, English witchcraft trials were conducted under the assumption that forensic examination of the body would ineluctably uncover the truth.

The influence of anatomical science on early modern English witchcraft proceedings is evident in Goodcole's trial pamphlet, a work that the author takes pains to distinguish from the "most base and false ballets" and "ridiculous fictions" that have proliferated in the wake of the Sawyer case. Indeed, Goodcole explicitly states his intention to report the whole truth about Sawyer's physical and verbal examination during the trial. The trial pamphlet's focus on the discovery of the truth offers us a perspective from which to read the Renaissance play that was based on it, *The Witch of Edmonton* (1621) by Thomas Dekker, John Ford and William Rowley. Although the playwrights used the Goodcole record rather than other more spurious sources, their attempt to stage the 'truth' about Sawyer's nefarious activities seems doomed to fail because unlike Goodcole, the *Edmonton*-playwrights could not relate to their audience the discovery of the witch's teat. Quite understandably, this sordid scene - in which midwives search the accused witch's naked and shaven body for her demonic teat - could not have been enacted on the Renaissance stage. To convey to the play's audience Elizabeth's Sawyer's dabbling in the magical arts, the playwrights staged spooky spectacles that, while engaging and exciting, were a whit the less graphic than the discovery of the teat. Taking issue with these stage substitutes for the witch's teat, Diane Purkiss argues that they compromise the play's representation of the epistemological protocols represented in the Goodcole trial pamphlet (1996, p 243).

Rather than regard *The Witch of Edmonton* as a compromised rendition of the Sawyer trial because the playwrights could not display the witch's teat, I propose that Dekker, Ford and Rowley intentionally invoke the limits of dramatic staging in their stage portraits of this graphic scene. Simply put, the playwrights tacitly urge their audience to rethink the trope underlying empirical discourses, that 'seeing is believing.' By alluding to the visual evidence against Sawyer that they cannot stage, the playwrights call into question the validity of contemporary scientific disciplines based on spectacles, that is, anatomical investigations of the human body. Although we would expect Renaissance medical practices to be more credible than magical superstitions were, we must keep in mind that such scientific empiricism offered grounds for witch hunters to search for the accused witch's body for the demonic teat and to regard it as damning evidence against her. In the *Edmonton*-playwrights' 'inaccurate' rendition of the Sawyer trial, they critique the trial's inaccuracies that were borne of, ironically enough, its reliance on forensic science and empirical evidence.

In Part I of this article, 'Witches' Teats and Women's Secrets,' I examine how the playwrights portray contemporary medical discourse about the female body's capacity to birth and nurse. Scientific curiosity about these 'women's secrets' sheds light on the valence accorded the witch's teat. In addition to being a forensic marker of the accused witch's guilt, the teat was also encoded with cultural retaliation against the female body for its perceived pre-eminence in shaping individual identity. As I have noted, the playwrights could not stage the demonic nursing or expose the witch's teat on Elizabeth Sawyer's body. As they rework the scene of demonic nursing and relocate the teat to accommodate theatrical limits, however, they call attention to approximations in the trial's epistemological procedure as well as the female body's own resistance to scientific attempts to understand its "secrets." Progressing deeper into my analysis, I turn my attention to the body's interior. In Part II, 'The Anatomical Theatre and the Theatricalized Anatomy', I examine the playwrights' response to invasive medical procedures. Anatomical science presumed the female body's interior subverted and thus invited empirical investigation of the secrets occulted therein. The playwrights reflect on these medical investigations that idealized the female body's vulnerability by portraying the witch's body as nothing but a costume that the devil can penetrate and wear. In depicting the devil's adoption of these 'costumes,' the playwrights draw attention to demonic possession that, like the demonic nursing, was a popular magical trope that they could not stage. Furthermore, Dekker, Ford, and Rowley illustrate how dissections in the anatomical theatre, while valorising empirical evidence, also enlisted the body in a gross theatrical display that would seem to undercut the dispassionate pursuit of scientific truth.

Part I: Witches' Teats and Women's Secrets

Who's your daddy?

Before I begin my discussion of *The Witch of Edmonton*, I will first briefly note a salient and relevant trend in early modern cultural discourse. A great number of Renaissance texts interrogated individual identity - where it resided, what factors constructed and changed it. The amount of energy invested in such Renaissance self-fashioning indicates an anxiety about personal identity, an anxiety that was manifest in a wide variety of cultural conversations. Throughout the play, the *Edmonton*-playwrights tend to root identity in the body. In doing so, they not only evoke Renaissance texts that proposed an individual's essence resided in his physical form or its various parts, such as the heart. They also speak to early modern medical science that designated the human body as a site of epistemological inquiry, a discourse reflected and reworked in the English witchcraft trials such as the proceedings against Elizabeth Sawyer.

In the play's very opening, individual identity is linked with biological conception, particularly, the father's role in it. This is apparent when the wealthy ne'er-do-well Frank Thorney assures his pregnant lover Winnifride: 'Thou needst not /Fear what the tattling gossips in their cups/ Can speak against thy fame. Thy child shall know/Who to call dad now' (I.i.2-5). Frank means that he will marry Winnifride and thus legitimize their child. Replying to this enshrinement of the father's name, Winnifride recalls an event no less auspicious than the moment of ejaculation: 'You have discharged the true part of an honest man' (I.i.5-6). Winnifride's motivation behind making this touching yet cryptic remark becomes clear when her other lover, Sir Arthur, comes on stage to reveal that he is the child's father. Winnifride's overstated attempt to secure patrilineage in Frank's body and the event of conception calls attention to the indeterminacy of biological fatherhood, which is soon paraded as falsifiable. Frank's subsequent exchanges with his own father also speak to early modern anxieties about identity as it is rooted in birth, particularly, the father's role in conception. Mr. Thorney is aware - albeit to a limited extent - of Frank's relationship with the servant-girl Winnifride. He threatens to disown Frank unless he marries the higher-class honey, Susan Carter. While Mr. Thorney's warning to Frank evokes class-based prejudices, it also suggests the ability of paternal relationships, a motif that pervades the play's first act.

Of woman born?

In early modern England, the relative indeterminacy of biological fatherhood seems at odds with a widely-held cultural assumption about the superiority of patrilineal relations, which were not dependent upon the female body or the mother's role in reproduction. Attending to this antifeminist thinking, Gail Kern Paster (1993, p 20) argues for the popular acceptance in Renaissance England of the "leaky" female body the grotesqueness of which offset the classical perfection of the male body. Such popular ideas about the female body's depravity find their authorization in medical sources. As Katharine Park (2000, p 24) points out, the mid-thirteenth century gynaecological manual *Women's Secrets* subscribes to Aristotelian medical theories predicated upon paternal agency in generation, which 'always intends to produce a male,' an operation that unfortunately goes awry about half the time. *Women's Secrets* does not explicitly label these 'imperfect males' with the term 'monsters' as one of its later commentators did. Yet, as Park (2000, p 34) notes, the text treats female births and birth defects together in its section on monsters. To the Renaissance reception of such earlier discourses on female imperfection, Ian Maclean (1980, p 31) responds: "none but satirical or facetious texts support the proposition of monstrosity." He adds that after 1600 the majority of doctors rejected Aristotelian notions of female degeneracy in favour of each sex's unique function.

Although medicine had putatively rejected theories of female monstrosity, fears about matrilineality still fuelled the popular fantasies that fixed a child's legitimacy in its resemblance to its father, that is, his maleness uncorrupted by female influence. What Janet Adelman (1992, p 212) calls a Renaissance 'parthenogenesis fantasy', the mother's exclusion from biological birth, underpins the resolution of Shakespeare's *Macbeth* in which Macduff's ascendancy depends exclusively on his mother's effacement. The witches tell Macbeth that he will be conquered by a man 'not of woman born' (IV.i.88). While this prediction seems to guarantee Macbeth's invincibility, it actually alludes to the circumstances surrounding the birth of Macduff, who was delivered by a Caesarean section. This theatrical predicament posed in *Macbeth* responded to and undoubtedly invigorated fantasies of patrilineal parthenogenesis that afforded escape from the mother's immediate yet detrimental influence over her offspring.

In *The Witch of Edmonton*, socially unacceptable and effaced maternal relationships resonate with cultural notions about biologically driven identity that privileged fatherhood over a degenerate motherhood. Winnifride carries an illegitimate child and misidentifies its father. The witch Elizabeth Sawyer has an unconventional maternal relationship with her animal familiar, the dog Tom. Mr. Thorney and Mr. Carter hammer out their children's marriage agreement while the play does not even mention Mrs. Thorney and Mrs. Carter. The playwrights use a paradigm of maternity to express the lability of identity itself, and thus, disclose their reservations about the female body that shapes identity so unreliably. When the townspeople are trying to track down Elizabeth Sawyer's familiar, they give a start when they think they hear the dog's voice. Cuddy Banks, a fool character who has taken a liking to the dog Tom, tries to cover up for him. He disingenuously asks his father, Mr. Banks: 'The voice of a dog? If that voice were a dog's, what voice had my mother? So am I a dog; bow, wow, wow!' (IV.i.251-2). The play's audience could not but be surprised by the dog's power of speech, a marvel that fetishizes language acquisition, and by extension, a pre-eminent form of human cultural initiation that is directed by the child's mother. Cuddy's invocation of his absent mother through his slapstick transformation into a dog evokes a troubling paradox about motherhood: it is degraded yet central to identity. Thus, the playwrights reflect a cultural prejudice against the female body, so awful and suspect for its influence on identity.

This problematic relationship between the maternity and identity depicted in Renaissance plays finds authorization in medical writings about the mother's influence on her child's development. For example, Park observes that *Women's Secrets* frequently remarks on the child's vulnerability to the mother's physical and psychological states, a preoccupation that later medical manuals would share (2000, p 34-5). Indeed, Ambroise Paré devotes four entire chapters of *Des monstres et prodiges* (1573) to implicating mothers in monstrous births. In addition to cataloguing baleful influences a pregnant woman can exert on her child, late 16th and early 17th-century gynaecological texts also authorize the widely held belief that the mother's milk affected the child's identity. *The Witch of Edmonton* playwrights gesture toward contemporary attitudes about breast-feeding when Mr. Carter coaches his future son-in-law Frank: 'Get me a brace of boys at a burden, Frank./ The nursing shall not stand thee a pennyworth of milk' (I.ii.211-2). Mr. Carter's endorsement of Frank's viripotence fosters a homosocial relationship that excludes his daughter Susan; the desired patrilineage will yield a 'brace of boys' untainted by the female sex. While Frank's hire of a wet-nurse will permit a faster turn-over due to nursing's alleged contraceptive effect, Susan's exclusion from nursing her children strikes an animating tension with early modern encomia on a mother's duty to breast-feed. Since Renaissance medicine viewed the nurse's milk as just as influential on the child as its very conception, wet-nursing exacerbated concerns about biologically determined identity. Even nursing as an upper-class privilege had fallen into desuetude due to the connections between milk and social status. Wet-nursing not only facilitated or interrupted genealogical transmission of identity but also created a threatening alternative genealogy that undermined biologically ordained identity. Mr. Carter's ambition to self-aggrandize through a great quantity of sound grandsons would thus be undercut by the deleterious influence of the lower-class nurse. Thus, in its first act, the play foregrounds the importance of patrilineal relations only to expose these as tenuous and to suggest the mother's terrible, unspoken power over her child.

"Mother Witch"

Early modern apprehensions about normative maternal agency transpire most awfully in the witch who nursed her familiar with her blood. Scholars have argued for the mutual influence of the cultural anxieties surrounding maternal nurture and those that produced the witch. Adelman (1992, p 131) sees in *Macbeth* the dual fantasy of a destructive maternal agency, embodied in Lady Macbeth and the witches, as well as an escape from this agency made possible through Macduff who is 'not of woman born.' Deborah Willis (1995, p 43-7) invokes a Kleinian psychosocial model to explain the maternal body's persecutory power wielded by the witch, the "bad mother" who deprived nurture to her neighbours. Paster (1993, p. 249) likewise argues for the conflation of witches and mothers in the early modern English cultural consciousness: 'Not only do witches resemble lactating mothers, but thanks to the witch-hunters' fetishistic attention to the witches' teat, lactating mothers come to resemble witches.' In addition to proving the accused witch's guilt, the teat serves another function in the witch trials; it attests to malevolent maternal nature, the monstrous distortion of a female capability.

The *Edmonton*-playwrights represent this misogynist paradigm in their characterization of Elizabeth Sawyer as a "bad mother." When the fool Cuddy Banks first meets Sawyer, she immediately identifies herself as a witch. Cuddy reassures her, '[W]itch or no witch, you are a motherly woman' (II.i.198-9) and fondly calls her "Mother Witch" throughout the play. Sawyer enters the stage at the beginning of Act Two lamenting the societal exclusion that has forced her into witchcraft. She ends the list of victims on whom she hopes to exert pernicious influence with 'babes at nurse' (II.i.13). References to nursing bracket the catalogue of skills she hopes to learn in the "art" (II.i.34): 'I have heard old beldams/ Talk of familiars in the shape of mice/ Rats, ferrets, weasels, and I wot not what,/ That have appeared and sucked, some say, their blood/ …………………../ So I might work/"Revenge upon this miser, this black cur /That barks and bites, and sucks the very blood/Of me and of my credit' (II.i.102-5; 115-8). Nursing an animal familiar with her blood tops the list of occult abilities that Sawyer wishes to acquire. Last but not least, she hopes to retaliate against Mr. Banks, the blood-sucking 'cur' who has beaten her for collecting sticks on his land. As soon as she articulates her desire to punish this cur as a "bad mother" would her suckling, the devil appears in the form of a dog, Tom. Sawyer and Tom seal their pact when he sucks blood from a spot on her arm that substitutes for a witch's teat, the bodily mark distinctive to the English witchcraft trials.

Bad Women's Bad Ends

This episode in which Sawyer seals the demonic pact is one of two moments in the play in which the *Edmonton*-playwrights allude to the fantastic scene of the familiar sucking the witch's teat, the evidence that the trial pamphlet author Henry Goodcole extrapolates from the 'teat' discovered on Sawyer's body. In his introduction to his pamphlet, Goodcole foregrounds the significance of the witch's teat, the 'private and strange marke on her body, by which their [the townspeople's] suspicion was confirmed against her' (B3r). Women who have been 'sworne thereunto to deliver the truth' (B3v) search for and discover the teat on Sawyer's body. Although Goodcole has verbally examined Sawyer, he notes expressly that he has not seen the teat and wonders even how his 'pen would forbeare to write these things for modesties sake' (B2v-B3r). The pen of the modest Goodcole manages somehow to bear forth and record the women's testimony to the teat's discovery: 'And they all three said, that they a little above the fundament of Elizabeth Sawyer the prisoner, there indited before the Bench for a Witch, found a thing like a Teate the bignesse of the little finger, and the length of halfe a finger, which was branched at the top like a teate, and seemed as though one had sucked it, and that the bottom of it was blew and the top of it was redde' (B3v). The teat-like thing, which looks, surprisingly enough, 'as though one had suckt it' (B3v), stands as the only empirical evidence against Elizabeth Sawyer as it did for many suspected witches in England.

Diane Purkiss (1996, p 232) argues that this interpretation of the 'teat' as a legible sign attests to the Sawyer trial's admission of 'the truth of the body' over other forms of proof. Indeed, Goodcole himself dismisses the 'old ridiculous custom' (A4r) of burning thatch from the suspect's house; if she appeared at the scene, which Elizabeth Sawyer did, she was deemed guilty of witchcraft. Although the significance attached to the witch's teat seems no less ridiculous, it illustrates the body's use in evidentiary procedure and thus speaks to how the "culture of dissection" in the 16th and 17th centuries conceptualized the body as imminently explorable; the body was even featured as complicit with its own exploration. Sawyer's body, particularly the teat encoded with its own history, affords an easy legibility that also characterizes the medical drawings of corpses that, quite generously, lifted their flayed skins to facilitate their own inspection. These drawings comprise a long tradition of "self-demonstration" that extends from Andreas Vesalius and his contemporaries such as Juan de Valverde (ca.1525-ca.1588) to Adrian van den Speighel (1578-1625). Jonathan Sawday (1995, p 57) argues for the increased frequency and visibility of anatomical dissections as well as the increased likelihood that bodies would be executed criminals'. Thus, Sawday (1995, p 114) observes in anatomical dissections the overlap of legal and medical procedures; the criminals' bodies "confessed" the truth by surrendering the ocular evidence hidden in their interiors.

Sawday envisions the mutual influence of legal and medical procedures, partly due to the circumstances by which anatomical corpses were acquired. Surely this practical association was but one variable that influenced the construction of the body as a site of epistemological certainty. Sawday's paradigm well accommodates *The Witch of Edmonton*, which drew upon a trial expedited by bodily autopsy. The playwrights make an off-handed reference to the anatomical vogue when Mr. Carter sniffs at the meagre fare served at 'slender city-suppers' and jokes that after three days of them 'you might send me to Barber-Surgeons' hall the fourth day to hang up for an anatomy' (I.ii.30-2). In Barber-Surgeons' Hall, they invoke a major centre for dissections that, as Sawday points out (1995, p 56), had been guaranteed a quota of corpses of criminals for anatomization since 1540. The author of the Sawyer trial transcript, Henry Goodcole, would report in *Heavens Speedie Hue and Cry Sent after*

Lust and Murder (1635) the trial and execution of a woman who 'after her execution was conveied to Barber Surgions hal for a Skeleton having her bones reserved in a perfect forme of her body which is to be seene, and now remaines in the aforesaid Hall' (C3r). Goodcole does not note the fate of Elizabeth Sawyer's corpse in his trial transcript. Sawday would argue, however, that the growing number of dissections in the 17th century raised both the probability and also the public's awareness that criminal corpses, such as Sawyer's, would wind up on the dissecting table. *The Witch of Edmonton* playwrights did not just borrow from the trial pamphlet, but rather, bought into the complex conversation on the body's use as evidence.

(Re)locating the Witch's Teat

I wished to contextualize the play within the medical culture that engendered the witch's teat. To recognize *The Witch of Edmonton* as a Renaissance play, however, problematizes its neat relationship to epistemological procedures. Most notably, stage substitutions for the ocular evidence of the witch's teat seem to undercut the playwrights' investment in the discovery of truth. In Act Two, Sawyer offers the dog her arm to suck because, as Paster (1993, p 258) delicately puts it, 'the more intimate relationship revealed in the sources is beyond the bounds of dramatic representation. When Tom later begs for the teat, Sawyer forestalls him with the physiological explanation that she is 'dried up with cursing and madness' (IV.i.154-5). She proposes instead, 'Let's tickle!' (IV.i.160) to placate the whining dog and satisfy the curious audience's desire for a spectacle. The playwrights cannot stage the animal familiar 'creep[ing] under an old witch's coats and suck[ing] like a great puppy' (V.i.173-4), a grim off-stage reality that is singled out by Cuddy as one of the 'beastly things' (V.i.174) that he has heard about Tom. Because the play relies on physical and verbal substitutes for the witch's teat, 'a bodily truth that is difficult to show on stage,' Purkiss (1996, p 242) contends that the performance fails to convey the discovery of truth presented in the trial transcript. The playwrights' limited ability to display empirical evidence tends toward an 'insensitivity to the protocol of epistemology' (p 240). They resort to spectacle, which, as Purkiss rightly notes, was 'usually an index of falsity' (p 232) on the Renaissance stage.

The playwrights do present a theatricalized spectacle when they displace the demonic nursing onto alternative affection between Sawyer and Tom. Indeed, the dog's feeding from Sawyer's arm seems plainly to advertise this theatricalized substitution for the "truth of the body." Tom's menacing words and a clap of thunder punctuate this highly melodramatic moment when Sawyer seals her pact with her blood. The *Edmonton*-playwrights could not possibly replicate on stage the damning discovery Goodcole records in the trial transcript. Yet, I ask what kind of relationship can be drawn between the play, circumscribed by staging limits well-known to the playwrights, and the Sawyer trial, predicated upon bodily ocular evidence. I invoke the word 'autopsy' which, as Jonathan Sawday (1995, p 14) reminds us, means 'inspection,' and propose that the playwrights do not display the discovery of witchcraft but rather an 'autopsy' of the early modern English body and the scientific discourses that attempted to guarantee its legibility.

The theatrical displacement of the witch's teat to Sawyer's arm calls attention to its location 'a little above the fundament' during her trial. As Purkiss (1996, p 131) rightly notes, the English witchmark was 'a teat or nipple inappropriately displaced into a part of the body associated with pollution.' A sceptical observer would have recognized this 'teat' as a body part wilfully mistaken by an empiricist over-zealous in his desire to interpret facts as evidence. Even the witch-hunter Matthew Hopkins would admit in *Discovery of Witches* (1647) that old women had 'natural excressencies, as Hemerodes, Piles' (Haining, 1974, p 179), protuberances that bore serendipitous likeness to witches' teats. The playwrights address the body's potential for misreading through Cuddy, who worries about his vulnerability to demonic attack: 'And her little devil should be hungry, come sneaking behind me like a cowardly catchpole and clap his talons on my haunches!' (II.i.239-40). Cuddy has defined Sawyer's affiliation with Tom in terms of sucking. The dog's disappearance "under an old witch's coats" is the "beastly" item on which Cuddy fixates as he tries to rehabilitate Tom. Likewise, in his parting words to Tom, Cuddy characterizes Tom's intentions toward him in terms of perverse nurture: 'I'll give no suck to such whelps, therefore henceforth I defy thee. Out and avaunt!' (V.i.179-80). In his vision of the demonic feeding in all its lurid detail, Cuddy imagines the 'little devil' will satisfy his hunger by attacking his 'haunches,' the rear part of the body exposed and inspected for the witch's teat in the trials. The teat's misplacement onto Cuddy Banks' male 'haunches' calls attention to the teat's prior relocations: from 'under an old witch's coats' to Sawyer's arm and, more importantly, from its usual spot on the female body to 'a little above the fundament.' Through Cuddy's anxiety that his body too can "give suck" to the devil, the playwrights expose the trial's medicalized legal procedures as but ridiculous approximations.

The Male Witch's Teat?

Context for understanding Cuddy's fear about demonic feeding can be found in another Renaissance play based on a witch trial transcript, Thomas Heywood and Richard Brome's *Late Lancashire Witches* (1634). As does *The Witch of Edmonton*, this play invokes the male witch's teat in a comedic context in order to address the witch trials' routine misreadings. The Lancashire witches' disruption of marital arrangements leaves the newly wed Parnell frustrated by her young husband Lawrence's inability to perform. The suggestion that a jury of women examine her body to see if she's still a virgin recalls the 1613 Frances Howard divorce suit against her husband, the Earl of Essex, who was allegedly rendered impotent by witchcraft. Inspections of these women to guarantee their integrity evince another means by which the discovery of witchcraft hinged upon evidence culled from the medicalized female body. In an understandable attempt to defend his masculinity, Lawrence asserts that the 'jurie of women' (1949) should search him instead: '[L]et me be searched as never a witch was searched, and finde ony thing mor or lesse upon me than a sufficient mon should have, and let me be honckt by't' (1960-62). Lawrence desires to prove his sexual parts are not 'lesse' than optimal yet fears that empirical investigation will misidentify his penis for a witch's teat. He worries that he will be 'honckt' for some physical infelicity, wrongfully hanged for his hanging manhood, as a witch was when a 'natural excressence' was misread as a significant token.

In *The Late Lancashire Witches*, the tendency to misidentify the witch's teat is tellingly imbricated with sexual misidentification. Although Cuddy's fear about the vulnerability and delectability of his 'haunches' might be dismissed as a fool's ridiculous ranting, *The Witch of Edmonton* playwrights invoke the fool as a sexually ambiguous character to disclose contemporary medical uncertainties about bodies that defied biological legibility. The Galenic one-sex model that patterned the female body on the male had organized centuries of medical thinking as well as present-day critical attitudes toward the Renaissance body and medicine. Cuddy's hypothetical ability to feed Tom might revise with a feminized difference the orthodox homology that had fallen out of fashion by the late 16th century. Yet, as Kathryn Schwarz (1997, p 147) argues, the female breast in English Renaissance literature was 'an inescapable site of difference' that gendered bodies undeniably female, their procrustean refashioning for the androcentric model of genitalia notwithstanding. As the belief in demonic nursing dispensed at the witch's teat attests to misogynist attitudes toward the female body, Cuddy's potential to 'give suck to such whelps' cannot but trouble the conventional episteme that associates nursing with the "leaky" female body.

Pre-Modern Gender Bending

Cuddy's speculation on his body's female capability evokes lively medical investigation into the existence and biological development of individuals who eluded neat sexual classification. In his *Des monstres et prodiges*, Paré provides witness to hermaphrodites, androgynes and females who turned into males when their organs 'hidden within the body' became 'exposed outside' (1573, p 32). Before Renaissance medical opinion endorsed the specific function of each sex, the Aristotelian view advocated the notion of female imperfection; women's bodies lacked the heat necessary to push out the internalized sex organs. The female body thus harboured the potential to turn male, a mutation governed by Nature's tendency toward what Paré calls 'what is most perfect' (p 33). The female body's innate hermaphroditism and proclivity for change incurs malevolent connotations in *The Late Lancashire Witches*. The fool Whetstone offers his insights on witches' ability to shape-shift: '[T]is sayd Hares are like Hermaphrodites, one while Male, and other Female, and that which begets this yeare, brings young ones the next; which some think to be the reason that witches take their shapes so oft' (ll.657-660). The projection of sexual ambiguity onto the witch's terrible body attests to the role of determinate sexual identity in qualifying bodies as human. Yet, the witch's opportunistic hermaphroditism but exaggerates a hidden capability that all female bodies possess. This admission of natural female hermaphroditism potentially circumscribed all women in the realm of the abject. The association of witches with sexually ambiguous bodies in *The Witch of Edmonton* and *The Late Lancashire Witches* reveals how the procedures designed to discover witches resonate with an early modern cultural obsession with the norms of female anatomy. The desire to feature all female bodies as deviant speaks to the witch trials' empirical procedure that could interpret any protuberance for a teat. Both sexological discourses and witch trials were predicated upon suggestible epistemes able to justify female degeneracy with biological proof.

The medically endorsed belief in female hermaphroditism reveals how women's bodies were associated with a changeability that stymied their intelligibility. Early modern medicine invested all bodies with a mutability, which, on one hand, edified the self. Michael Schoenfeldt (1997, p 243) argues that the body's processes of change, liquefaction and rarefaction, the conversion of blood into semen and breast milk were all regarded acts of self-fashioning in early modern England. Yet, on the other hand, as Sawday (1995, p 18) points out, these 'fluid processes (literally the movement of fluids)' of the 'ever-changing body' posed the greatest problems to post-Vesalian science. Women's bodies in particular fostered this changeability that tended toward inscrutability. The playwrights exploit the female body's mutability to account for the shortcomings of their art. Since the teat cannot be displayed on stage, Sawyer must apologize to Tom for her inability to nurse: 'I am dried up/ With cursing and with madness, and have yet/ No blood to moisten these sweet lips of thine' (IV.i.154-6). As the teat displaced onto Sawyer's arm indicted questionable epistemological methods, so Sawyer's demurral reveals that the female body's mutability proscribes its reliability. The playwrights also blur the lines between witches and ordinary women whose lactating bodies are subject to abrupt physiological change. Lactating women, unlike Sawyer, convert their blood into milk through a normative process of change that 'masks' the likeness of their bodies to witches'.

What's the bloody point?

Since this mutability was strongly associated with women and transmogrified in the body of the witch, it is significant that Frank Thorney takes to describing his own physiological changes. In the play's domestic plot, Frank is Sawyer's human analogue; both are tempted by the devil and executed at the play's end. When Susan Carter is unable to interpret Frank's sudden disenchantment with her, he attributes the cause to biological changes: 'In mine own bosom, here the cause has root. The poisoned leeches twist about my heart, and will, I hope, confound me' (II.ii. 114-6). These 'poisoned leeches' will indirectly 'confound' Frank, for in his changed mental and physiological state he will kill

Susan and be executed for her murder. The leeches also evoke the demonic familiar that feeds on the witch's blood. Given the cultural gendering of the breast and the playwrights' attention to the witch's fetishized practice, locating the source of his changed mood in his 'bosom' speaks to the widely held belief in feminine changeability. Frank remarks to Susan later that same conversation on the body's unreliability: 'But we, as all things else,/ Are mutable and changing' (II.ii.142-3). He identifies medically documented mutability as the body's defining characteristic that ironically precluded its comprehensive definition.

In their portrait of Frank's discovery as Susan's killer, the playwrights represent how Sawyer's trial drew its evidence from her body. The witch's teat that the playwrights could not show as evidence of Elizabeth Sawyer's witchcraft is metonymically transferred onto Frank's knife. The 'evidence' (IV.ii.165) of Tom's demonic influence on him is the knife, the 'bloody point' (IV.ii.167) that calls to mind Goodcole's description of Sawyer's teat: 'the top of it was red' (B3v). At the very end of the previous scene Sawyer has lovingly called Tom her 'bloodhound' (IV.i.268), a pet name that evokes not only the bloody demonic feeding but also evidentiary procedure and discovery. Frank draws the 'bloody point' from his pocket to cut a chicken in a gross re-enactment of Susan's murder made palatable for the stage. He eats the chicken as he recuperates from self-inflicted wounds allegedly dealt him by the robbers who killed Susan. Tellingly, the discovery of Frank's guilt is couched in repartee that medicalizes the body. Frank asks Mr. Carter: 'Do the surgeons say my wounds are dangerous then?' (IV.ii.131) and ruefully adds, 'Would he were to open them' (133). This proposed bloodletting evokes his criminal act as well as Sawyer's demonic feeding. When the townspeople bring in the corpse of Susan 'sick to the death' (IV.ii.145) to force a confession from Frank, Mr. Carter characterizes him as a doctor, 'an excellent rascal for letting blood' (IV.ii.145-6). Frank's interpolation into medical discourses precedes the discovery of his crime and resonates with Sawyer's physical examination that eventuated in her execution. Through his just punishment, *The Witch of Edmonton* playwrights wryly comment on the miscarriages of justice by witch hunters who regarded guilt in a felicitously placed 'bloody point.'

To this point in my paper, I have contextualized *The Witch of Edmonton* within contemporary medical discourses to understand better the admission of bodily evidence in witch trials such as Sawyer's. In Part II, I continue to consider the playwrights' autopsy of medical discourses, specifically, the investigation of truths interred within the body. The second half of the play exhibits a preoccupation with bodily invasion; this comes as no surprise since the play was based on a capital trial, many of which ended in dissection. Critiques of anatomical dissection are encoded in the devil's insidious penetrations of the body. Thus, the playwrights' remark upon the construction of the body, the female body particularly, as 'naturally' open to invasion.

Part II: The Anatomical Theatre and the Theatricalized Anatomy

A Womb with a View?

Through various Renaissance disciplines, Katharine Maus tracts an investment in 'inwardness.' The body's interior was putatively endowed with an authenticity that would evanesce when noted or exteriorized. Theatre could only refer to this 'inwardness' that defied display; hence the commonplace accepted by Renaissance dramatists first and foremost that their art was derivative. On the stage, this genuine 'inwardness' was encased by a theatricalized exterior, the actor's costume that Maus (1995, p 31) identifies as a 'fictional surface' that rankled the antitheatricalists for its ability to 'counterfeit' and to trick its audience with mere appearances. I would like to contextualize more than Maus does this trope of 'inwardness' alongside scientific discourses that focused on the gap between interiority and exteriority. As Sawday argues, the 'culture of dissection' likewise featured the body's insides as the ultimate site for investigation. Yet, this new focus in the 16th century on invasive dissections would undoubtedly revise this bodily episteme that relied on a distinction between interior and exterior. The body's interior became exteriorized in medical dissections, and thus, Luke Wilson (1987, p. 63) argues, it 'lost forever its definitive epistemological resistance.' *The Witch of Edmonton* playwrights invoke the theatrical trope of 'inwardness', particularly through costuming, to remark upon invasive medical procedures and their effects on 17th century English notions of the body, reconfigured by the very discourses designed to study it.

This campaign to exhume the truths interred inside the body would target women's bodies particularly. Renaissance anatomists and artists featured the female body, especially its reproductive functions, as an avatar for epistemological resistance to be mastered by investigation. For its occulted location in a 'private' spot, the witch's teat seemed to instigate the aggressive inspection that discovered it. Likewise, the medical text *Women's Secrets* presumes the purposeful resistance to interrogation of all female bodies, poised to withhold their 'secrets' from men. As Park (2000, p 34) points out, *Women's Secrets* 'specifically identifies women's "secrets" with generation and reproduction, and it characterizes these not merely as incidentally "hidden" (*occulta*) in the sense of pertaining to the internal organs, or "secret" (*secreta*) because of the shameful nature of the sexual parts, but also as powerful and important knowledge available to women and purposefully kept from men.'

The cultural investment of the female body with deep secrets tended toward reduction of the female body to its womb. Renaissance medical opinion did not still regard the womb as an animal that wandered about the body, yet defined it as the seat of female unpredictability that warranted its own field of study, hysteriology. The womb not only enjoyed widespread celebrity in blazons that carved up women's body. Sawday (1995, p 206) goes so far as to argue that the wombs 'were precisely the topoi of the blazon', the endpoint in the dismemberment of the female body. *The Witch of Edmonton* playwrights illustrate that the womb epitomizes the female body when Cuddy suits up for the Morris dance. He jauntily exhorts the dancers: 'Let the hobby horse provide a strong back. He shall not want a belly when I am in 'em' (II.i.84-5). Although 'belly' can be a gender-neutral term, it also denotes specifically the female womb. As Sawday (1995, p 198) notes, Renaissance male writers referred to the female 'stomach' as a metonymy for women's enviable generative capability. Cuddy reveals that the 'belly' qualifies bodies as female. Although he refers to the Hobby Horse with male pronouns, Cuddy also expressly notes it is the only 'woman's part' (III.i.9) in the Morris except Maid Marian. The gross externalization of the Hobby Horse's womb draws attention to Maid Marian's presumed bodily integrity, and by extension, her religious analogue whose virginal womb was focus for religious devotion.

Demonic Possession is a Drag

Cuddy's theatricalized animation of a female sex organ calls to mind Renaissance carnivalization of the female body, particularly its lower half. Paster (1993, p 20) tracts the early modern English conception of women's bodies as 'leaky vessels' that were both verbally and physically incontinent. Enshrinement of the female body as an avatar for scientific investigation invokes a variation on this biological paradigm, one that classifies the female body as essentially vulnerable, 'open' to penetration. Cuddy's costuming introduces a series of episodes in which the female body is penetrated in a theatricalized context. These other penetrations tellingly address medical dissection through demonic possession, itself described in demonological treatises as a physical invasion of the body. The playwrights' conflation of demonic and anatomical discourses not only demonizes anatomical penetration of the body, but also speaks to the medical basis for the 'discovery' that exposed the witch's congress with the devil.

When the townspeople try to force Frank's confession with display of Susan's body, dissection of this 'carcass' (III.iii.99) is not discussed. Yet, the very next scene depicts an instance of demonic invasion characterized in medical terms. Sawgut, a Morris dance performer whose very name suggests dissection, asks of his mute fiddle 'not a word in thy guts? I think, children, my instrument has caught cold on the sudden… I'll lay mine ear to my instrument that my poor fiddle is bewitched' (III.iv.37-8, 43-4). Sawgut fears that the 'devil [that] has been abroad amongst us today' (III.iv.69-70), provoked Susan's murder and has also jinxed the Morris dance. He locates the fiddle's inability to play in its 'guts', a pun that evokes both the instrument's catgut strings as well as the body's insides. Sawgut's lament for his fiddle, rendered silent by the devil, draws attention to Susan's dead body, which Mr. Carter identifies as a mute performer when first he sees it: 'she's none of mine./ Bob me off with a dumb-show? No, I'll have life.' (III.iii.101). The fiddle substitutes for Susan's body, the real object vulnerable to demonic invasion and conceivably dissection. Susan's body will indeed be penetrated, not by dissection, but by Satan when he reanimates her body to torture Frank (IVii).

In Sawgut's penetrated fiddle, demonic and medical invasion elide as they do when Anne Radcliffe confronts her tormentor, Elizabeth Sawyer. In the scene following the fiddle's bewitchment, Anne, eulogized as 'witch[ed] unto death' in the trial transcript, lunges for Sawyer on stage. Anne couches her threats to Sawyer in anatomical terms: 'I prithee let me scratch thy face, for thy pen has flayed off a great many men's skins' (IV.i.184-5). She depicts Sawyer wielding the dissector's flaying pen, and thus reverses the paradigm operative in the trial in which Sawyer was the object of autopsy. This affiliation of the witch with dissection invokes the medicalized witch trials and also demonizes anatomical flaying of the body. This anatomical flaying would have included the face that, as Park (1994, p 21) argues, undoubtedly added a frightening dimension to dissection for its effacement of the person's recognizability. Sawyer co-opts anatomical discourse in her promise to 'tear to pieces' her enemies, a punishment with which the devil and the jury have threatened her. The devil conventionally makes this threat; yet, in the context of this play, demonic possession is a trope for anatomical invasion. The disaggregation of the body is also an eerie harbinger of what may have happened to Sawyer, the post-mortem 'punishment' that continued on the dissecting table where medical and legal procedures combined. Through Anne's demonic invasion, the playwrights even suggest that bodies are encoded with the proclivity for their own dissection. Possessed by the devil, Anne mourns her body's disintegration: 'O, my ribs are made of a paned hose and they break....Welcome, devil! Hands, hands! Hold hands and dance around, around, around' (IV.i.190, 193-4). The playwrights anatomize Anne's body through the 'paned hose'; this article of costume that will 'break' calls to mind how the ribs were cracked open in dissection to permit inspection of the body's insides.

The playwrights introduce medical dissection through demonic invasion to exaggerate the body's suitability for dissection. In demonic possession, an invisible agent can render the 'open' body 'opened'; thus, all bodies verge toward anatomical objects. Tom boasts of such physically invasive yet surreptitious entrance in his final meeting with Cuddy: 'I'll stretch myself/ And draw this bulk small as a silver wire,/ Enter at the least pore tobacco fume/ Can make a breach for' (V.i.187-90). Tom describes himself as a metal instrument entering the body, an image that evokes dissection. Yet, what makes this vision so disturbing is that he can penetrate a body unawares. The devil's invasion of a body-as-costume, a recurring motif in the play's last two acts, conveys the body's vulnerability tends toward susceptibility to penetration. When Elizabeth Sawyer criticizes the justice system that overlooks the nefarious activities of the wealthy and persecutes poor women as witches, she characterizes this class difference via the costumes the devil chooses to inhabit. If poor people are the 'coarse witches', the rich are 'the fine,/Spun for the devil's own wearing' (IV.i.122-6). Although their appearance belies and such sordid traffic, the rich are perhaps more given to evil. As does Sawyer, Tom argues every body is open to the devil's invasion. He warns Cuddy Banks that when he intends or does evil, '[h]e's [the devil's] within thee' (V.i.136). Tom enters the stage at the beginning of Act V with a whole new look. His change from a black to a white one grimly portends, he tells Elizabeth Sawyer, the 'winding sheet' in which her dead body will be wrapped (V.i.36). In the Goodcole trial transcript, the dog appeared white when Elizabeth Sawyer was praying. *The Witch of Edmonton* playwrights intend for the white "costume" to pique the audience's interest in what becomes of Sawyer's dead body.

Tom's final exchange with Cuddy subtextually reveals the fate of her corpse. Curious about Tom's physical change, Cuddy inquires, 'I do not then wonder at the change of your garments, if you can enter into the shapes of women, too' (V.i.114-5), and probes further, 'where do you borrow those bodies that are none of your own? The garment-shape you may hire at a broker's' (V.i.122-4). Cuddy uncovers the devil's preference for female corpses. In a long soliloquy, Tom details his penetration of dead female bodies: 'The old cadaver of some self-strangled wretch/ We sometimes borrow, and appear human./ The carcass of some disease-slain strumpet/ We varnish fresh and wear as her first beauty' (V.i.139-43). The devil's insidious penetration of these helpless "costumes" exposes the body's post-mortem vulnerability. Dissectors were able to bridge the hallowed gap between interior and exterior quite easily when they came to possess the dead body. More accurately, this female corpse-as-costume trope lays bare the false distinction between "natural" bodies (blank slates) and "cultural" bodies (inscribed with cultural meaning). The playwrights expose that the anatomical gaze presumes a "natural" demarcation between the body's inside and outside; yet, this barrier, like a costume, is artificial. As were the female sex organs' "secrecy," the body's epistemological resistance was not natural, but naturalized. What the devil's costuming reveals is that human bodies are in fact man-made, products of an episteme that naturalizes the body's resistance to invasion in order to legitimize the cultural impetus for investigation.

Conclusion

This paper began as an inquiry into the admission of the witch's teat as evidence in early modern English witch trials. Other criticism on the teat, such Willis' and Paster's studies, had focused on early modern gynaecology to explain medically sanctioned animus toward the maternal body. While I might have situated the teat in this more immediate medical context, I could not ignore the playwrights' sustained attention to dissections, encoded so trenchantly in the trope of demonic invasion; these I regarded as part of a necessary framework for understanding ways of knowing predicated on the human body. Medical images in *The Witch of Edmonton* always arise in the context of theatricality, a trend for which I accounted from a defensive standpoint: theatre can address empirical ways of knowing despite the limits of display, and in fact, invoke these limits to expose the blind spots and failings of medical knowledge. More provocatively, what the playwrights disclose is the suitability of theatrical display to address empirical sciences. I invoke again the definition of the word 'autopsy' to characterize the playwrights' enterprise. Theatre was discredited for as nothing but externalised display; yet, the play calls attention to the medical impetus to externalise and deliver for an audience. The anatomical stage legitimises its spectacle, empiricizes display as ocular evidence, by appealing to the truth it has posited within the body.

References

Adelman, J., 1992, *Suffocating Mothers: Fantasies of Maternal Origin in Shakespeare's Plays*, Routledge, New York and London

Dekker, T., Ford, J., and Rowley, W., 1980 [1621], *The Witch of Edmonton: a Critical Edition*, ed. Etta Soiref Onat, Garland Publishers, New York and London

Goodcole, H., 1621, *The Wonderful Discoverie of Elizabeth Sawyer, late of Edmonton, her conviction and condemnation and death*, London

Goodcole, H., 1635, *Heavens Speedie Hue and Cry Sent after Lust and Murder*, London

Haining, P. (ed.), 1974, *The Witchcraft Papers: Contemporary Records of the Witchcraft Hysteria in Essex, 1560-1700*, Robert Hale, London

Heywood, T. and Brome, R., 1979 [1634], *An Edition of The Late Lancashire Witches by Thomas Heywood and Richard Brome*, ed. Laird H. Barber, Garland Publishing, New York and London

Maclean, I., 1980, *The Renaissance Notion of Woman*, Cambridge University Press, Cambridge

Maus, K. E., 1995, *Inwardness and Theater in the English Renaissance*, University of Chicago Press, Chicago

Paré, A. 1982, *On Monsters and Marvels*, trans. and intro by Janis L. Pallister, University of Chicago Press, Chicago

Park, K. 2000, 'Dissecting the Female Body: From *Women's Secrets* to the Secrets of Nature,' in J. Donawerth and A. Seeff (eds.), *Crossing Boundaries: Attending to Early Modern Women*, University of Delaware Press, Newark, Delaware, 29-47

1994,'The Criminal and Saintly Body: Autopsy and Dissection in Renaissance Italy', *Renaissance Quarterly*, 47, (1), 1-33

Paster, G. K., 1993, *The Body Embarrassed,* Cornell University Press, Ithaca

Purkiss, D., 1995, *The Witch in Histor,* Routledge, New York and London

Sawday, J., 1995, *The Body Emblazoned: Dissection and the human body in Renaissance Culture*, Routledge, London and New York

Schoenfeldt, M., 1997, 'Fables of the Belly in Early Modern England', in D. Hillman and C. Mazzio (eds.), *The Body in Parts: Fantasies of Corporeality in Early Modern Europe,* Routledge, New York and London, 243-61

Schwarz, K. 1997, 'Missing the Breast', in D. Hillman and C. Mazzio (eds.), *The Body in Parts: Fantasies of Corporeality in Early Modern Europe,* Routledge, New York and London, 147-69.

Shakespeare, W., 2004 [1605], *Macbeth*, Cambridge University Press, Cambridge and New York

Willis, D., 1995, *Malevolent Nurture*, Cornell University Press, Ithaca, NY.

Wilson, L., 1997, 'William Harvey's *Prelectiones*: the Performance of the Body in the Renaissance Theatre of Anatomy', *Representations*, 17, (1), 62-95

The Re-enchantment of the Medical: *an* examination of magical elements in healing.

Penny Lowery

Introduction

In 1971, Sir Keith Thomas's monumental work *Religion and the Decline of Magic* documented the 'disenchantment' of popular belief systems that accompanied and followed the Reformation in early modern England. Over the three decades since, however, historians and cultural critics have begun to question this assumed loss of the magical and occult, reconfiguring it rather as a displacement or change in status of many of the superstitions that Roman Catholicism supported. Alex Walsham, for example, in *Providence in Early Modern England* (1999), examines what she calls 'the intrusion of the supernatural in the secular sphere', arguing that Protestantism, rather than being wholeheartedly resisted, 'gradually implanted itself in the hearts and minds of the Elizabethan and early Stuart populace' (p 3). It did so, she suggests, by incorporating and reclassifying – rather than, as was first thought, eliminating – the magical and mystical elements of the receding practice of Catholicism, so that 'monstrous' births and other miraculous happening became, in post-Reformation ideology, part of 'providence' – the finger of God at work to punish or admonish the sinful.

The putative 'rationalisation' of the English world view at that time, then, was not so complete as once imagined; post-Reformation 'disenchantment' was, it seems, not a disenchantment at all but more accurately a rehabilitation of witchcraft, astrology, and the miraculous and magical in general. Walsham suggests that the rationalist imperatives of the eighteenth century were not necessarily, after all, an organic progression from the Reformation, which thus loses its status as 'a kind of halfway house on the road to "the age of reason"' (1999, p 334). Indeed, the Enlightenment itself has undergone systematic re-evaluation in recent years. It is evident that most systems of learning underwent a change in status during the eighteenth century, which tended to lend the respectability of 'objectivity' to sites of knowledge which were once the province of the occult: chemistry disowned its origins in alchemy, astrology was supplanted by astronomy, and medicine, devoid of its humours, potions, chants and spells, became 'science'. However, Terry Castle and others have suggested that 'the Uncanny', Freud's term for the mysterious and intuitive in the collective imaginary, was rather, during the so-called 'age of reason', temporarily driven into the 'cultural unconscious' (Castle, 1995, p 6), to emerge in literary forms such as fairytales and ghost stories, the sentimental and the Gothic novel, which enjoyed an unprecedented surge in popularity at that time.

Something similar, I shall argue, has taken place in contemporary times; that is to say, rationalist imperatives are at work, but their effect is not complete, tending to displace and reclassify much that is intuitive, uncanny or metaphysical rather than eliminate it. Medical discourses and practices, the subject of my enquiry, seem to have undergone a certain disenchantment during the latter third of the twentieth century (though arguably this process began much earlier); during this period, while medicine claimed to become more scientific, magical and marginal forms of healing were separated off from hegemonic medical discourse, but still retained a certain power and following. The scientific rationale of contemporary medicine, I will argue, both tolerates and supports a cultural underbelly of what Julia Kristeva has called the 'in-between, the ambiguous, the composite' (1982, p 4). In this paper I question what has happened to the human desire for the magical in medicine, and suggest that, like the superstitious rituals of Catholicism during the Reformation, or the uncanny elements of literature in the Age of Reason, it has not gone away: Magical elements emerge in the present day in forms of 'alternative' medical practices which have an ascending popularity and often a longer pedigree than the 'rational', 'scientific' system which supplanted them. Furthermore, one of the forms of complementary medicine which has developed most rapidly in the west, Chinese medicine, shows a surprising number of parallels in both its theory and practice with the Galenic or Hippocratic model used in early modern times, indicating, it would seem, that if the magical is eliminated from a culture's hegemonic medical practices, it will seek and find them somewhere else. Chinese medicine and acupuncture have proved themselves eminently suitable for import, coming as they do from a culture where metaphysical and orbisconographical[1] aspects of medicine have enjoyed a greater longevity than in Europe.[2] Furthermore, the performative aspect of acupuncture cannot be ignored: a certain showmanship – or do I mean showpersonship? – accompanies its practice, and the insertion of needles under the skin – causing surprisingly little discomfort – and the resultant reduction in pain and other symptoms has an undeniably magical aspect. The technological conjuring tricks of scans, stem cell treatment and keyhole surgery may perhaps compete with that of acupuncture, but the latter remains remarkable as a low-tech example of wizardry, requiring as it does no equipment but a few filaments of stainless steel.

I intend to examine in detail the intertextuality between the manuals of Galenism and Chinese medicine (CM), and this intertextuality will show just how closely linked is the genealogy of this popular form of alternative treatment with the medical practices of our early modern English predecessors. The theory of CM is familiar to me, since I have practised acupuncture for some two decades; and it has the further advantage of being an ancient system which demonstrates clearly the aspects of energetic therapies which have been lost from medicine as currently practised in the West. In comparing it with Galenism, however, it will become clear that neither system relies upon magic as much as may first appear; both models have their own internal logic, which merely differs from the 'scientific' medicine to which we have become accustomed. They are both also, given the closeness of the interaction between practitioner and patient, inseparable from the social practices of the Symbolic order.

The instability of the human body has meant that, since the earliest recorded times, the efforts of certain human beings to heal others in various ways have formed an important part of social organisation (Buckman and Sabbagh, 1993, p 12). Roy Porter argues that in early modern times the apparently rigid hierarchy encompassing physicians, barber-surgeons, apothecaries, cunning folk and others was in reality a 'fluid and heterogeneous' system (2001, p 172); indeed it could hardly be described as a system at all. This gave rise, he suggests, to 'public unease – or at least uncertainty – at who was who, and who was meant to be doing what, within the healing business' (*Ibid.,* p 173). Surgeons were generally also barbers, and surgery – the setting of bones, amputation of limbs, lancing of venereal sores and extraction of teeth, for internal procedures were not yet possible without anaesthetic or sterilisation – was considered a manual skill. Only in 1745 did the Barber Surgeons Company of London become bifurcated into the two separate specialties of haircutting and surgery (*Ibid.*, pp 173-4). The public had a poor opinion of surgeons, who featured often in the pejorative jokes and caricatures to be found in the material culture of the age (*Ibid.*, p 175). Apothecaries underwent a change in status, from shopkeeper to practitioner, which was legalised in the early eighteenth century: in 1747 Robert Campbell wrote of them that some 'practise surgery, man-midwifery and many times officiate as Physicians, especially in the country' (quoted in Porter, 2001, p 193). Alongside medical astrologers and other miscellaneous healers, this dizzying array of practitioners must have been almost as confusing as today's range of specialists. The main difference is that now we can be fairly certain that the expert we consult holds a piece of paper issued by a medical school; and our confusion is perhaps alleviated by the fact that a general practitioner is responsible for referrals, leaving us little room for manoeuvre in choosing a consultant unless we have the means to pay for private treatment. At least in the past this choice was a free one; and arguably the increasing popularity of complementary techniques is in part due to the increase of choice they offer.

Whatever the reasons, and confusion and anxiety may well have been among them, by the nineteenth century the Age of Reason had done its work, and members of the medical profession had reached a point in their development where they could consider themselves scientists. The transition in the status of medics from mediaeval priests, herbalists, astrologers, wise women and cunning men to the specialists of today appeared to be complete, helped on its way by René Descartes, who in the early 1600s re-introduced and consolidated the Platonic notion of the mind/body split, a theoretical development that brought about 'the rise of scientific medicine [and] the fall of the patient' (Buckman and Sabbagh, 1993, p 25). The Medical Act of 1858 brought all practitioners of what is now considered orthodox medicine under one umbrella and onto one list, the Medical Register (Porter, 2001, p 254). There were a number of repercussions from this act: women were excluded from practising until the late nineteenth century, although, previous to the formalisation of training, women were active as midwives and herbalists; the mystical, magical and spiritual were largely displaced from medical practice; and with them went, in part, a certain social element, much of the human contact involved in seeking help for a troubling ailment, and the alleviation of anxiety that may accompany this social transaction. As the simple prescribing of a pill became the answer to acute infection, and x-rays and scans were required for more stubborn conditions, the need for prolonged contact between doctor and patient was removed, and a certain distance replaced it. One of the closest contacts between doctor and patient was on the operating table, where bodily boundaries were transgressed to an unprecedented degree: however, once anaesthesia was developed the patient's unconscious state removed any possible intimacy from the transaction. Was there a displacement of magic, at this point, onto the site of an inchoate medical technology that would later bring us transplant surgery, MRI scans and the genome project? In any event, from the 1930s it seems that patients became dissatisfied with doctors (Buckman and Sabbagh, 1993, p 26), and doctors became frustrated with patients, who half the time (more according to some studies) presented with some vague dis-ease that the scientific approach was powerless to rectify. This vacuum opened up the space for a range of alternative techniques during the course of the twentieth century; or, more accurately, these have always been a part of medical culture, but were pushed to the margins as scientific medical discourse gained hegemony. These alternative methods have increased in popularity as it became clear that they fulfilled certain needs that orthodox medicine failed to meet – a need, I argue, for both the magical and the social – and as people began to question the apparent omnipotence of the scientific doctor. Curiously, some of the complementary treatments have a good deal in common with the Galenic model used by physicians until the eighteenth century. Some of these have become defined as 'fringe' or 'alternative' only recently, just as, as Buckman and Sabbagh point out, for a long time in early modern Europe the two systems – the orthodox and the 'fringe' – were indistinguishable. Similarly, in China, 'in the early stages medicine and magic were indistinguishable and were practised by shamans (*wu*) who are still active… Shamans and doctors were referred to together as "*wu yi*" (shamans and doctors)' (Ho and Lisowski, 1997, . 11). Thus in both systems it is 'conventional medicine that is the recent upstart, the brash new kid on the block… the medical establishment as we now know it became established by the act of establishing itself' (Buckman and Sabbagh, 1993, pp 9, 24). In other words, the power relations of the modern medical environment emerged for reasons more political than scientific, and the knowledges used in that environment are a construct like any other.

Interestingly, at the same time as the interaction between doctor and patient lost some of what has often been called the 'healing factor', that is to say, the apparently inexplicable positive benefit brought about by close contact between practitioner and client (often dismissed in clinical trials as a 'placebo effect'), Western medicine began to develop certain magical elements which may have gone some way to compensate. Following closely on X-rays which reveal the internal bony structures of the body, Ultrasound, MRI and CAT scans found ways to show other living tissues invisible to the naked eye, and to show them both three-dimensionally and mobile; and keyhole surgery has meant that intricate manipulations of bodies may take place with minimal cutting. I have personally undergone a bone density scan, which involved lying on a couch while a large bracket emitting light passed over my body – as an experience, a little like a hybrid between going through a carwash and being photocopied – and seen the results, including a detailed image of my spine, on a computer screen minutes later. This kind of twenty-first century magic, I would argue, has in part replaced the enchantment of a more personal variety provided by orbisconographical models of medicine. As patients have become disaffected with doctors, the godlike powers of the medical profession are seen to be on the wane: providing technological wizardry to dazzle us may serve to reinstate the medic as magician, but perhaps remains somewhat lacking in the area of social contact and reassurance.

Insiders and Outsiders

The magical is provided in present day medical care, then, in two different ways: by 'alternative' methods which, despite their insistence on 'wholeness', rather attempt to reinstate the human subject as a complex being functioning on a number of levels; and by means of the more reductive magic of technological scans, a sort of radiographical panopticon. Rosalind Pollack Petchesky has commented on the surveillance of the internal aspect of female bodies that has come routinely to accompany pregnancy and birth, showing, after Foucault, that such technology constitutes a troubling aspect of power relations in obstetric medicine, or what she calls 'a kind of *panoptics of the womb*' (in Herrmann and Stewart, 1994, p 411, italics in original). It is perhaps in part to avoid the problematics of power in high-tech orthodox medicine that a good many people with health problems consult complementary practitioners; and the division between those who opt for hegemonic medical practices and those who are drawn to the complementary or marginal, in terms of practitioners as well as service users, is significant in political terms. For, as Porter suggests, the General Medical Council is most important for whom it excludes: like all systems, it knows itself and its boundaries by those it relegates to the margins. It is no accident that women in this country were excluded from medical training until 1870, (Conrad, 1995, p 235) or that in contemporary Britain women are much more likely to work as, or consult, alternative practitioners than are men.[3] In her book *Enlightened Absence,* Ruth Salvaggio (1988) suggests that the result of rationalist imperatives of the 'age of reason' was an exclusion not just of women but of 'feminine material', that is to say, human elements seen as irrational, intuitive, emotional, mystical or supernatural (Salvaggio, pp 20-21). Energetic or orbisconographical medicine, then, has come to be seen as 'irrational', the 'other' from which Cartesian medicine seeks to distance itself, at the same time as it requires this other to establish its parameters. This political necessity was even enshrined in law by means of the so-called 'Quack's Charter' of 1542, which ordered that 'at all times from henceforth it shall be lawful to every person being the King's subject having knowledge and experience of the nature of herbs roots and waters or of the operation of the same by speculation or practice… to practise use and minister in and to any outward sore, wound, swelling or disease, any herb or herbs ointments bathes poultices and emplasters, according to their cunning experience or knowledge…' (quoted in Porter, 2001, p 196). To this day, it is legal in the UK to set oneself up as a practitioner of almost anything, the only limitations being in terms of the diseases one claims to be able to cure. Thus the medical profession, surrounded by marginal elements who are safely excluded from hegemony, can be sure of knowing where its boundaries lie.

Galenism and Chinese Medicine

Galenism, despite its close resemblance to more marginal therapies of today, was the medical model which reigned supreme in Western Europe from the time of the Roman Empire until the eighteenth century, just as Chinese Medicine was hegemonic in China until recently, despite its currently marginal status in the west.[4] (Such categories are subject to a good deal of ambiguity and slippage over time and space.) Galen was a Greek physician and philosopher: born in Pergamum in Asia Minor around 130 AD, he was a prolific writer of medical and pharmacological texts, basing his theories on those of Hippocrates, that other great Greek physician who lived and worked a few centuries earlier (Temkin, 1973, pp 12-13, 103). Like Chinese medicine, Galenism embraces the principle of the microcosm and macrocosm: that is to say, the human body is seen as functioning in ways that reflect the workings of the wider universe. In Galen's system, the four elements, earth, air, water and fire, are represented in the body by the four humours, yellow bile, black bile, phlegm and air; blood is a combination of all four (*Ibid.*, p 17). Individuals show the psychological characteristic of their predominant humour: choleric, phlegmatic, sanguine and melancholy (Macdonald, 1981, p 186). In Chinese medicine the elements are five in number: metal, water, wood, fire and earth. The internal organs function in pairs: the heart and small intestine are an aspect of the fire element, the liver and gallbladder of wood, stomach and spleen of earth, kidneys and bladder of water and lungs and colon, curiously enough, of metal. There are several 'essences' which exist in the body, rather like Hippocrates' humours: they are yin and yang, qi, jing and blood (Maciocia 1989, pp 38-41). In both models, imbalance in the elements, essences and humours results in illness, either physical or emotional. The language of the Galenists has entered the English language and remained with us to the present day: we speak of people as 'bilious' or 'phlegmatic', or of 'venting one's spleen' on an object of rage. Chinese medicine also has an emotion to accompany each element: wood is associated with anger, fire with joy, metal with grief, water with fear, and so on. In the Galenic system, the more advantageous emotional states are joy, sorrow, grief and compassion, since fear, anger and envy shorten life (Katz, in Featherstone and Wernick, 1995, p 64); similarly, in Chinese medicine over-work injures the kidneys, over-thinking injures the spleen – academics beware! – and so forth. In both methods, looking carefully at the patient is of prior importance, for persons with imbalances in a particular element will magically manifest the related colour on the face: red, white, green, yellow or blue, depending on the humour or essence that is out of kiltre. Hence close physical examination, based on the notion that, 'like the label on a bottle, bodily appearance advertise[s] contents' (Porter, 2001, p 91), is crucial to diagnosis in both systems.

Intertextualities: theory, diagnosis and treatment

Both models, then, were 'established on the basis of naturalistic and relationalistic principles, but [consider themselves] neither scientific, magical, nor superstitious' (Lee, 1974, p 219). Both are based on an orbisconographical reasoning which is quite coherent given the information available at the time. What is curious is that the two models are so similar, given their emergence from such different cultures. Both models of health and disease rely on a balance of essences or humours in the body, combined with a complex – and connected – interaction of internal organs. The Renaissance physician Vesalius asserted that '[t]he liver, workshop of sanguification... takes chylus from the stomach and the intestines and purges the black bile humor into the spleen' (quoted in Temkin, 1973, p 140). Maciocia, quoting from a Chinese classic, the 'Simple Questions', describes the digestive functions of the liver thus: 'If Liver-Qi flows smoothly, the Stomach can ripen and rot food and the Spleen can extract Food-Qi. In disease, if Liver-Qi becomes stagnant it may invade the stomach preventing the downward movement of Stomach-Qi... If it invades the Spleen, it obstructs the transformation and transportation of food and prevents Spleen-Qi from flowing upwards, resulting in diarrhoea' (1989, p 79). The language used in both texts sounds rather like a spell or incantation, a little archaic to twenty-first century ears. It is perhaps the latter statement, about Chinese medical physiology, that now sounds most bizarre; and yet this system of medicine has a growing number of followers in the west, whereas if I were to set myself up in practice as a Galenist I suspect that I would be considered rather eccentric, to say the least, and attract few, if any, paying customers. The language of modern medicine, on the other hand, is another kind of construct and mystifies in another way, with Latinates and technological terms designed to exclude service users from understanding the workings of their bodies.

Both models consider that the qualities of heat and cold, dryness and dampness affect well being. Galen suggested that temperaments were determined by the precise combination of these qualities, often coupled, as in hot and moist, hot and dry, and so on (Temkin, 1973, p 19). Compare this with the Chinese medical model, which sees acute illness as caused by invasion of damp-heat, wind-cold, or even on occasion wind-cold-damp; and similarly views internal disease as due to such causes as liver-yang rising, phlegm misting the heart, liver insulting the lungs, stomach yin deficiency or kidneys failing to grasp the qi. (It seems probable that the elements/essences described in acupuncture text books could have been more accurately translated as 'humours', if the word did not have such archaic overtones.)

Arguably much folk-medicine depends on phenomena observable in nature, and is based on the idea that in rural cultures the human body, so dependant on the elements for its survival, is composed of and internally influenced by those same elements. Both systems, however, amounted to rather more than folk-medicine, remaining hegemonic for an extraordinary length of time: acupuncture for at least three millennia, and Galenism for some 1600 years. Unsurprisingly, the taking of the pulse – one bodily function palpable from outside without technological intervention – is another diagnostic tool common to both models. What is more compelling evidence of their similarity is that the *quality* of the pulse was paramount in both, the precise character of the pulse being considered to reflect the state of the body's workings, or indeed of a specific organ. Writers on both systems assert that it takes years of assiduous practice to detect pulse qualities accurately. In the *Ars Medica*, Galen writes that a warm, dry heart manifests a pulse that is 'hard, big, rapid and frequent', and suggests that people with this condition have dispositions 'ready for action, courageous, quick, wild, savage, rash and impudent' (quoted in Temkin, 1973, p 103). Giovanni Maciocia lists twenty-eight pulse qualities, including rapid, empty, full, slippery, choppy, overflowing, tight, wiry, hollow, floating, hasty, knotted, scattered and hidden (1989, pp 166-171). Galen's 'hard, big, rapid and frequent' pulse probably corresponds with Maciocia's 'wiry', 'overflowing', 'rapid' and 'hasty'. Subjective as these descriptions may seem, and difficult as they are to differentiate even for practitioners of some experience, they have a coherent logic within their respective models. It was only in Renaissance Italy that Galileo, and later the physician Santorio, developed the modern practice of *timing* the pulse and suggested that this process might be diagnostically useful (Reiser, 1978, pp 96-7). (The idea was first suggested by Nicholas of Cusa in 1450, but was considered rather bizarre, and was laughed at and largely dismissed (*Ibid.*, p. 96)). Timing the pulse did not really catch on until the English physician Sir John Floyer, who was probably aware of Santorio's work, suggested it as a more objective method of pulse diagnosis. Even he was much opposed by contemporaries (*Ibid.*, p 98).

Both Chinese and Galenist models recognised the heart as the most important of the internal organs: the metaphor of the heart as king or emperor of the other organs (subjects) runs through their respective literatures. An Elizabethan surgeon, Thomas Vicary, wrote that 'he [the heart] is set in the middest of the brest seuerally by him selfe, as Lord and King of al members' (quoted in Porter, 2001, p 230). Not only is the heart considered the emperor in the Chinese medical model, but Chinese herbalism depends on a system in which the various herbs in a prescription are considered as ministers, chancellors and messengers, both constructs reflecting the ruling hierarchies of the cultures which produced them. Perhaps more remarkable is that the condition of 'possession', the invasion of the human organism by demons, occurs in both Chinese medicine and in the medical lore of early modern England. Even taking into account the problem of translation, which sometimes makes similarities appear where there are none because of the difficulty of finding a corresponding concept in another language, when we consider that these two models sprang from quite different theological environments, the parallels are compelling. In early modern England, 'the assault of devils might either be external... or from inside the patient's body' (Thomas, 1971, p 570). The notions of 'internal' and 'external' possession are also quite clear in writings currently used for the teaching of Chinese medicine in the UK, with two different combinations of seven acupuncture points recommended to 'unleash the seven dragons upon the seven demons' (Worsley, 1982, p 287). (Dragons are a force for good in the mythology of China, in contrast to that of Western Europe where they are most often evil creatures to be slain by the virtuous. Seven, however, seems to be a magical number in the numerology of both cultures.) When being taught the methodology of this treatment in the early 1980s, we fledgling acupuncturists were told to leave the window of the room open, so that the evil spirit could escape (and presumably not choose us as its next residence, but instead a hapless passer-by!) This instruction is perhaps not so bizarre when we consider that Pentecostal churches are to this day offering 'deliverance' – a reclassification, it seems, of exorcism – to those afflicted with incurable pain and other ills, including children. This can be somewhat dangerous, unlike the relatively harmless, if bizarre, view of 'possession' in Chinese medicine. Joanna Service, author of the documentary *The Possessed*, witnessed a serious exacerbation in the condition of her own father through this procedure: he had a degenerative disease of the spine, but was nevertheless instructed by the pastor/exorcist to get up and walk after his 'deliverance', which, predictably, did him no good at all. Service's investigations reveal people 'crying, vomiting, spitting and screaming… it's very upsetting to watch'. The reliance on this process was also tragic in the case of Victoria Climbié, where an inexperienced pastor intent on exorcising her 'demons', failed to realise that she was actually being abused (Service, *The Possessed*, Channel 4, 10.05.02) The Christian and the Buddhist models of possession, however, are similar insofar as the embodied human subject is seen as a site for the enactment of a struggle between the forces of good and evil.

Similarities occur between acupuncture and Galenism not only in their diagnostic theories but also in treatment. The use of herbs is an obvious link, but it is also found in every folk-medicine in the world. For systems which developed without the benefit of microscopes or a complete understanding of immunology or physiology – for example, dissection was taboo in China until recently – it is to be expected that their 'therapeutic rationale lay in expelling toxic substances from the body' (Porter, 2001, 21). For the Galenists this meant 'purging, sweating, vomiting and the ritual of bloodletting... aiming thereby to restore 'balance' and fortify the constitution' (*Ibid.*, p 21). It will come as no surprise that Chinese medicine shows a similar preoccupation with the expulsion of wind, damp, heat and other undesirables. Special needles are manufactured for the deliberate bleeding of points in some conditions; I was taught that acute back sprain can be relieved by bleeding the congested blood vessels at the back of the patient's knee (JCM seminars, London, 1986). The accidental loss of a little blood after needling (which is relatively unusual) is sometimes thought to clear heat, or inflammation, from the body. This blood loss is of course not on the same scale as venesection; however, the principle of treating disease by the expulsion of toxins from the body is widespread in systems such as naturopathy, which uses skin-brushing, diet and enemas as well as urine therapy to achieve detoxification (Keel, 2002).

The judicious application of heat is seen as beneficial in both Chinese and Galenist models. 'The use of cautery for complexional disorders... was predicated on the notion that [it] could be used to direct good or bad humors to different parts of the body' (Siraisi, 1990, p 129). The practice of 'scarring moxibustion' – burning a herb on the skin until it blisters – has been part of Chinese medicine for centuries, but has never, to my knowledge, been recommended in this country, much less on litigious American clients. Moxibustion is still common, but the herb is removed as soon as the patient feels the heat, or otherwise is placed in a clump on the end of a needle. Cupping is also a feature in both models: the acupuncturist creates a vacuum in a glass cup by the burning of cotton wool dipped in surgical spirit or a similar inflammatory substance, and the cup is immediately placed on the skin, to which it adheres, sucking a small mound of flesh into the vessel if the vacuum is strong enough (Maciocia, 1989, p 294). This is said to expel a virus (wind-heat) before it can develop, and can also relieve pain and congestion, and the procedure must be common to a number of folk-medicines: a patient once told me that 'cupping' is still commonly practised in her homeland, Barbados. She was delighted when I performed the technique to help her backache.

This practice must also have been carried out in early modern England: woodcuts bear witness to the method, sometimes described as 'potential' cautery (Siraisi, 1990, p 129) – that is to say, the cups were warm but not hot enough to burn. This, of all the processes I have described, appears the most magical, rather like the experiment I remember from physics lessons, where a vacuum is formed in a milk bottle by burning off all the oxygen therein, and as a result a hard boiled egg (minus its shell) can be sucked dramatically into the bottle. There is also a ritualistic element to these processes, comparable to the rituals to be found in modern medicine-as-science, where patients and doctors are often required to wear special clothing (surgical greens, gloves and masks, gowns to facilitate examination) and undergo 'purging' rituals – signified by the 'nil by mouth' sign above the bed before surgery – to prepare for undergoing certain procedures.

Afterword

The parallels which indicate the continuity of orbisconographical medicine are myriad, and cross the boundaries of cultures and epochs.

Naturopaths still tell their patients that the equinoxes are the most propitious times for detoxification (Keel, 2002), and medical astrology can predict what we will die of and when we are most likely to conceive. I have even discovered a website which claims that 'paper' homoeopathy – the writing of the name of a remedy on a scrap of paper which is carried in a pocket on the left side of the body, often thought by healers to be the side that is most readily absorbent of energy – is as effective as the physical variety, if not more so (Naumann, 1998, pp 1-40). This practice does not seem far removed from the early modern Catholic habit of wearing a piece of paper 'inscribed with verses from the gospels or with the sign of the cross' (Thomas, 1971, p33); both signify a belief in the magical power of objects. In *The Alchemist,* Subtle's recommendations for the layout of Drugger's shop (Jonson, 1983, p 27) are an irresistible reminder of Feng Shui, the art of organising ones environment most propitiously. Chinese herbalism, or, more accurately, 'Chinese Medicinal Substances', once contained prescriptions including a length of rope that had been used to hang someone (JCM Seminars, London, 1987); similarly, Roy Porter reports an old English custom of causing a goitre or other deformity to be touched by the hand of a person just hanged, in the belief that it – the goitre, not the hand – would be cured (2001, p 61). In these cases, the correlation with magical objects, charms, and incantations is self-evident; and the belief that words or objects either hold intrinsic power or power conveyed to them by magic has not died out. Reformation attempts to divest such objects – whether sacramentals or superstitions – of their power merely resulted in displacement and reclassification, a shifting of cultural anxieties from one area to another, and arguably this process continues today, as, for example, the substitution of 'deliverance' for 'exorcism' to deal with cases of 'possession'. To place one's faith in the power of magical ritual, words or objects is not bizarre or irrational to those who do so. Perhaps, then, though we may laugh at our early modern forebears for carrying fragments of communion wafer in their pockets for good luck, it is not so bizarre that many twentieth-century subjects are suspicious of the technological 'magic' of orthodox medicine, and have turned to gentler and more relational methods of healing as offering a dimension missing from their contemporary counterpart. Indeed, it seems likely that the aggressive and interventionist medical practices of today will seem risible a few centuries hence, just as later physicians, seduced by 'science', condemned the teachings of Galen, the orthodox medicine of its day, as a 'heathnish Physicke' (Temkin, 1973, p 167). Buckner and Sabbagh, in discussing the assiduous blood-letting applied to a certain English monarch, suggest that 'some of the heroic interventions being made by modern medicine (keeping alive 800-gram neonates, mega-doses of chemotherapy with autologous bone-marrow transplants for drug-resistant common cancers and so on) might one day appear as barbaric as what happened to King Charles' (p 23). Or, as Keith Thomas muses, 'how are we to classify the status of 'scientific' remedies, in which we place faith, but which are subsequently exposed as useless? This was the fate of Galenic medicine... but it will also be that of much of the medicine of today' (1971, p 799). Research indicates that by the end of the twentieth century some 30% of patients in hospital were there for the treatment of iatrogenic diseases, that is to say, those caused by medical intervention. The website of a respected journal, *What Doctors Don't Tell You,* asserts that 'The drugs industry is the most profitable in the world. It is probably also the only industry in the world that kills so many of its customers. Around 107,000 Americans and 40,000 Britons die every year from a drug reaction, and these figures are based on gross under-reporting' (WDDTY, 2004). The statistics given, I would also point out, do not include deaths as a result of surgery. Whether current medical practices are actually any more effective than Galenism is impossible to speculate, a set of unknowable statistics beyond the grasp of epistemology; I suspect that there is little to choose between them. What is certain is the dependence of both constructs on ritual, and this may be another site of medicine to which the missing magical element of older, more traditional methods has been displaced. Clinician Wendy Rogers, writing of the treatment of menopausal women, comments that '[d]efining menopause as an estrogen-deficiency disease with extensive symptomatology and serious long-term sequelae requiring treatment is a very powerful ritual, the obverse side of which is necessarily abject' (in Komesaroff, 1997, p 235). Rituals to cast out the abject or unwanted in humanity – ageing, loss of fertility, the female subject as no longer sexually attractive or docilely reproductive – which Rogers argues have been instated in order to control the bodies through normalising techniques, seem to me to have certain parallels in the casting out of wind, damp, phlegm, bile or demons, or indeed the ancient custom of excluding women from church after childbirth for a number of weeks.

If we examine the further hierarchy between body and mind, the body itself becomes seen as abject, or at least inferior. Fiona Mackie suggests that the separation of mind and body in the thinking of individuals begins early:

'From the moment of birth, a child of modernity imbibes an externalized form of knowledge and control deemed objective and associated with "mind". Thus begins the long progression in which "mind" becomes detached from "body" and installed as emperor over all that lies below the neck... "Body", deemed part of "nature", is thus relatively put out of play' (in Komesaroff, 1997, p 17). The inextricable character of the relationship between mind and body was an important feature of Galenism which the dualistic model of Cartesian thinking attempted to displace. The medicine of early modern times was more holistic than is generally realised: mental strain could affect the humours and cause physical ills, but conversely melancholy and other emotional illness might have a physical aetiology (Macdonald, 1981, p 186). Porter describes the medicine of the Galenists as 'rhetorical and performative... an art (or mystery) transcending the narrow confines of a science or technique' (2001, p 25). In describing one of the advantages of orbisconographical medical constructs Porter has also identified one of the problems of scientific medicine: alongside a vast widening of learning has somehow come a narrowing of knowledges and practices. In mediaeval and early modern times, the boundaries between science and religion as well as between medicine and the mystical were more porous. The endeavours of medical orthodoxy to render these boundaries watertight has not been entirely successful; its effect has largely been to displace the magical and the social, which are so important to healing interactions, to other parts of medical culture. To some extent the magical and the mysterious are now embodied in the technologies of scans, x-rays and advanced surgery; for those mistrustful of technology, enchantment in medicine is to be found in alternative treatments. Wherever this aspect of medicine has been displaced to, the binary thinking and scientific 'advances' of recent centuries have reconfigured medical discourse in a particular way: 'western medicine over its history has gradually separated itself from spiritual matters' (Douglas quoted by Porter, 2001, p 31). The result has been that the need for the spiritual in healing has been met elsewhere, by practitioners who are outside the hallowed realms of orthodoxy. These practitioners, however, like the witches of the past, have not entirely ceased to be persecuted: lay acupuncturists in France (i.e. those without a medical training) are still liable to imprisonment,[5] and the Sangoma of South Africa, practitioners of folk medicine and other occult methods, lead a dangerous existence on the margins of that culture (Binsbergen, 2002).

Of course, not all aspects of the continuity of 'spiritual matters' are positive: one that is somewhat troubling is the propensity for blaming the patient for his or her misfortunes, an extension of the emphasis on self-help found in both past and present systems (Conrad, 1995, p 181). Their belief in Providence, the notion that everything was sent by God, encouraged those of earlier ages to see illness, including madness, as divine punishment for sins committed, or else as the result of bewitching. The first encouraged an exaggerated sense of personal responsibility, and the latter a complete lack of it. (In either case, the magical powers of the priest or magician might yield some relief). For the human psyche, both attitudes seem preferable to the randomness that actually seems to determine who gets ill and who stays healthy. The power of the imagination has been acknowledged for centuries: sometimes, however, this idea has often been used to apportion guilt where there is none. One example is the attribution of foetal abnormalities to the power of the mother's imagination (Wilson, 1993, p 69). The tendency to blame the victim is an unfortunate component of New Age thinking: the ideas of radical surgeon/guru Bernie Siegel, whose book *Love, Medicine and Miracles* (1988) suggests that cancer can be overcome by those who really want to survive, now pervade popular thinking about cancer to the point where people who struggle in vain against the disease feel they must be doing something wrong (Buckman and Sabbagh, 1993, p 239). This is unhelpful, for surely feeling guilty never made anyone get better; yet the body is a semiotic site, and failure of the body is seen as personal failure, for 'the flesh is eloquence itself' (Porter, 2001, p 35). The English word for an ailing body, 'invalid' also means, with a slight shift of emphasis, 'without legal force' or 'out of date'.

On a more positive note, the 1990s saw some tentative moves towards a destabilisation of the binary between orthodox and complementary medical practices. Jackie Stacey comments on the emergence of partnerships between the NHS and the (hitherto exclusively private) sector of alternative medicine: she cites the existence of the Homoeopathic Hospital in London, and some referral systems whereby cancer patients have access to massage or art therapy. To this I would add the trial of a scheme sponsored by Lewisham Hospital in south east London during the nineties, which offered acupuncture, osteopathy and homoeopathy free of charge to patients referred by their GP. The demand was overwhelming, and funding soon ran out. The ambiguity of modern medicine, which promises miracles but does not always deliver, and people's ambivalence to it, explains in part the success of alternative practices, despite their outsider status and the fact that clients must generally pay for them, in the UK over and above the contribution already made to state health care. Stacey also points out the advantages of complementary medicine in terms of power relations between practitioner and client, for in this system '[p]atients are customers and, in paying for this service, expect quite different treatment from practitioners than from the usual medical staff... Indeed, practitioners are dependant on clients for their income... Thus, there are financial, as well as moral or medical, motivations for treating patients with respect in this mutually beneficial exchange' (1997, p 214). She goes on to identify the aspects of alternative treatments that clients value: patients are 'typically encouraged to participate actively in their recovery'; they also have 'more time with the practitioner, a more caring approach to healing, a sense of understanding the treatment process and a feeling of being involved in the healing' (*Ibid.*, p 215). It is to be hoped that the culture of 'treating patients with respect' will seep into orthodox medical practices, and that, if this osmosis between the two systems continues, each will derive some benefit from the association. Stacey does not mention the appeal of 'magical' or intuitive elements in complementary medicine: such aspects are rarely emphasised, for 'fringe' medicine tends to aspire to the respectability of the scientific.

However, the human desire for magic and the mystical in matters of health care manifests across both historical and geographical divisions. Keith Thomas suggests that '[i]f magic is to be defined as the employment of ineffective techniques to allay anxiety when effective ones are not available, then we must recognise that no society will ever be free from it' (1971, p 800). I would suggest, rather, that, because of the very complexity of the human organism, what may at first glance seem like magic may well not be 'ineffective' at all, but actually have a positive effect on health. Rationalist imperatives have sought, at various times and in various guises, to eliminate the magical, in religion, in literature, and in medical discourses. In the late twentieth and early twenty-first centuries, as much as at any other time, a 'disenchantment' like those described by Thomas, Walsham and Castle has taken place, but in response to it – or, perhaps more accurately, concurrently with it – we have also experienced a re-enchantment of culture both medical and literary; the extraordinary popularity of the Harry Potter books bears witness to the latter. Looking back to early modern times, Keith Thomas asserts that 'the evidence of the sixteenth and seventeenth centuries suggests that the common people never formulated a distinction between magic and medicine' (1971, p 800). Later medical historians added: 'The true pre-history of medicine is magic' (Buckman and Sabbagh, 1993, p 10). I would argue that, although the distinction between the two has become clearer, magic remains today as an aspect of most medicine, morphed into either the alternative or the technological. Furthermore – and I suggest that the two aspects are almost impossible to disentangle – the social aspect of healing, the role we take on when we ask another human being for help, and the relationship built upon that transaction, are all as important as the spell the cunning person incants, the point where the needle is inserted, or the choice of antibiotic or surgical tool. Theo Brown comments: 'However sensible and obvious the cult of science appears on the intellectual level, there is awareness in man [sic] of belonging to the other world which revolts against such a closed system of existence. Hence, in our scientific age, we have a boom in science fiction and the occult, expressing the popular fantasies of the masses, which appear frivolous to 'serious' people' (1979, p 91).

I suggest that we are all part of 'the masses', and that, however 'serious' we may be, the need for mysticism and human contact in the healing arts is as strong as ever. Not finding these in the clinical domain of orthodox medicine, or finding them only in unacceptable, hi-tech forms, we have constructed forms of 'alternative' medicine, or imported them from other cultures, in which these features are central. Chinese medicine is a robust system, which has survived the transition to the west with some success. The reasons for this are several: it involves regular contact between practitioner and client; it is often very effective; and it incorporates a generous measure of the mystical in its practice and beliefs. Indeed, it is in part the intervention with the body's energy systems by means of the insertion of needles that lends the practice and performance of acupuncture its magical quality, and which often prompts the question 'how does it work?'; and any attempts to explain the results by means of endorphin theory or the function of synapses only serves to undermine the magical and performative character of the technique. The social and relational should not be underestimated in this regard: acupuncture therapy, as with most alternative methods, requires weekly consultations and treatments, and not just for the five minutes allowed by a GP but for anything up to an hour, thus fulfilling the need for human contact. The displacement of the magical from conventional medical practices means that magic needs to find a new site: acupuncture and other complementary or energetic systems offer themselves readily to fill this vacuum. Furthermore, an awareness is growing that the powerful drugs and invasive surgery of orthodox medicine as practised in western cultures can do harm; we are learning to question the assumption that 'earlier generations [of doctors] had faulty access to truth and that ours is far superior' (Sybylla, 1997, in Komesaroff, p 203). Perhaps, however, there is another reason why so many people of this culture have embraced it so readily: the remarkable resemblance it bears to the medical practices of our forebears. In opting for acupuncture or Chinese medicine as their primary form of health care, a growing number of people are reclaiming the orbisconographical, and thus reconfiguring medicine as magic once more.

Notes

1. 'Orbisconography' is a translation of the Chinese term *tsang-hsiang*, which is difficult to render in English. It means an imagistic view of the internal workings of the body (Porkert, 1974, pp 67-8).

2. Western orthodox medicine is now also available in China; patients attending a hospital have a choice as to whether to consult a western or traditional doctor. We would do well to imitate this system in the west.

3. Information from the Foundation for Integrated Medicine, UK.

4. I have not included a comprehensive history of Chinese medicine here: for those interested, there is an excellent overview at http://healthy.net/asp/templates/article

5. In France acupuncture is considered an unlawful activity, and those who wish to train in this specialty must look elsewhere for courses. This information has been confirmed by Roger Hill of the Department of Complementary Health Studies, Exeter University. I was unable to gather any further intelligence from the French embassy in London or the British embassy in Paris.

References

Bennett, Gillian, 1986, 'Ghost and Witch in the Sixteenth and Seventeenth Centuries', *Folklore*, 97

Brown, Theo, 1979, *The Fate of the Dead*. D.S. Brewer Ltd., Ipswich and Cambridge

Buckman, Dr. Robert, and Sabbagh, Karl, 1993, *Magic or Medicine? An Investigation into Healing*, Macmillan, London

Bynum, W. F. and Porter, Roy, (Eds.), 1987, Medical *Fringe and Medical Orthodoxy 1750-1850*. Croom Helm, London, Sydney, & Wolfeboro, New Hampshire.

Castle, Terry, 1995, *The Female Thermometer: Eighteenth Century Culture and the Invention of the Uncanny,* Oxford University Press, New York & Oxford

Chellow, Ross, 2002, 'Health: Chinese Medicine, Ancient and Modern', *Connect,* April-May,12

Collins, Terah Kathryn, 1996, *The Western Guide to Feng Shui: Creating Balance, Harmony and Prosperity in Your Environment,* Hay House, Inc., Carlsbad, CA.

Conrad, Lawrence I., Neve, Michael, Nutton, Vivian, Porter, Roy, and Wear, Andrew, 1995, *The Western Medical Tradition 800 BC to AD 1800,* Cambridge University Press, Cambridge, New York and Melbourne

Ernst, Edward, (ed.), 1996, *Complementary Medicine: an objective appraisa,* Butterworth-Heinemann, Oxford, Boston, Johannesburg, Melbourne, New Delhi, Singapore.

Featherstone, Mike and Wernick, Andrew, (eds), 1995, *Images Of Aging: Cultural Representations of Later Life,* Routledge, London and New York.

French, Roger and Wear, Andrew, 1989, *The Medical Revolution of the Seventeenth Century,* Cambridge University Press, Cambridge & New York

Freud, Sigmund, 1961, Civilization *and its Discontent,* Translated by James Strachey, W. W. Norton & Co., New York & London.

Freud, Sigmund, 'The Uncanny', in Rivkin, J and Ryan, M. (eds), 2001, *Literary Theory: an anthology*, Blackwell, Malden, Massachusetts and Oxford, UK

Graham, Helen, 2001, *Soul Medicine: Restoring the Spirit to Healing,* Gill & Macmillan, Dublin

Herrmann Anne C. and Stewart, Abigail J., 1994, *Theorizing Feminism: Parallel Trends in the Humanities and Social Sciences,* Westview Press, Boulder and Oxford.

Ho, P.Y. & Lisowski, F.P., 1997, *A Brief History of Chinese Medicine,* World Scientific, Singapore, New Jersey, London, Hong Kong.

Jonson, Ben, *The Alchemist,* Edited by Douglas Brown, 1983, Ernest Benn Ltd., London

Kieckhefer, Richard, 1976, *European Witch Trials,* Routledge & Kegan Paul, London & Henley

Komesaroff, Paul, Rothfield, Philipa, and Daly, Jeanne, (eds.), 1997, Reinterpreting *Menopause: Cultural and Philosophical Issues,* Routledge, London and New York

Kristeva, Julia, 1982, *Powers Of Horror: An Essay on Abjection*, translated by Leon S. Roudiez, Columbia University Press, New York

Lee, Rance P. L., 1974, 'Interaction between Chinese and Western Medicine in HongKong: Modernization and Professional Inequality', in Kleinman, Arthur, Kunstadter, Peter, Alexander, E. Russell, and Gale, James L. (eds.), *Medicine in Chinese Cultures: Comparative Studies of Health Care in Chinese and Other Societies* Geographic Health Studies, Washington

Lindemann, Mary, 1999, *Medicine and Society in Early Modern Europe,* Cambridge University Press, Cambridge, New York & Melbourne

MacDonald, Michael, 1981, *Mystical Bedlam: Madness, Anxiety and Healing in Seventeenth-Century England,* Cambridge University Press, Cambridge, London, New York, New Rochelle, Melbourne, Sydney

Maciocia, Giovanni, 1989, *The Foundations of Chinese Medicine* Churchill Livingstone, Edinburgh, London, Melbourne & New York

Marland, Hilary and Pelling, Margaret, (eds), 1996, *The Task of Healing: Medicine, religion and gender in England and the Netherlands, 1450-1800,* Erasmus Publishing, Rotterdam

Petchesky, Rosalind Pollack, 1994, 'Fetal Images: The Power of Visual Culture' in *Theorizing Feminism: Parallel Trends in the Humanities and Social Sciences,* Herrmann, Anne C. and Stewart, Abigail J. (eds.) Westview Press, Boulder, San Francisco and Oxford

Porkert, Manfred, 1974, 'The Dilemma of Present-Day Interpretations of Chinese Medicine' in *Medicine in Chinese Cultures: Comparative Studies of Health Care in Chinese and Other Societies,* Kleinman, Arthur, Kunstadter, Peter, Alexander, E. Russell, and Gale, James L (eds.), Geographic Health Studies, Washington

Rogers, Wendy, 'Sources of Abjection in Western Responses to Menopause', in Komesaroff, Paul, Rothfield, Philipa, and Daly, Jeanne (eds.), 1997, Reinterpreting *Menopause: Cultural and Philosophical Issues,* Routledge, London and New York Porter, Roy, 2001, *Bodies Politic: Disease, Death and Doctors in Britain, 1650-1900,* Reaktion Books Ltd., London

Porter, Roy (ed.), 1985, *Patients and Practitioners: Lay perceptions of medicine in pre-industrial society,* Cambridge University Press, Cambridge & New York

Reiser, Stanley Joel, 1978, *Medicine and the Reign of Technoloy,* Cambridge University Press, Cambridge & New York

Salvaggio, Ruth, 1988, *Enlightened Absence: Neoclassical Configurations of the Feminine,* University of Illinois Press, Urbana & Chicago

Scarre, Geoffrey, 1987, *Witchcraft and Magic in 16th and 17th Century Europe,* Macmillan, Basingstoke & London

Service, Joanna, 2002, *The Possessed,* [Documentary film], Broadcast by Channel 4, UK, Friday 10-05-2002

Shanghai College of Traditional Medicine, 1981, *Acupuncture: a comprehensive text,* Translated and edited by O'Connor, John and Bensky, Dan. Eastland Press, Chicago

Sharpe, James 1996, *Instruments of Darkness,* Hamish Hamilton, London

Siegel, Bernie, 1988, *Love, Medicine and Miracles,* Harper & Row, New York

Siraisi, Nancy, 1990, *Mediaeval and Early Renaissance Medicine: an Introduction to Knowledge and Practice,* The University of Chicago Press, Chicago and London

Stacey, Jackie, 1997, *Teratologies: A cultural study of cancer,* Routledge, London and New York

Sutherland, William Garner, 1990, *Teachings in the Science of Osteopathy,* Rudra Press, London & Edinburgh

Sybylla, Roe, 1997, 'Situating Menopause within the Strategies of Power: a Genealogy', in Komesaroff, Paul, Rothfield, Philipa, and Daly, Jeanne (eds.), Reinterpreting *Menopause: Cultural and Philosophical Issues,* Routledge, London and New York

Temkin, Owsei, 1973, *Galenism: Rise and Decline of a Medical Philosophy,* Cornell University Press, Ithaca and London

Thomas, Keith, 1971, *Religion and the Decline of Magic,* Penguin, London & New York.

Walsham, Alex, 1999, *Providence in Early Modern England,* Oxford University Press, Oxford and New York

Weber, Max, 1965, *The Sociology of Religion,* Methuen, London

Wilson, Dudley, 1993, *Signs and Portents: Monstrous Births from the Middle Ages to the Enlightenment,* Routledge, London & New York

Worsley, Jack R., 1982, *Traditional Chinese Acupuncture: Volume I - Meridians and Points,* Element Books, London

Websites consulted

Binsbergen, Wim van, 30-03-2002, *The Sangoma Tradition Of Southern Africa,* http://www.come.to/sangoma

Keel, Dianna, 03-04-2002, *The work of Coach Dianna Keel – Naturopath,* http://www.coach.tc/Health_dk.htm

Naumann, Eileen, 30-04-1998, *Paper Remedy Experiments Report,* http://www.medicinegarden.com/Homeopathy/PaperRemedies.html

The History of Acupuncture in China, 12-10-2003,

http://www.healthy.net/asp/templates/article.asp?PageType+article&ID=1819#THe%20History%20of%20Acupuncture%20in%20China

The Journal of Chinese Medicine, 2-04-2002: www.jcm.co.uk/

What Doctors Don't Tell You, 19-10-2004,

http://www.wddty.co.uk/factsheet/PRESCRIPTION%20DRUGS/index.asp

Lectures

Journal of Chinese Medicine Seminars, 1986-7, London

Apparitions, Ghosts, Fairies, Demons and Wild Events: Virtuality in Early Modern Britain

Dr. Jonathan Paul Marshall

Apparitions are common throughout the world, with many local ways of classifying them, explaining them and of allocating them powers. Despite this, it seems rare for historians to show much interest in them. There are probably thousands of pages considering witchcraft for each one considering apparitions, yet the two are often linked in contemporary sources. This paper explores how apparitions were used in religion, politics, morality and philosophy in 16th and 17th Century Britain. The range of sources shows that interest permeated all parts of society.

Writings about apparitions inform us what various people think is important about their psyches and selves, about truth, error, mystery and the constitution of the world. Apparitions are made to conform to, or confirm, existent worldviews and political positions, and may be subject to dispute by different groups of people - cultures may not present a coherent view on this subject. The categories involved are not pre-existently clear, but make different linkages to suit the positions being utilised. Lack of system and variegated categories may give apparitions some of their magical and ambiguous appearance. The word 'virtual' in the title is a reminder that explanatory objects often cannot be perceived directly but are inferred or imagined, sometimes forming almost parallel worlds, and also that problems of veridicity, experience and illusion have a long history.

Apparitions in General

The term 'apparition' in this period does not only apply to ghosts, but to all strange appearances. As John Webster wrote 'the large extent of the word' includes 'the appearing of new Stars, Comets, Meteors and other Portents, and Prodigies' (1677/2004, p 302), and it is in this wider sense the term is used here.

Apparitions need not be 'phantasmal' or visual alone. The apparition, in the booklet *the most strange and wonderful apperation of blood in a poole at Garraton*, is quite clearly a concrete 'appearance' - the water of a large pool becoming red and thick and being shunned by cattle. Other apparently supernatural apparitions are also concrete, for example the 'strange Apparitions' in the pamphlet *Horrid and Strange News from Ireland*, have to enter through open doors or windows and can be punched and hit with a sword, even if they can change shape. Nor does the event have to be classified as supernatural. The apparition of a dragon in the sky, according to Gadbury was a meteorological phenomenon (1661, pp 135-8).

Reports of apparitions are not always meant to be true. Some tales are clearly satirical or told for amusement. One 17th Century satire treated as 'real' in at least two modern sources (Thompson, 1930, pp 103-4;

Haining, 1987, p 46) is the Smithfield's ghost, reported in the *Mercurius Democritus ... Communicating many strange Wonders, Out of the World in the Moon, The Antipodes, Tenebru, Fairy Land, Green-land and other adjacent countries. Published for the right understanding of the Mad-merry-People of Great-Bedlam'*. The source's title might be something of a give away. It states:

> 'There is a great report of a Ghoast that walkes every Night amongst the Butchers at Smithfield Barrs.. in the Habit of Mallet the Lawyer,[1] pulling the meat off the Butcher's Tainters; many have adventured to strike at him with Cleavers and Chopping-Knives, but cannot feel anything but Ayre, every Saturday at Night between 9 and 12 he walkes his stations… doing more mischief to the Butchers then ever Robbin Goodfellow did to the country Hindes.
>
> 'A young maid meeting his on Valentines Day in the morning in Moor-fields made him a low Cursey, bidding him Good morrow Valentine, whereupon he saluting of her eat her up alive' (Feb 8-Feb 15, 1654, p 467).

Although the satire may be obvious, the events referred to are not. Perhaps this vagueness makes it appear real?

Ambiguity is often present and we cannot assume tellers of stories of apparitions were without scepticism. John Aubrey writes: 'It is certain that there are Houses that are haunted: tho not as many as reported: for there are a great many cheates used by Tenants' (1972, p 201). Believers could hold that many reports stemmed from superstitious fear or lack of knowledge of Nature (Glanvil, 1700a, p 27; Taillepied, nd, chapters

3-7). Perhaps the most famous haunting of late 17th Century England, the Drummer of Tedworth, seems to have been widely discussed and widely disbelieved.[2] Issues of perception, deceit and validity circle around apparitions at all times. Displaying awareness of the possibility of error is one way the reporter shows they are trustworthy.

Catholic and Protestant Theory up to the Seventeenth Century

It is agreed by most scholars that the Reformation and the abolition of purgatory affected stories of apparitions. Easily the best recent account is Peter Marshall (2002). After the 12th Century, Church theory held that ghosts originated from purgatory where most souls go after death, returning to ask for help, to reduce their suffering, or to give warnings of the fate faced by others. Ghosts were usually portrayed with symbolic accoutrements displaying their sins and their punishments and could be put to rest by religious rituals (Finucane, 1982, p 65, 81ff), although there are occasional accounts of animated corpses causing havoc and resisting easy theological explanation (Caciola, 1996).

Thomas Aquinas argued that no one could leave heaven or Hell absolutely, although with the dispensation of God they could go forth for a time. The Saints could appear when they willed but not the damned, while those in purgatory may seek our prayers (1952, p 885ff). The English text *Dives et Pauper* says that ghosts are sometime sent by God "for to have help: Sometime to show that souls live after death to confirm them that be feeble in faith" (quoted in Thomas, 1973, p 79). When the ghost ascended from Purgatory, it could repay the favour by praying for those who had prayed for it. Purgatory was a world which resulted from the interaction of Religious dogma with general morality. Implicit in its conception is the idea that most of us are neither virtuous enough to attain heaven nor bad enough to deserve hell; that God and others can help us to become better, and that there must be some other place in which this can occur.

To Catholics, ghosts represented the continuity of obligations between family and friends and the community of believers stretching into the hereafter (Brown 1979, pp 15-16). Protestants placed the emphasis on individual salvation rather than on communal responsibility for each other. The fate of the dead depended on their own actions in life and unpredictable grace, not on the actions of those left behind. It is possible the idea that the living could help the dead was dropped by Luther even before the idea of Purgatory was (Linton, 2002, p 19).

Purgatory, and the selling of indulgences which reduced time in Purgatory, became a focal point of Protestant attack. Indulgences were portrayed as unfair to the poor, a waste of money, and a method by which the Church extorted wealth. Protestants also attacked contradictions in Catholic descriptions of Purgatory and its location, but to some extent this was a dangerous argument due to vagueness about the agreed locations of Heaven and Hell. This attack, Marshall argues, 'facilitated, even if it did not primarily intend, a process of "despatialising" the afterlife, of abstracting it or even internalising it' (2000, p 129). In a way this current life became Purgatory. The Church of England formally dropped the doctrine of Purgatory in 1563 (Greenblat, 2001, p 235). Under Elizabeth, the bishops and clergy 'hunted purgatory to extinction' (Marshall, 2002, p 124). Although Catholic apparitions of the Virgin and the Saints, faded with remarkable rapidity (Brown, 1979, pp 3-9), British Protestants still encountered ghosts and had to account for them, or sermonise against them (cf Marshall, 2002, pp 235, 248, 241).

Without purgatory, Protestants had to deny ghosts originated there, even when using traditional sources. Zacharie Jones felt he needed to apologise for the Catholicism of de Loiyer when translating the latter's *Treatise of Spectres* – 'Herein therefore your discretion must supply the partialitie and particularitie of his opinion' (1605/2004, p 8). Early Protestants denied ghosts were apparitions of the dead as it was theologically impossible, and thus other explanations had to be found. At one extreme, Reginald Scott denied ghosts completely, claiming apparitions arose from melancholy, timidity, imperfection of sight, drunkenness, false reports, and that:

> 'In all ages moonks and preests have abused and bewitched the world with counterfet visions; which proceeded through idlenes, and restraint of marriage, wherby they grew hot and lecherous, and therefore devised such meanes to compasse and obteine their loves… Through ignorance of late in religion, it was thought, that everie churchyard swarmed with soules and spirits: but now the word of God being more free, open, and knowne, those conceipts and illusions are made more manifest and apparent, &c…. Where are the soules that made such mone for trentals, whereby to be eased of the paines in purgatorie? Are they all gone into Italie, bicause masses are growne deere here in England?' (Scot, 1930, pp 268-9).

Other Protestants shifted the cause to demons, like Thomas Browne, who wrote:

> 'those apparitions and ghosts of departed persons are not the wandering soules of men, but the unquiet walks of Devils, prompting and suggesting us unto mischief, bloud, and villany, instilling and stealing into our hearts; that the blessed spirits are not at rest in their graves, but wander, solicitous of the affairs of the world' (1645/2002, p 81 #37).

Taillepied, a French Catholic writer of the late 15th Century, confirms the connection by writing that: 'All those writers who have drunk at the muddy and stinking waters of the Lake of Geneva incline absolutely to deny apparitions and ghosts' (nd, p 6).

The most common Protestant arguments were that ghostly apparitions arose through melancholy delusions, dreams, fear, religious ignorance,[3] the actions of demons,[4] or papist trickery. However, the interpretation of ghosts as the returning dead never completely died (cf. Marshall, 2002, pp 247-8, 251-2, 253) and was to return as shall be explained later.

Shakespeare famously mades use of these explanatory ambiguities. The ghosts in *Macbeth* are possibly hallucinations from guilt, other apparitions are conjured by witches. In *Richard III* and *Cymberine*, ghosts appear in dreams. The ghost in Hamlet clearly states that it comes from Purgatory - yet the audience is Protestant (as is probably Hamlet a student of the University of Württemberg), and perhaps with a tendency to disbelieve this statement. Horatio is sceptical but becomes convinced something strange is happening. Hamlet tests the ghost to discover if it is telling the truth, or if it is a 'goblin damn'd'. Even so, ghosts are let out of purgatory for redemption - not for revenge and the messy consequences perhaps imply the ghost was a demon after all.[5]

Apparitions in politics and morality

Apparitions might be seen as manifestations of disorder in the world.[6] John Gadbury wrote 'Prodigies are (not only the Antecedents, but the ordinary and usual) Antecedents of worldly changes' (1660, p 39), giving a forty page list of such historical prodigies, including comets, rains of blood, multiple suns, sounds of trumpets, and armies fighting in the skies. These events might be portrayed, in our terms, as both natural and supernatural. Gadbury's naturalistic explanation of eclipses, did not prevent him from proposing they could have astrological significance, and Lilly argued that although some weird sights could perhaps be explained by the natural actions of planets, they were more likely caused by angels (Lilly, 1644, p 6; 1645, pp 10-11).

People everywhere seek meaning in the progress of the cosmos and its relation to their lives, and see disruptions of what is perceived as normal as particularly meaningful. There is no inherent reason why an apparition should be meaningful. However questions of why something occurred, or questions of what will occur, imply intention and meaning, and these kind of questions seem to be the first response to apparitions. People who hold that God is omnipotent are likely to see all events as manifestations of His will. Alexandra Walsham writes that '[a]ccording to lay and clerical commentators alike, apparitions were sermons inscribed by the finger of God in the sky. They were "heralds" and "trumpeters" of His wrath and indignation' (2001, p 58). Here apparitions are subsumed under a more general theory, Providentialism, which assumed God was 'an assiduous, energetic deity who constantly intervened in human affairs... He regularly stepped in to discipline sinners and bestow blessings'. Providentialism was 'part of the mainstream, a cluster of assumptions that enjoyed near universal acceptance' (1999, p 2). Walsham suggests that early Protestantism was particularly prone to this mode of interpretation which 'stemmed in large part from their expulsion of all intermediaries between God and the individual soul' (ibid, p 5), as we have seen acting with the abolition of purgatory. Protestantism was not initially a move towards Weberian 'disenchantment of the world', but a move to seeing God's actions and messages everywhere. However, what is important here is not that apparitions can be put into a Providentialist framework, but that doing so without control of dispersion of the story, or with religious factionalism, evokes contestation of interpretation due to apparitional ambiguity - reports can be used by different groups to give cosmic backing to quite different views or indeed, to live in different 'virtual worlds'.

A booklet published after the execution of Charles I, in parallelling Charles and Jesus, is overtly political and religious arguing that:

> 'when our saviour suffered there were terrible signs and wonders over all the land. So during the time of our sovereign's martyrdom, there were strange signs seen in the sky in divers places in the kingdom... They have overthrown the order of God and Nature' (quoted in Friedman, 1993, p 35).

Supporters of the Parliament tended to argue that the prodigies were signs from God that Charles should make peace with them. Later, after the Restoration some Puritans claimed there were apparitions signifying God's indignation, while Anglicans denied the prodigies were miracles or signs from God (Friedman ,1993, p 247ff).

The most famous apparition of the early Civil War, occurred after the battle of Edge Hill where, starting in January 1643, the battle was reputedly re-enacted by ghostly armies for weeks on end. King Charles sent no less than six men to observe the sights. These gentlemen were reported as seeing among the apparitions 'divers to their appearance that were then slaine as Sir Edward Varney' (*New yeares Wonder; A great wonder in Heaven*; Thompson, 1930, pp 256-9). In this case, both pamphlets, while claiming ignorance of what is presaged, use the visions to call for general peace to avoid the wrath of God, and yet the first seems to blame the apparitions on the deaths while the second blames it on demons.

Another well known political haunting occurred when a supposed demon, drove out the Parliamentary commissioners from the ex-royal residence of Woodstock, as they were trying to sell its effects. After the Restoration, one of the Clerks to the Commissioners confessed to engineering the demon, but this confession might have been self interested in siding with the eventual victors (*The Woodstock Scuffle*, Thompson 1930, pp 73-6; Aubrey, 1972, p 52).

The pamphlet *Signs and wonders from heaven* claimed that apparitions resulted not from particular sins but general sins, just as the separation of King and Parliament resulted from everyone's sins (rather than say the King or Cromwell's sins). The Astrologer on the Parliamentary side, William Lilly, disagreed writing that 'I am of this opinion, the Heavens never send forth any great figures which have not a particular relation to some great personage: for doubtless they are the Universal Cause (God permitting) of all things' (1645, preface). Allocating responsibility is vital for interpretation.

People were interested not only in local but foreign apparitions, especially when they resonate with local concerns. There are numerous English pamphlets describing apparitions in France, or in the Hague.[7] The ballad *A Lamentable List, of certaine Hideous, Frightful and Prodigeous Signes* illustrates the prodigies supposedly seen over Germany between the years of 1618 and 1638 (roughly the time of the thirty years war and of grave concern to Protestants), such as a blazing star, armies fighting in the air, three rainbows and three suns, a battle of crows, and monstrous births (Rollins, 1927, pp 21-5).

Fictional Apparitions could also be used politically, as with the ghost of Jack Straw who warns in *The Just Reward of Rebels* that the souls of those who rebel against the king will not rest easy. The ghost of Wolsey, in a piece supposedly by Archbishop Laud (*Canturburies Dreame*), warns Laud against ambition and vanity. The ghost of Cromwell laments his murder of good king Charles in *A New Meeting of Ghosts at Tyburn*.

Some such stories reinforce social morals, as in the Ballad *A Warning for Engrossers of Corn* (c.1643) which tells how a man selling corn at a very high price was undone by selling it to the devil (Rollins, 1927, pp 31-5). Another story shows how a woman swearing by God she had not committed theft was swallowed by the earth (*Ibid*, pp 62-6). Others tell how a man drinking a health to the devil dropped dead while the devil appeared (*Ibid.*, pp 76-9), and how a loan shark was tormented by devils (ibid, pp 216-18). Such moral violations can be political, as when *A Wonderful and Strange Miracle* implies that drinking healths to the devil is part of standard cavalier practice, or when a *Relation of a Strange Apparition* implies that the devil's appearance is likely at Catholic meetings.

Sometimes writers did not claim to know what was indicated by these signs or that 'prodigious Apparitions in the Heavens' simply forewarn us 'from proceeding into our daily vice' (*Ireland's Amazement* 1641, p 1, cf Rollins, 1927, pp 84-5). A particularly odd example is described in the 1646 pamphlet *Sad Newes from the Eastern Parts,* of which this is an excerpt:

> 'There was a Pillar of a Cloud obscure to ascend from the Earth with the hilts of a great Sword in the bottom of it, which Cloud fashioned it self into the forme of a sharp steeple, which was encountered by a Pike or Sphear coming down point blanck from Heaven and threatened by another Lance or Pike, with very sharp points descending out of the Skye, standing ready to interpose, but did not engage its self....
>
> 'The like Spire Steeple with a Lance or Pike descending from above, and encountering it... was beholden by many persons, Inhabitants at Brandon in Norfolk, and by others who travelled those parts at the same time, lying between Cambridge and Botsam there was seen a broach or sharpe

steeple ascending out of a Cloud like a Church which removed from place to place: This steeple afterwards did split itself into three parts of three distinct colours; the one red; the other yellow: and the third blew; one of which being highest sunck down lower, and out of it went forth a great Ball of fire towards the two Townes in Cambridgshire, the one called Sopham, the other Sopham Bullbark, scorching and singing the grass and the grain as it went, and left a very hot and strong scent of brimstone behind it'.

All the author can manage to say about these dramatic apparitions is that they 'for-warn us of further troubles in or about the Church and Church Affaires'.

Explanations of wild events varied: they could be portrayed as indications of divine wrath, the licensed actions of demons, mirrors of the disruption of the natural order, or as without specific meaning. Others, such as the *Mercurius Democritus,* could see them as evidence of foolishness and stupidity. In general, the meanings of apparitions were more contested than their actuality, and interpretation was a politico-religious act.

Apparitions and Philosophy

Apparitions were a source of philosophical dispute and evidence. There is no necessity for a theoretical split between mind and body, or spirit and body, even in Western Religion. In the Hebrew Scriptures '*nephesh*' is distinguished from '*ruach*' (other distinctions are possible such as *neshamah*) and in the Greek Bible '*psyche*' is distinguished from '*pneuma*', and both are distinguished from what we might call flesh. Augustine points out that humans are created in the image of a triune God. Plato, unsystematically divides the psyche into three parts located in different bodily organs. Lullian alchemy argued that the distinction between spirit and matter is one of degree, that matter can be etherealised and spirit concentrated. Paracelsus argued that humans have a spirit, a soul and a body:

> 'there are in man two bodies one compounded of the elements, the other of the stars... In death the elemental body goes to the grave together with its spirit, but the ethereal bodies are consumed in the firmament, and the spirit of the image of God goes to him whose image it is'.

The sidereal (star) body can become a ghost until it is consumed (Jaffe, p 66, cf Webster, 1677/2004, p 326).

However, sometime during this period these complexities became lost, and the self became associated with a single mind. This is usually blamed upon Descartes, who separated the mind from space, gaining an elaborate physics while leaving the psyche to theologians. In response, many English philosophers either thought Cartesian atomism deprived the soul of a function within the world, or tried to explain everything through a single cause.

Famously, Thomas Hobbes not only appeared to deny the existence of the soul but the reality of apparitions. He alleged that apparitions resulted from the difficulty of telling dreams from waking, especially when 'full of fearful thoughts', or were engineered to support religious power and thus conflicted with monarchical power:

> 'And for Fayries, and walking ghosts, the opinion of them has, I think, been on purpose either taught, or not confuted, to keep in credit the use of Exorcisme, of Crosses, of Holy water, and other such inventions of Ghostly men' (Hobbes 1985, pp 91-2; cf chapter 29, 44, 45).

Hobbes, took the Protestant argument further, and associated all talk of incorporeal spirits, witches and ghosts with Catholicism.

> 'what is all the legend of fictitious miracles in the lives of the saints; and all the histories of apparitions and ghosts alleged by the doctors of the Roman Church, to make good their doctrines of hell and purgatory, the power of exorcism, and other doctrines which have no warrant, neither in reason nor Scripture; as also all those traditions which they call the unwritten word of God; but old wives' fables?' (1985, p 702).

Hobbes claimed that anxiety over our future and ignorance of causes lead us to propose the existence of invisible causes like our own souls (*Ibid.*, pp 170-1) and also proposed that the idea of incorporeal substance was incoherent and contradictory (*Ibid.*, pp 171-2). He allowed that angels could be formed of 'Substances, endued with dimensions, and take up roome', but they were probably just the impressions of the thoughts of God on our fancies (*Ibid.*, pp 434-5). Hobbes objections were primarily based on rationalism, on deductions from obvious truths, rather than from any empiricism, and it could be argued his atomic plenum of hard matter was equally imaginary.

Denial of spirits and apparitions, became particularly problematic during the Commonwealth when various religious sects became associated with disorder, rebellion and atheism. A pamphlet of 1647, *Hell Broke Loose*, alleged that some religious sects not only claimed that all religious ordinances came from the devil, but that 'the soul of man is mortal, as is the soul of beast' (quoted in Friedman, 1993, pp 91-2). This made the soul and apparitions a political and religious issue. Philosopher Henry More closed *An Antidote against Atheisme* (1653) by remarking, 'that Saying is not more true in Politicks, *No Bishop, no King;* than this in Metaphysics, *No spirit, no God*' (More, 1662, Vol.1, p 142).

After the Restoration, there seems to have been a deliberate movement to suppress religious dissent and to channel the experience of God and Spirits into orthodox, controlled and hierarchical forms. This tended to reverse earlier Protestant denials of ghosts as spirits. British philosophers after the Restoration commonly argued that we cannot determine the possible existence of spirits or apparitions from reason alone, but must look at the data. As Joseph Glanvil wrote: although the 'Philosophick Arguments' for God and immortality are cogent they 'are many of them speculative and deep requiring [too] great an attention and sagacity... for the common sort.. [who are] best convinced by the Proofs that come nearest the Sense' (Glanvil, 1700a, p D3v).[8] Atheism resulted from prejudice and ignorance, and the denial of spirits; 'those that dare not bluntly say "There is NO GOD" content themselves ... to deny there are SPIRITS or WITCHES'. The puritan preacher Richard Baxter plainly stated on the title page of his *The Certainty of the Worlds of Spirits* (1691), that it was 'Written for the Conviction of Sadduces & Infidels'. He continues that 'almost all the Atheists, Sadduces and Infidels, did seem to profess, that were they but sure of the Reality of the Apparitions and Operations of Spirits, it would cure them [of disbelief]' (1691, p A5).

Glanville claimed that this denial was especially common amongst those a 'little above the vulgar and among most of the looser Gentry' (*Ibid.*, Preface, pp 2-3). Class is related to testimony. The implication is that lower orders are too simple to lie and the upper orders too noble. Witchcraft

> 'being matter of Fact is only capable of the Evidence of Authority and Sense; and by both these the being of Witches and Diabolical Contracts is most abundantly confirmed... We have the attestations of Thousands of Eye and Ear-witnesses... of wise and grave Discerners; and that when no interest could oblige them to agree together in a communitie' (Glanvil, 1700a, pp 3-4).

Glanvil argued that it was improbable that so many unlikely stories would be invented by different people (1700a, pp 6, 16). Furthermore, claiming that spirits cannot do something because we think it impossible, was foolish, as was shown by the new science; 'we know many things may be done by the Mathematicks and Mechanick Artifice which common heads think are impossible', and the knowledge and capability of spirits may be well beyond our own. We cannot argue from ignorance into impossibility, any more than we could argue that because we do not understand how a foetus is formed it is therefore impossible (ibid, p 7). His argument, that we need to observe the facts rather than proceed solely from reason or prejudice, is similar to the arguments he had used against rationalism as a mode of scientific knowledge, and to the way

Robert Boyle was arguing against Hobbes' objection to the existence of a vacuum (Shapin & Shaffer, 1989).

Glanvil not only read reports about apparitions, but also went to investigate some of these events - particularly the Drummer of Tedworth. This case arose when, shortly after the Restoration, a Mr Mompesson heard of an 'idle Drummer', who demanded money to cease from drumming outside people's houses, and claimed to have a pass allowing him to behave so. Mompesson saw that the pass was forged and had the Drummer arrested and the drum confiscated. The Drummer was released by the local Law officers before the trial. Shortly afterwards drumming was heard in Mr. Mompesson's house, and normally inanimate objects began to move. The Local minister was asked to come and pray, and while the noise stopped during the prayers, it came back afterwards. 'In sight of the company the chairs walkt about the room of themselves' (Glanvil, 1700b, p 51). The Drummer was later accused of witchcraft and sentenced to Transportation, but escaped.

Glanvil visited the house with a friend 'on purpose to enquire the Truth of those Passages'. He talked to the neighbours who confirmed events which they had observed. He heard 'a strange scratching' in the children's bed room. The children's hands were visible and it was apparently not them making the noise moving about the room. Glanvil 'made all the search that possibly I could to find if there was any Trick, Contrivance or common cause of it; the like did my Friend, but we could discover nothing'. The noise changed to panting, 'like a Dog out of breath' (ibid, p 55). 'The motion it caused by this panting was so strong, that it shook the Room and the Windows, very sensibly'. He also saw 'something (which I thought was a Rat or a mouse) moving in a Linen-Bag, that hung up against another Bed that was in the Room', but 'found nothing at all in it' (*Ibid.*, p 56). Later that night his horse became sick dying several days later.

The King sent two gentlemen to look over the house but during their visit the house was quiet. Some used this fact to show the house was not haunted, but Glanvil suggested that this was similar to the argument that as he had never been mugged in London the city had no thieves (*Ibid.*, p 61).

Glanvil claimed the Tedworth case was well evidenced because it was extraordinary (so it could not be 'natural'), contemporary, and witnessed by numbers of people who were not melancholy or superstitious with no party interest in the stories. However, the Drummer's good fortune and constant escapes does suggest that there was some factionalism and interest in the town, whatever Glanvil might think. The tales were not "passages of a Day or Night, nor the vanishing glances of an *Apparition*; but these Transactions were *near* and… *publick*, *frequent*, and of *diverse years continuance*" (1770b, p 62).

Witnessing is also of importance in the more popular pamphlets. Thus *Strange Newes From France*, claims to be 'the Copie of a Letter, which was sent from thence to the Ordinary Ambassador for the King of France unto his Majesty of great Brittaine', *A Great Wonder in Heaven*, claims to be 'Certified under the hands of William Wood Esquire, and Justice of the Peace in the Said countie, Samuel Marshall Preacher. and other persons of qualitie', *A Wonderful and Strange Miracle*, claims to be 'Attested by Mr. Adam Nicholson, Cler. P & Co., Mr Dudley Silvester, Clericus', and so on. Lilly claims to be an eyewitness of the events he describes in

Supernatural Sights and Apparitions (Lilly, 1644), although it is surprising that so few of these strange accounts claim to be by eyewitnesses. They are nearly all reports of things heard from supposed witnesses, or even more distant.

Material of Apparitions

The question arises: if apparitions are real, what are they made of, and how can they be seen?

In some instances it was possible to ask. In a French case in the city of Dole in 1628, Jesuit interrogators trying to decide if a ghost was what it claimed to be, or an evil spirit, asked the woman who saw the ghost (Huguette) the following questions, and she reported the ghost's ambiguous answers:

> 'It is asked, "Are you a pure spirit?"
>
> "Yes I am," it says. "Don't doubt this at all."
>
> Huguette: "Are you a completely spiritual substance?"
>
> The spirit: "I don't understand the question that's being asked me."
>
> "Are you a spirit who gave shape to a body in another time?"
>
> "I'm a spirit who once gave life and movement to a body."
>
> Huguette: "Where is this body?"
>
> The spirit: "It's dispersed." ....

"And this body which you have now, is it the one that you had while you were alive on earth?"

The spirit: "No, because it's dissipated and reduced to ashes, as I have already said."

Huguette: "Of what matter is it then, and where did you get it?"

The spirit: "I get it as God gives it to me when I come here. I am so comforted and pleased to be clad in it in order not to feel the fire of Purgatory during this time that I pay no attention at all to the matter from which it is made!'" (Edwards, 2002).

Such interviews were not often possible, and in Britain the most common explanations made use of the air or airy substances. Kirk in his account of elves and fairies, written in the late 17th Century, wrote that fairies had 'light changeable bodies (lik those called Astrall) somewhat of the nature of a condens'd cloud... congealed air', and so consequently could shift shape (1979, p 51). However he acknowledges that there are other theories. Some say, he claims, that fairies are 'departed souls attending a while in this inferior state' their bodies bought by alms giving in this life, while others say that wraiths are

> 'only exuvious fumes of the Man approching death, exhal'd and congeal'd into a various thickness (as Ships and armies sometime shapt in the air) and called Astral Bodies, agitated as wild fire with wind, and are neither souls not counterfeiting spirits' (ibid, p 58).[9]

Fairies, in his view, are the natural inhabitants of the Air and made of air, just as we are inhabitants of the Earth, and made of earth (cf Glanvil, 1700a, p 5; Baxter, 1691, p B2 verso). Scaliger apparently suggested that we should not be surprised at the ability of spirits to make bodies out of air, for surely this was easier than nature's ability to generate mice from waste matter (Yardly, 1929, p 234).

Burton quotes Origen, Tertullian and Bodine as arguing that demonic spirits have coarser aerial bodies than angels and can deceive human senses (1972 I, p 182), and writes that "Paracelsus of our late writers stiffly maintains that [spirits] are mortal, live and die as other creatures do." (ibid, p 185). However Burton seems to be of the opinion that

> 'They may deceive the eyes of men, yet not take true bodies, or make a real metamorphosis; but as Cicogna proves at large, they are... mere illusions and cozenings...
>
> [Spirits] deceive all our senses, even our understanding itself at once. They can produce miraculous alterations in the air, and most wonderful effects, conquer armies, give victories, help, further, hurt, cross and alter human attempts and projects ...' (*Ibid.*, pp 185-6).

Burton divides sublunary spirits into 'fiery, aerial, terrestrial, watery, and subterranean devils, besides those fairies, satyrs, nymphs, ... ' (*Ibid.*, p 190). Each type explains various observations: fiery spirits produced St.Elmo's fire and counterfeit suns; Airy spirits cause tempests and counterfeit armies in the air; Terrestrial spirits make goblins or counterfeit ghosts and so on. Yet again this is not always clear, the perception of spirits, like the miracles of Catholicism, can be caused by phantasy:

> 'Never any strange illusions of devils amongst hermits, anchorites, never any visions, phantasms, apparitions, enthusiasms, prophets, any revelations, but immoderate fasting, bad diet, sickness, melancholy, solitariness, or some such things, were the precedent causes, the forerunners or concomitants of them' (1972 III, p 343).

More claims that spirits have 'a faculty and right to move of themselves, provided there be no express Law against such', 'they have a power of appearing in their own personal shape to whom there is occasion'. He implies that desire in the beholder, or a sense of justice in the spirit, can also be important for the apparition (1700b, p 27). More uses his apparitional data to oppose Descartes' proposition that spirit does not occupy space, and is consequently nowhere. Spirit and matter, he argues, both have extension but are different types of substance, and one of the types of extension possessed by spirits is different from that of matter. Spirit also differs from matter in that it is penetrable and indivisible (More 1700a, pp 26-32). More also recognises the existence of spirits other than the human soul, there are animal spirits in the body, and spirits can have different types of vehicle Aethereal, Aereal or Terrestrial corresponding with apparitions of gods, daimons and fairies. On the whole the spirits we witness make their bodies out of air (1662 II, pp 34, 98, 118). More also proposes that a Spirit of Nature guides the functioning of the world, causing things to fall towards the centre of the Earth and so on (1662 I, pp xv, 43).

Glanvil suggested (1700a, pp 22-3) that it was painful for spirits to compress themselves into a visible substance which is why there are so few apparitions and why they hastily depart. He also suggested that spirits must have some kind of body as sense depends upon excited matter, and spirits perceive. Furthermore, Nature makes gradations, not precipitate jumps (ibid, pp 23-4). Similar views also, although less commonly, reached the pamphlet literature. *A Great Wonder in Heaven* claims that demons are 'dispersed in the empty regions of the ayre as thicke as motes in the Sunne... It is evident besides, that the divell can condense the ayre into any shape he pleaseth (pp 3-4).

Webster accepted the notion of there being two ethereal parts in humans: the soul and the spirit - the spirit acting as a bridge between the soul and the body, and also possibly having the emotional and imaginative faculties within it. The spirit also carried the pattern which organises the material of the body into its correct shape, and operates in the alchemical resurrection of plants from ashes, and in other alchemical experiments where images of humans are produced by working on human blood, or on earth mould from graveyards (1677/2004, pp 326-34). Therefore apparitions arise as a result of natural and common possesses and Webster slightly inclines away from the existence of demons, or from giving intentional meaning to apparitions. As a result More seems to have considered Webster's explanations as fantastic conceits (1700b, p 6). It seems to have been hard for those in favour of spirits of some kind to agree on much. More was also to vehemently dispute with Baxter on different grounds (More, 1683).

Saving the Appearances

Theories usually have ways in which they can be saved, especially when most of the writers have never witnessed what they describe. Burton, says that although people will be declared 'a melancholy dizzard, a weak fellow, a dreamer, a sick or a mad man' for doing so, many have claimed to witness spirits, and it can be experienced:

'Leo Suavius, a Frenchman, *cap.* 8, in *Commentar. lib. I. Paracelsi de vita longa*, out of some Platonists, will have the air to be as full of them as snow falling in the skies, and that they may be seen, and withal sets down the means how men may see them: [by looking steadfastly at the sky in bright sunshine without blinking] and saith moreover he tried it... and it was true... Paracelsus confesseth that he saw them divers times, and conferred with them, and so doth Alexander ab Alexandro, "that he so found it by experience, whenas before he doubted of it."' (1972 I, p 183).

For Burton, the testimony is so voluminous it must be believed, even without this experience. Thomas Browne argues that atheists wanting to see apparitions are already damned and won't see any, as apparitions are produced by the devil who has no interest in changing their views (1645/2004, p 64 #30). James I was of the opinion that spirits can only haunt where there is 'grosse ignorance, or.. some grosse and slanderous sinnes' (1597, p 58), which would explain why the learned or virtuous rarely witnessed evidence themselves. Indeed to claim to witness an apparition was to put oneself in moral doubt. Finally it was always possible to claim that although any individual case might be a fake or an illusion, cases in general, or specific, were not. As Baxter argues, although deceits occur 'he forfeiteth the Benefit of his own Eye-sight, who thinks that none see, because some Beggars counterfeit Blindness' (1691, p B2).

Addison, at the end of this period (1711-12), implied that apparitions were the product of a fearful feminine mind, by describing the terrors which arise in women:

> 'I know a Maiden Aunt, of a great Family, who is one of these Antiquated _Sybils_, that forebodes and prophesies from one end of the Year to the other. She is always seeing Apparitions, and hearing Death-Watches; and was the other Day almost frighted out of her Wits by the great House-Dog, that howled in the Stable at a time when she lay ill of the Tooth-ach.'

Such Fears can be consoled by rational reflection on God, so a moral person, by implication will not perceive apparitions (Spectator no.7, see also No.s 12, 421). However, he thinks it unreasonable to dispute the testimony of reputable people to the existence of spirits, especially when there are some (possibly female or lower class) 'who by Instances of this Nature are excited to the Study of Virtue' (Spectator no.110). Although reasonable men won't see such sights it is moral to believe. Glanvil, More and Baxter's desire to convince sceptics of religion's truth so as to support its social utility has been reduced to social utility only.

Conclusion

The way of arguing in favour of spirits alters over the 17th Century. We begin the Century with arguments from reason and from classical authority, we finish the Century with people arguing from what they considered contemporary matters of fact and the overt usefulness of belief in spirits to religion and morality. Protestant accounts seem to be less prone to dismiss ghosts has having something to do with the dead. Witnesses, shift from deceased philosophers to living people of supposed reputation. This probably first arises in popular accounts of apparitions, where it is frequent to append a list of witnesses, or claim that the curious can go and visit the place of the events and either talk to witnesses or see for themselves.

However, witnessing was fraught. Not only was the deluded or deceived witness part of the apparitional tradition, but it was part of the arsenal for fighting reports of miracles which confirmed other religions, denominations or heresy. In Seventeenth Century Britain this discrediting was particularly directed at radical 'Enthusiasm', or claims of direct contact with God and spirits; which break from the authority of the established church was largely blamed for the Civil War. Henry More, used the charge of Enthusiasm and delusion against alchemists, something which was not uncommon. This left the status of witnesses for apparitions, or any other not universally perceived phenomena, in doubt as well. Conventions of trustworthiness had to be constructed, and toward the end of this period these tended to be based on class, honour and familiarity. Most of the reports of apparitions given by More, may have been recorded by honourable, sober men, but the actual witnesses were largely unknown and of uncertain gentility. Witnesses were not generally questionable by readers of the right class and it was rarely possible to delete the intermediary authority. Many apparitions could only be seen by one person and so further avoided group reality, and they could not be displayed in a public place. Finally, by claiming to have witnessed apparitions, something which was extremely uncommon, a person put themselves in the category of those who perceived the unusual and should be investigated to discover if delusional.

Apparitions had strong religious associations and it was hard to separate them from Religious or moral fields. In some ways those fields called these apparitional worlds forth to give meaning to the cosmos, and evidences of God, demons and souls. The new science, while supporting established religion, generally did not investigate religious issues. So, if apparitions were not delusional then it was appropriate and safer to leave them for theologians, especially if they were the work of the devil. The growth of empiricism relates to issues of trusting the senses, not particularly of privileging them. It seemed clear that senses could deceive. This was, as we have seen, a religious issue as much as a 'scientific' issue, as visions, prodigies, apparitions and marvels could generate and promote religion which might be uncontrollable by the Churches. Church as well as intellectual needed some way to silence unorthodox testimony of the senses, or a method which helped choose whether testimony was good. The New Philosophy decided on a juridical procedure: would a reasonable audience in the same circumstances, untouched by biases which might affect perception, perceive the same things? Can the circumstances be replicated? The religious problem of interpretation could only be solved by restricting testimony to those of the same poltico-relgious faction, and this was difficult in 17th Century Britain.

Although, people usually tried to fit their views of apparitions into their views about Religion, the inclination of Early Protestants to dismiss the possibility of ghosts being the spirits of the dead to attack Catholicism, did not survive for long, and there may have been an increase in intellectual attention paid to ghosts, apparitions and spirits, in the face of politically radical Protestants and perceived disbelief. However ghosts were fairly easy to tie to local worlds, and hence while preserving local continuities between the living and the dead, had little wider political repercussions. Discussion of large scale visions may have declined because of issues of control of interpretation.

Discourse about apparitions tends to focus on problems of life. For philosophers and theologians this centres on the vicissitudes of the soul, its structures and materials, and the corruption of reason through imagination, dreams, fear, ignorance, deceit, trickery. For almost everyone it involves the role of God in the world, what happens after death, and what kinds of meaning the world is invested with. The issues of ghosts and Purgatory involved moral issues about communality, individuality and the placability of God. Popular writers focused more on the meaning of a particular apparition than on apparitions in general. Apparitions are a reading of meaning into the world, but the meaning, cause and witnessing is uncertain, and depends on the reader. Apparitions can be the work of devils as well as the work of God, the World Spirit, angels or the dead.

Finucane points out that these Seventeenth Century ghosts tend not to be wreathed in flames, or blackened showing their state after death, but often represent the condition at death. They generally do not float through walls or just appear, but open and close doors, pull back bed curtains, most are quite normal in appearance. 'The dead were still functioning in society, were concerned with ongoing trivial and familial problems... two thirds were personally known to their percipients' (1983, pp 149-50). Henry More tells us that ghosts were active pin detecting the Murtherer, in disposing their estate, in rebuking injurious Executors, in visiting and counselling their Wives and Children, in forewarning them of such and such courses, with other matters of like sort (1662 II, p 130), which is they cannot be demons - he also clearly expects ghosts to be male.

Although narrators of apparitions sometimes report that witnesses felt terror, there is little or no attempt to convey that terror in the narrations, which tend to be very matter of fact. There is also little evidence for a theory that apparitions are inevitably anomalous, or threats to ways of thinking - they may even support for ways of thinking. We cannot assume that apparitions are generated by social stress and dislocation (and hence the apparently increasing numbers of apparitions in the period of the Civil Wars), it may simply be that distribution of reports increases. It is also clear that people of the time also interpret these apparitions as evidence of what we would call social, or personal, stress, and thus the explanation is not separate from our history.

The apparent explosion in popular apparition stories in those stressful times of the Civil Wars and Commonwealth correlates pretty well with the massive increase in the number of printers in the 1640s and 1650s. This also correlates with the increase in the number of regular newsletters during the same period. The suppression of news sheets by Charles II on the restoration (Friedman' 1993, pp 3-4), may also be the reason why most of the later stories come from books, by reputable authors.

This suppression may also explain why apparitions, in the more general sense of seen prodigies, appear to become less of interest as the century moves on despite the continual interest by some people, in apparitions till this day. There has been little religious or political motive for defenders of the establishment to discuss these kinds of apparitions with varied, and possibly dangerous, political implications. The use of apparitions for politics has probably been confined to oppositional groups and become more marginal with time.

Here the connection between apparitions, and ideas of substance, psyche, space, religion, politics, morality and philosophy, has only briefly been sketched. Much work remains to be done in these fields to get some idea of the richness of experience and discourse during this period.

Notes

1   Rollins (1927, p 87) claims this is Sir William Mallet.
2   Aubrey (1972, p 428); Pepys June 15 1663. Glanvil reports that many people said he was lying (1700b, p 1).
3   After seeing a ghost in Ireland, Lady Fanshawe and her husband 'concluded the cause to be the great superstition of the Irish, and the want of that knowing faith, which should deffend them from the power of the Devill, which he exercises among them very much' (Loftis, 1979, p 125).
4   James I implied that demons animated dead bodies and impersonated the dead (1597, pp 59, 60- 67).
5   Such remarks are now commonplace but seem to have been first mooted by Spalding (2004/1880, pp 58-60).
6   The ghost in Shakespeare's *Julius Caesar* may be more an example of the world's disruption than of Caesar's desire for revenge - again ambiguity is present.
7   The apparitions seen at the Hague in May 1646 are described in *Several Apparitions Seene in the Ayre at the Hague in Holland*, in *Good Newes from Oxford*, and in *Sad Newes from the Eastern Parts*. The *Several Apparitions*

pamphlet warns against incredulity, as in the time of Noah, implying that not everyone believed these signs.

8   Glanvil was a clerical defender of the Royal Society and its new philosophy, and although the Society never issued formal support for Glanvil's work, many of its members helped him compile his relations, in the spirit of empiricism. Even Increase Mather wrote: 'I have often wished, that the Natural History of New-England might be written and published to the World; the Rules and method described by that Learned And excellent person Robert Boyle Esq being duely observed therein' (2004/1684, p 17).

9   These views imply that fairies had a fairly strong association with the dead in some people's minds. Kirk also reports that the 'mountain people… superstitiously' believe that the 'souls of the predecessors' dwell in fairy hills (1979, p 61).

References

Anonymous Pamphlets, with Thomasin Tract number.

Canturburies Dream, 1641, E180(19)

Good Newes from Oxford, 1646, E340 (23)

A Great Wonder in Heaven 1643 E85(41)

Horrid and Strange News from Ireland, 1644, E78(1)

Ireland's Amazement, 1641, E181(41)

The Just Reward of Rebels / The Ghost of Jack Straw

Mercurius Democritus

    Feb 1-8, 1654, E728(4)

    Feb 8-15, 1654, E728(30)

The Most Strange Apperation of a Poole of Blood, 1645, E303 (45)

A New Meeting of Ghosts at Tyburn, 1660

New Yeares Wonder 1643, E86 (23)

A Relation of a Strange Apparition

Sad Newes from Eastern Parts, 1646, E344(16)

Several Apparitions at the Hague, 1646, E340(33)

Signes and Wonders From Heaven, 1645, E295 (2)

Strange News From France, 1642, E136 (15)

A Wonderful and Strange Miracle, 1642, E126(36)

The Woodstock Scuffle, 1649, E587 (5)

Addison, Joseph, nd, *The Spectator*, Routledge, London

Aquinas, Thomas, 1952, *Summa Theologica, Vol.2*, Encyclopedia Britannica Inc, Chicago

Aubrey, John, 1972, *Three Prose Works*, edited by John Buchanon-Brown, Southern Illinois UP

Baxter, Richard, 1691, *The Certainty of the Worlds of Spirits*, Cheapside

Brown, Theo, 1979, *The Fate of the Dead*, DS Brewer, Cambridge

Browne, Thomas, 1645/2001, *Religio Medici*, [On-line].

http://penelope.uchicago.edu/relmed/relmed1645.pdf

Burton, Robert, 1972, *The Anatomy of Melancholy*, Everyman's Library, Dent, London

Caciola, Nancy, 1996, 'Wraiths, revenants and ritual in medieval culture', *Past & Present*, 152, 3-45

Edwards, K., 2000, 'Female Sociability, Physicality, and Authority in an Early Modern Haunting', *Journal of Social History*, 33, 601-21

Finucane, R.C., 1982, *Appearances of the Dead: A Cultural History of Ghosts*, Junction Books, London

Friedman, Jerome, 1993, *Miracles and the Pulp Press During the English Revolution: The Battle of Frogs and Fairlord's Flies*, UCL Press, London

Gadbury, John, 1660, *Natura Prodigiorum: or, a Discourse Touching the Nature of Prodigies...*, London.

Glanvil, Joseph, 1700, *Saducismus Triumphatus*, London:

(1700a), 'Some Considerations about witchcraft in a Letter to Robert Hunt' in Glanvil, 1700.

(1700b), 'Saducismus Triumphatus the Second Part' in Glanvil, 1700

Greenblat, Stephen, 2001, *Hamlet in Purgatory*, Princeton UP

Haining, Peter, 1987, *Ghosts: The Illustrated History*, Treasure Press, London

Hobbes, Thomas, 1985, *Leviathan*, Penguin, Harmondsworth

Jaffe, Aniela, 1979, *Apparitions: an Archetypal Approach to Death Dreams and Ghosts*, Spring, Dallas

James I, 1597, *Daemonology, in forme of a Dialogue*, reprint Edinburgh, ed G.B. Harrison, Bodley Head, London

Jones, Zacharie, 1605/2004, trans. *A Treatise of Spectres*, London

Kirk, Robert, 1976, *The Secret Common-wealth*, edited by Stewart Sanderson, DS Brewer, Cambridge

Lilly, William, 1644, *Supernatural Sights & Apparitions*, London E4 (5)

1645, *Starry Messenger*, London, E288(17)

Linton, Anna, 2003, 'Blithe Spirits: Voices from the Other Side in Early Modern German Lutheran Funereal Poetry' in John Newton (ed.), *Early Modern Ghosts*, Centre for Seventeenth Century Studies, University of Durham

Loftis, John (ed.), 1979, *The Memoirs of Anne, Lady Halket and Ann, Lady Fanshaw*, OUP

Marshall, Peter, 2000, 'The Map of God's Word: Geographies of the afterlife in Tudor and early Stuart England' in Bruce Gordon and Peter Marshall eds. *The Place of the Dead: death and remembrance in late medieval and early modern Europe*, CUP

2002, *Beliefs and the Dead in Reformation England*, OUP

Mather, Increase, 1684, *Remarkable Providences: An Essay for the Recording of Illustrious Providences,* [On-line], http://history.hanover.edu/texts/matherrp.html

More, Henry, 1662, *A Collection of Several Philosophical Writings*, London 1683, 'Annotations upon the Discourse of Truth', in Joseph Glanvil, *Two Choice and Useful Treatises, the one Lux Orientalis....*, London

1700a, 'The Easie, True and Genuine Notion and consistent Explication of the Nature of a Spirit', in Glanvil, 1700

1700b, 'Dr. Henry More's Letter', in Glanvil, 1700

Purkiss, Diane, 2000, *Troublesome Things: A History of Fairies and Fairy Stories*, Allen Lane

Rollins, Hyder, E., 1927, *The Pack of Autolycus*, reprint Kennikat Press, New York

Scot, Reginald, 1972, *Discoverie of Witchcraft*, Dover, New York

Shapin, Steven and Shaffer, Simon, 1989, *Leviathan and the Air Pump*, Princeton University Press

Spalding, Thomas A., 2004/1880, *Elizabethan Demonology*, [On-line] http://www.gutenberg.org/etext/12890

Taillepied, Noel, n.d., *A Treatise Of Ghosts*, trans Montague Summers, Fortune Press, London

Thomas, Keith, 1973, *Religion and the Decline of Magic*, Penguin University Books, Harmondsworth

Thompson, C.J.S., 1930, *The Mystery and Lore of Apparitions*, Harold Shayler, London

Walsham, Alexandra, 1999, *Providence in Early Modern England*, OUP

2001, 'Sermons In The Sky - celestial visions reported across early modern Europe', *History Today*, 51, (4), 56-63

Webster, John, 1677/2004, *The Displaying of Supposed Witchcraft*, London

Yardley, Mary, 1929, 'The Catholic Position in the Ghost Controversy of the Sixteenth Century', in Lewes Lavatar, *Of Ghostes and Spirites Walking by Night (1572)*, edited by J. Dover Wilson and May Yardley, Shakespeare Association, Oxford

'A half-choked meep of cosmic fear': Is there esoteric symbolism in H.P.Lovecraft's *The Dream-Quest of Unknown Kadath*?

David Geall

'A tale of paths between the spheres, dim corridors leading to equally dim and conjectural lands of elder myth ...'

Introduction
H.P.Lovecraft (1890-1937), an American writer of 'horror' fiction in the tradition of Poe, has been claimed by many modern occultists to be one of their own, a truly occult author with a good knowledge of magical lore, even if - suggests Kenneth Grant - gained unwittingly by a 'natural adept'. They include Aleister Crowley's heir, Grant and his followers in England; Michael Aquino, Anton La Vey and Michael Bertiaux in the

USA; and Wolfgang Muller in Germany, who dubs Lovecraft 'The Alchemist of Providence', and sees him as an adept of the highest rank.

I have always found this intriguing but unsubstantiated, feeling that these occultists were reading into Lovecraft things that he would not have been aware of, and indeed would have denied any knowledge of. John Gonce (2003, p 85) discusses the apparent reluctance of Lovecraft scholars to consider HPL's knowledge of the occult, leaving a lacuna in which occultists can wildly speculate. In what follows I shall suggest that a reading of *The Dream-Quest of Unknown Kadath* raises the intriguing possibility that Lovecraft was aware of the symbolism of occultism; in a discussion following the analysis I shall consider how well substantiated that claim may be.

The Dream-Quest of Unknown Kadath, according to August Derleth (1966, p 7), 'was very probably conceived and written ... sometime in the early or mid-1920's, but ... it was evidently never extensively revised'. It was never revised, or considered a commercial proposition – 'it is composed under no illusion of professional acceptance', wrote Lovecraft in a letter on 19 December 1926. As a result, we are able to study the original imagery of *The Dream-Quest*. S.T.Joshi's chronology (1980, p 37) dates its writing more precisely, and later, from autumn 1926 to 22 January 1927. This puts it just after *The Call of Cthulhu* and just before *The Case of Charles Dexter Ward*, part of what Burleson (1983, pp 115-160) calls the 'Homecoming Burst of Creativity' - the creation of the Mythos by Lovecraft, back home in Providence from New York, from 1926 to 1928. That period certainly shows also Lovecraft's literary interest in the occult: *The Call of Cthulhu* begins with a voodoo cult in Louisiana, while in *The Case of Charles Dexter Ward* Lovecraft uses some cabbalistic incantations and the lunar nodes known as the Dragon's Head and Tail.

The Dream-Quest of Unknown Kadath is a strange and yet seminal text in that it pulled together many themes begun in earlier short texts of the 'dream-cycle' - *Polaris, The White Ship, The Statement of Randolph Carter, The Cats of Ulthar, Celephais, Nyarlathotep, The Other Gods, The Hound, Pickman's Model.* These texts are generally thought of as belonging to the period in which Lovecraft was influenced by the Irish fantasy writer Lord Dunsany, whose writings were popular following the success of *The Gods of Pegana* in 1904. If S.T.Joshi's chronology is correct, it contradicts the common perception that this Dunsanian 'Dreamlands' period was over and done with before Lovecraft began work on his 'Mythos' cycle.

As a fantasy story, *The Dream-Quest of Unknown Kadath* – to adopt the terms used by Clute and Grant (1997) - takes the form of a Quest for a Dark Tower, the haunt of a Dark Lord (in this case, Nyarlathotep). As Wetzel (1980, p 84) points out, while the world of *The Dream-Quest* is a dream-world explored by the sleeping Randolph Carter, it is also an afterworld, where one might meet the dead (as one sometimes does in dreams too), with both an Elysium and a Tartarus, where Carter meets, for example, King Kuranes and Pickman the ghoul, respectively. Wetzel compares *The Dream-Quest* to the ancient Greek otherworld, with which Lovecraft was familiar through his reading; Dante also comes to mind - perhaps the illustrations of Gustave Dore to Dante and Milton, which impressed so Lovecraft as a child (letter of October 24, 1936). In terms of the Cabalah, Tartarus or Hell is represented by *Olam ha-Qlippoth,* the world of empty shells or demons; and in some of the more unpleasant spots of Carter's dreamland the *Qlippoth* do indeed seem to appear.

An esoteric reading of *The Dream-Quest of Unknown Kadath*

Unlike Dante, Carter had no Virgil in the text of *The Dream-Quest* to guide him around the Dreamlands, which include sites that may be described as infernal, purgatorial and even paradisal. We may perhaps be justified in seeing Carter's journey as a sort of pilgrim's progress, into the sleeper's subconscious mind, through various vicissitudes, temptations and dangers, until he achieves true knowledge and reaches his own private paradise. But Carter was the persona of Howard Phillips Lovecraft, who may not have been composing as freely as we might suppose: in the analysis that follows, we see Carter following the Paths between the Sephiroth of the Tree of Life of the Cabalah. This gives a structure to the universe of *The Dream-Quest*, whether it is seen as the inner space of the subconscious mind, the outer space of the ascent to and return from Kadath, the interior of the Earth, or the other world of the after-life - for it can be all these things. There is, however, one major anomaly immediately obvious in this case: because it is giving a structure to the underworld, or the subconscious, the Tree of Life is growing upside-down. As Denning and Phillips (1988, p 100) say, 'a progress from the Malkuth to the Kether of the qliphothic Tree ... is really a descent ... It does lead to the Abyss.' Where the Qliphothic forces outweigh those of the Sephiroth, their attributes distort the usual character of the Sephira affected. To cite Wetzel (1980, p 84) again, 'It is in the novel, *The Dream-Quest of Unknown Kadath* (1926), that the Hell of H.P.L.'s Cthulhu Mythos is fully described and made the locale of a story.'

There is one other peculiarity which might be explained by the author's psychology, not unrelated to the previous breakdown of his short-lived marriage: there are no women, no goddesses, no females at all, not even apparently among the animals. All the paths of the Tree of Life linked to Tarot cards depicting female figures are somehow avoided, or not mentioned. There is, however, another explanation for this, whether a conscious or unconscious reflection of his personal situation. As Epstein wrote in 1969, 'An ever-functioning system of opposites, mediated by harmony, rules over the mental and physical universe, whose new creations emerge from their fusion. Balance and harmony through creation are perpetuated by means of sex. Equilibrium is thereby equated with love, and love is personified in the female form of the Shekinah, or the mystery of God's everlasting presence … It is the absence of the Shekinah that denotes the presence of evil … if a man cuts himself off from God, the Shekinah will leave him to Satan, who will drag him further into the pit until he suffers the torments of hell in his life. In this case the Sephiroth are reversed and form instead a "tree of death" whose roots emanate from the Kelipah *(i.e. the Qlippoth)*' (p 26-7 – my italics).

The journey begins on Earth, 'the waking world', which is the Sephira of Malkuth, or Kingdom. Carter is desperate to revisit and freely wander a marvellous city he has glimpsed thrice in his dreams, and prays in vain to the tyrannous, 'hidden gods of dream that brood capricious above the clouds on unknown Kadath, in the cold waste where no man treads. Finally, … Carter resolved to go with bold entreaty whither no man had gone before, and dare the icy deserts through the dark to where unknown Kadath, veiled in cloud and crowned with unimagined stars, holds secret and nocturnal the onyx castle of the Great Ones. In light slumber he descended the seventy steps to the cavern of flame ... ... and thinking shrewdly on his course, he boldly descended the seven hundred steps to the Gate of Deeper Slumber and set out through the Enchanted Wood' (*Dream-Quest* p 107).

The cavern of flame and the Gate of Deeper Slumber appear to be but way-stations on the Path between the Sephiroth of Malkuth and Netzach. The 70 and 700 steps may be a clue: Netzach is the seventh Sephira. In his *Sepher Sephiroth*, Aleister Crowley (1912) gives the following equivalences in Hebrew gematria: 70=Night; 700=The Veil of the Holy; 770=going forth, all of which, particularly the last, seem to be appropriate. Netzach is related in its symbolism to the planet Venus, and the Roman Venus is a typical example of the deities, usually goddesses, representing nature, life and fertility, which are typical attributes of the character of Netzach. The Enchanted Wood, inhabited by Zoogs (animals by name and nature), is thus appropriate for this zone, as is the colour green of the trees and mossy stones, for green is the colour of this Sephira. In the wood is a stone circle, suggesting that the Zoogs are perhaps the *Qlippoth* of Netzach, the *Seirim* or Satyrs.

Carter parleys with the Zoogs, accepting a gourd of moon-tree wine, 'grown from a seed dropped down by someone on the moon.' The reason for this reference (the word *moon* appears thrice here) is that the Path between the Sephiroth of Malkuth and Netzach is traditionally allocated to the Tarot trump The Moon, the image of which - a path between two towers - may also have suggested to Lovecraft the Gate of Deeper Slumber. The card depicts drops of dew falling from the moon, which may have suggested "the seed dropped down by someone on the moon". The Hebrew letter associated with the Path between Malkuth and

Netzach is Qoph, meaning 'the back of the head', and is particularly relevant to Carter's dreaming. As Case (1947, p 175) wrote: 'This is the part of the skull which contains the ... medulla oblongata ... The cells of this organ remain awake when the rest of the brain is asleep ... Sleep is the function assigned to Qoph. Sleep is the period ... during which the cells of the body undergo subtle changes which make the advancing student of occultism ready to experience and understand facts and phenomena concealed from ordinary men.'

Carter leaves the Enchanted Wood, leaving Netzach on the Path to Hod, the next Sephira. 'At noon he walked through the one broad high street of Nir ... and soon afterward he came to the great stone bridge across the Skai ...' (A glance at the diagram of the Tree will reveal the broad road crossing the river below: the Path from Netzach to Hod, which passes over that from Yesod to Tiphereth, represented in the story by the River Skai. Hod (or Splendour), related to the planet Mercury, is represented by Ulthar in the story. Carter heads for that "venerable circular tower" which crowns Ulthar's highest hill - the Path he has just taken is allocated to the Tarot trump of The Tower. There he confers with the old priest Atal, who advises him to see the mountain of Ngranek in the isle of Oriab, where there is a great carved face, perhaps bearing the features of the gods. Not knowing how to get there, he advises Carter to follow 'the singing Skai under its bridges down to the Southern Sea', to the port-city of Dylath-Leen. 'Then twilight fell, and the pink walls of the plastered gables turned violet and mystic ... and sweet bells pealed in the temple tower above': violet is the colour of Hod on the King Scale, and the bell is regarded as a suitable, although not exclusive, symbol of Mercury.

As he admired the pleasant scene, Carter 'swore that Ulthar would be a very likely place to dwell in always, were not the memory of a greater sunset city ever goading one onward' (*Dream-Quest* p 113). This temptation recalls the fact that, according to Denning and Phillips (1988, p 129), 'in its qliphothic ... aspect, Hod becomes the sphere of Samael, the Tempter of Eden.'

In the morning Carter joins a caravan of merchants, 'and for six days they rode on the smooth road beside the Skai ... the placid river': in terms of the Tarot, Temperance, which depicts an angelic figure standing beside a river (a road running off into the distance). (To get to this path, Carter presumably retraced his steps along the Tower path to the bridge of Nir, but Lovecraft does not dwell on this, getting him there in one short paragraph). 'On the seventh day a blur of smoke arose on the horizon ahead, and then the tall black towers of Dylath-Leen, which is built mostly of basalt. Dylath-Leen with its thin angular towers looks in the distance like a bit of the Giant's Causeway, and its streets are dark and uninviting' (*Dream-Quest* p 113). This is the next Sephira, Tiphereth or Beauty, related to the Sun: but here, on the inverted Tree, there is neither sunlight nor beauty. Perhaps Lovecraft has left us a clue, however: Tiphereth is the sixth Sephira, and basalt forms hexagonal, six-sided columns, as on the Giant's Causeway in Ulster. Moreover, the journey took six full days. The 'thin angular towers' may even suggest the acute angles between the many Paths that meet here.

Eventually one of the black galleys docks, bringing rubies from an unknown shore, and Carter tries some moon-wine on one of the merchants who came aboard it. He is hoist with his own petard, however, for after a sip of wine from a ruby bottle he loses consciousness, 'and as

Carter slipped into blackness, the last thing he saw' - but he awakes to find himself alive and fairly well on the deck of the galley. This *little death* is not surprising when one sees that they are sailing along the Path of the Tarot trump Death, past 'the charnel gardens of Zura.' Moreover, according to Sturzacker (1971, p 90), 'On this path the student or initiate is in the sphere of the "dark night of the soul" commenced in Temperance'. A ship is visible in the background of this card in the Rider-Waite pack, as are two pylons framing the setting sun in the background, which might account for this:

'before the day was done Carter saw that the steersman could have no other goal than the Basalt Pillars of the West' ...
which wise dreamers well know are the gates of a monstrous

cataract wherein the oceans of earth's dreamland drop ... and shoot through the empty spaces toward other worlds and other stars ...' (*Dream-Quest*, p 116).

The ship has now turned on to the Path of The Star, marked by a female figure pouring water from two jugs, and also by one large star and seven other stars. Carter 'soon saw that the helmsman was steering a course directly for the moon', and the Path of The Star leads directly to Yesod (or Foundation), the fifth Sephira, which is related to the moon. According to Sturzacker (1971, p 61), 'This path is the link between the "waters above the firmament" and the "waters below the firmament" of Genesis.' Carter finds the moon to be inhabited by creatures variously described as 'a sort of toad, toad-things, or toadlike moonbeasts', the toad being linked in magical symbolism with the moon. The toadlike moonbeasts may represent the Gamaliel, or obscene ones, the Qliphoth of Yesod. (Carter is then rescued by the cats of Earth and Ulthar, who spirit him back to Dylath-Leen on a furry bridge of cats, the second time Lovecraft sends him there in a few words).

Carter is once again able to take ship for the Isle of Oriab, 'and for two days they sailed eastward.' They are following the Path of The Devil on the Tree, but no reference is made to it until Carter reaches his destination. There he sees a wall-drawing in which there is 'a crowd of little companion shapes ... with horns and wings and claws and curling tails', which leaves little doubt of the source of his inspiration. The Devil card depicts not only a large traditional devil with all the attributes mentioned above, but also two smaller companions sporting horns and tails too.

The story continues: 'But on the third day they turned sharply south'; having sailed east and turned sharply south, they are now following the Path of The Hanged Man, which provides us with an origin for one of Lovecraft's most startling images. The ship drifts over the ruins of a sunken city, clearly visible in the moonlight: '... and Carter did not blame the sailors much for their fears. Then by the watery moonlight he noticed an odd high monolith in the middle of that central court, and saw that something was tied to it. And when after getting a telescope from the captain's cabin he saw that the bound thing was a sailor in the silk robes of Oriab, head downward and without any eyes, he was glad that a rising breeze soon took the ship ahead to more healthy parts of the sea' (*Dream-Quest*, p 123).

The Hanged Man of the Tarot is also hanging upside-down, and, although it is from a tree or cross, the Golden Dawn title for the trump is *The Spirit of the Mighty Waters*: it is linked astrologically to the element Water, and also to Neptune. Oddly enough, T.S.Eliot also represents the Hanged Man by a drowned sailor in the *Death by Water* section of *The Waste Land* (1922), raising the question of a possible common source.

Carter then arrives at the port of Baharna in the great isle of Oriab, where mount Ngranek rises jagged and snow-crowned in the distance. This is the next Sephira, Geburah, representing strength or severity, and related to the planet Mars. Ngranek is an extinct volcano, "thinly covered with ... ash trees", upon which a great carved face gleams red in the sunset. Carter has a good, curved scimitar in case of any trouble. Fire, the god Volcanus, the ash-tree, the colour red and the sword are all attributes of Mars / Geburah, as are the rubies carried by the black galleys on which Carter first attempted to sail here.

> 'As the ship drew into the harbour at evening the twin beacons Thon and Thal gleamed a welcome, and in the million windows of Baharna's terraces mellow lights peeped out quietly and gradually as the stars peep out overhead in the dusk, till that steep and climbing seaport became a glittering constellation hung between the stars of heaven and the reflections of those stars in the harbour' (*Dream-Quest*, p 124).

Lovecraft's description of Baharna may owe something to the Tarot card of The Chariot, which represents the next Path he attempts to take: a glance at the card shows towers on either side, perhaps the origin of the twin beacons, while the chariot is covered by a hanging awning made of cloth covered in stars. As in the background of the card, the city rises 'in great stone terraces.' Moreover, a mighty warrior in his chariot is also the magical image of Geburah. On the card the chariot is drawn by two sphinxes with zebra-striped head-dresses, which may account for the fact that Carter hires first one and then another zebra for transport. The first zebra is killed during the first night, 'with its blood all sucked away through a singular wound in its throat ... and all around on the dusty soil were great webbed footprints' - signs perhaps of the *Qetebim*, or Destroyers, the Qliphoth of Geburah, 'the pestilence that walketh in darkness'.

In the face carved on the far side of mount Ngranek Carter recognises the features of sailors he had seen (in previous dreams) in Celephais, and he decides to retrace his steps, via Dylath-Leen, the Skai, and Nir to the Enchanted Wood (i.e. via Tiphereth to Netzach), and from there northward along the river Oukranos to Thran, and thence to Celephais. A glance at the Tree will show that he could have taken a Path straight from Oriab / Geburah to Thran / Chesed. The reason why he did not is perhaps because the card linked to the Path to Chesed, Strength, features a lady dominating a lion: as noted above, Lovecraft has avoided feminine figures. Another reason may be that it is apparently the occult wisdom that, according to Sturzacker (1971, p 23), 'The foolish rise from Hod to Geburah only to fall back', so that Carter's progress at some points resembles a game of snakes and ladders. The question is academic, in any case, for Carter is whisked away from mount Ngranek by night-gaunts, which take him to the Abyss which lies between and below the Sephiroth.

As they flew over it, 'far below him he saw faint lines of grey and ominous pinnacles which he knew must be the fabled Peaks of Throk. Awful and sinister they stand in the haunted disc of sunless and eternal depths' (*Dream-Quest*, p 131). This 'haunted disc of sunless and eternal depths' is the hidden, occulted Sephira of Daath (Knowledge). 'As the band flew lower the Peaks of Throk rose grey and towering on all sides, and one saw clearly that nothing lived on that austere and impressive granite of the endless twilight.' Carter is deposited in the Abyss of the vale of Pnoth below the Peaks of Throk, but a rope-ladder lowered by his ghoul friends enables him to climb up to the top. There the ground is scattered with gravestones and other sepulchral monuments filched by the ghouls, 'and Carter realized with some emotion that he was probably nearer the waking world than at any other time since he had gone down the seven hundred steps from the cavern of flame to the Gate of Deeper Slumber' (*Dream-Quest*, p 133). Daath has a close relationship with Malkuth: in Cabbalist lore, but for the Fall, the Sephira of Malkuth would be in the position of Daath. If we imagine hinges at Hod and Netzach on the diagram of the Tree of Life, we can see how Malkuth could be easily swung up into the position of Daath. It seems that Lovecraft envisaged a three-dimensional model here: Malkuth above Daath, and Daath below the general level of the dreamlands, in 'the grey air of inner earth.'

Carter and a few companion ghouls surface in the city of the giant Gugs: 'they were in a forest of vast lichened monoliths reaching nearly as high as the eye could see ... and seen through aisles of monoliths, was a stupendous vista of cyclopean round towers mounting up illimitable into the grey air of inner earth' (*Dream-Quest*, p 135). They make their way to the biggest tower: 'this was the central tower with the sign of Koth, and those stone steps just visible through the dusk within were the beginning of the great flight leading to upper dreamland and the enchanted wood' (Lovecraft also speaks of the sign of Koth 'above the archway of a certain black tower standing alone in the twilight' in *The Case of Charles Dexter Ward*). They climb the spiral staircase of the Tower of Koth, and emerge through the exit, covered by a great stone slab in the Enchanted Wood. No Path corresponding to this route is visible on the Tree, but, according to Hulse (1994, p 333), there are also sixteen invisible paths running between the Sephiroth. The companions seem to have joined the one running from Inquanok / Binah to the Enchanted Wood / Netzach, which is linked to a Tarot Court card, the Queen of Cups: it may only be coincidence that *kathon* is Greek for a drinking cup. Lovecraft may give us a clue later, too: when Carter finally reaches Inquanok / Binah, he finds that 'on a hill in the centre rose a sixteen-angled tower greater than all the rest ... the Temple of the Elder Ones ... nothing was more splendid than the massive heights of the great central Temple of the Elder Ones with its sixteen carven sides' (*Dream-Quest*, p 152-3).

Back in the Enchanted Wood, Carter parts from the dog-like ghouls, 'shaking the paws of those repulsive beasts'; thinks sadly of the zebras he hired in 'far-away Oriab so many aeons ago'; and helps to forestall an attack by the Zoogs on the cats of Ulthar - all of which is perhaps appropriate in the realm of Netzach, relating to 'natural' animal life. He leaves the Enchanted Garden this time by way of 'the singing river

Oukranos', through a flowery paradise: 'Carter heard only the murmur of the great stream and the hum of the birds and bees as he walked onward under an enchanted sun.' This Path is linked to the Wheel of Fortune - *'the Lord of the Forces of Life'* - which is related to the element of water; the descending serpent on the card may also have suggested the winding river. The divinatory meaning of this card is 'good fortune and happiness', so it is appropriate that 'A blessed haze lies upon all this region ... so that men walk through it as through a faery place, and feel greater joy and wonder than they ever afterward remember' (*Dream-Quest*, p 142). It is also linked by some, such as Zain (1994, p 144), with the planet Uranus: remove the *k* from Oukranos and one has *Ouranos*, the Greek original of Uranus. In Greek Cabalah, according to Barry (1999, p 253-4) *Ouranos* has a value of 891; add the *k,* which has a value of 20, and 911 is the value of the words for *axle, wheel, joy, grace,* and *bloom of youth* - all highly appropriate here.

As the sun sets, Carter sees the white towers and gilded spires of the city of Thran, galleons of cedar anchoring at its marble wharves: cedar is an attribute of Chesed, or Mercy, the next Sephira, which Thran represents. Carter does not linger, but boards a galleon bound for Celephais the following morning. They continue down the river, past the perfumed jungles of Kled, to the port of Hlanith on the Cerenerian Sea. They are taking the Path from Chesed to Chokmah, which is related to the Tarot trump of The Hierophant, or High Priest: it is linked to the astrological sign of Taurus, and among its attributes are naturally bulls and all other bovines, plus the Taurean quality of strength. Carter goes ashore, and not surprisingly sees *ox*-carts, and *bull's*-eye panes in the tavern windows; while Hlanith is noted for its rugged granite walls and oaken wharves, and 'is prized for the solid work of its artisans' (*Dream-Quest*, p 145).

From there they sail across the Cerenerian Sea for two nights and two days. 'Then near sunset of the second day there loomed up ahead the snowy peak of Aran with its gingko-trees swaying on the lower slope, and Carter knew they were come to the land of Ooth-Nargai and the marvellous city of Celephais.' This is the Sephira of Chokmah, or Wisdom. Lovecraft had previously written of Celephais and its wise ruler, King Kuranes, in *Celephais* (1920), and in both that piece and in *The Dream-Quest* he mentions the turquoise temple of the deity Nath-Horthath: turquoise is one of the gem-stones attributed to Chokmah. 'On the following day Carter walked up the Street of the Pillars to the turquoise temple and talked with the High Priest': the High Priest refers back to the Path just travelled from Chesed to Chokmah, that of the Tarot trump of The Hierophant, or High Priest. Carter also visits the Lord of Ooth-Nargai, King Kuranes, with whom we may link the Path of The Emperor, which connects Ooth-Nargai / Chokmah with Dylath-Leen / Tiphereth. The Emperor is enthroned, just as Kuranes 'sat pensive in a chair'; the throne is decorated with rams' heads, and Carter, after leaving the turquoise temple, had 'sought out the market of the sheep-butchers' (*Dream-Quest*, p 146).

The colour violet is attributed to this Path, and in both texts (*Celephais* and *The Dream-Quest*) Kuranes, who was previously a dream-quester like Carter, meets with S'ngac, a being in the form of a violet-coloured gas. This Path is also related to the element of Air, and Kuranes is also Lord of the Sky around Serannian, where he reigns 'in the turreted cloud-castle of sky-floating Serannian.' Likewise, Chokmah is related to Uranus as the sky or heavens, the primeval god of Greek myth rather than the modern planet: according to Bias (1997, p 17), 'Chokmah is ... the Sphere of the Fixed Stars ... Uranus as the Starry Heaven'. Carter followed the River Oukranos most of the way from Netzach to Chokmah: as mentioned above, remove the *k* and one has *Ouranos*, the Greek original of Uranus.

'One starlit evening', a ship from Inquanok puts in: the sailors' faces resemble the face carved upon mount Ngranek, and, although excited by this, 'Carter did not hasten to speak with the silent seamen. He did not know how much of pride and secrecy and dim supernal memory might fill those children of the Great Ones'. The word *supernal* is an interesting choice: the three highest (or in this case lowest) Sephiroth are known as supernal, and Carter is about to sail from one of them, Chokmah, to another, Binah. (The word is also used in the opening paragraph: 'a fanfare of supernal trumpets', and towards the end: 'supernal Kadath in its cold waste'). The fact Carter is now in the supernal regions is symbolised in the story by polar symbolism and Poe-like reminiscences of Arctic exporation: 'night came with gorgeous stars, and the dark ship steered for Charles' Wain and the Little Bear as they swung slowly round the pole ... Each day the sun wheeled lower and lower in the sky, and the mists overhead grew thicker and thicker. And in two weeks there was not any sunlight at all, only a weird grey twilight ... ' (*Dream-Quest*, p 151). There seems to be some inconsistency here: the ship should be westering, too, if our interpretation is correct, and yet Inquanok appears 'to the east' ... perhaps, as in polar regions, the compass has become unreliable! More to the point, it may be that the ship took a long, curvaceous, route, rather than sailing straight across along the Path of The Empress, since the latter is (of course) never mentioned in any way.

After a voyage lasting twenty-two days (the number of the Tarot trumps and the visible Paths), they reach the black onyx city of Inquanok, with the sixteen-angled tower (the number of the invisible paths) of the Temple of the Elder Ones. Although the Path just taken (or avoided) is that of The Empress, it is not surprising, in view of Lovecraft's exclusion of the feminine from this text, that Inquanok is ruled by a Veiled *King*. Inquanok represents the Sephira of Binah, which is related to the planet Saturn - as are onyx and the raven, which are mentioned several times, while black is a colour related to both Binah and Saturn. As would be appropriate to Saturn, the planetary god of the seventh day, there is septenary symbolism: the Temple garden has seven gates, seven lodges, seven doors, seven paths, and seven columns of bowl-bearing priests. Binah is known as the Great Sea, and its symbols include the cup, the chalice, the well: In the garden of the great central Temple of the Elder Ones 'there are fountains, pools and basins ... all of onyx and having in them small luminous fish taken by divers from the lower bowers of ocean' (*Dream-Quest*, p 151).

But 'always to the east ... rose the gaunt grey sides of those topless and impassable peaks across which the hideous Leng was said to lie'. Carter hires a yak and proceeds north into the area of the onyx-quarries: Leng / Kether lies north-east from Inquanok / Binah in our scheme. He sees only the miners and an occasional raven, but is pursued and abducted by a 'squat slant-eyed trader of evil legend' who had spied on him in Dylath-Leen and Inquanok, 'leading on a noxious horde of leering Shantaks to whose wings still clung the rime and nitre of the nether pits'. The Shantak-birds - huge, horse-headed scaly flying beasts that lurk in caves in the mountain-sides - are a form of Qlippoth. According to Denning and Phillips (1988, p 103), 'The Cohorts of the Qlippoth beyond the Abyss are collectively known as the Sataroth, or Concealers ... the Sataroth have been compared to huge, foul, voracious birds brooding on the slimy and fog-covered steeps of an unscaleable cliff'.

Mounted upon a shantak, Carter and his captor fly over 'that haunted place of evil and mystery which is Leng ... finally they came to a wind-swept table-land which seemed the very roof of a blasted and tenantless world'. Seeing 'a squat windowless building, around which a circle of crude monoliths stood ... Carter surmised from old tales that he was indeed come to that most dreadful and legendary of all places, the remote and prehistoric monastery wherein dwells uncompanioned the High-Priest not to be described, which wears a yellow silken mask over its face'. The High-Priest represents The Magician, the Tarot trump related to the Path just taken, from Inquanok / Binah to Leng / Kether; its symbolic colour is yellow. Kether is the topmost Sephira (polarity having changed), and thus may be seen as the 'very roof of a ... world'. In the normal Tree of Life, Kether is the Crown, the fountainhead of all good; here, in this infernal Tree, it may fairly be described as 'that most dreadful and legendary of all places.' Instead of light, we have a windowless building, which is encircled by monoliths: a point within a circle is a symbol of Kether. 'There were no lights inside', so, ironically, a lamp, which is also a symbol of Kether, is mentioned several times in this episode, being much needed in the prevailing darkness (*Dream-Quest*, p 161).

Carter escapes from his captor and reaches Sarkomand, the city of dreadful night on the coast of Leng. Here he meets up again with the ghouls, and together they defeat more of the moonbeasts. The ghouls and their night-gaunt allies agree to escort him on the final stage of his journey from Leng to Kadath, 'approaching unknown Kadath either through the desert of carven mountains north of Inquanok, or through the more northerly reaches of repulsive Leng itself.' Crossing the Great Abyss to the Supernal Sephiroth changes polarity, so that what was formerly 'south' is now 'north', as Lovecraft makes abundantly clear: 'Everything focused toward the north; every curve and asterism of the glittering sky became part of a vast design whose function was to hurry first the eye and then the whole observer onward to some secret and terrible goal of convergence beyond the frozen waste that stretched endlessly ahead' (*Dream-Quest*, p 180).

As they fly north, they pass a range of mountains, carved into shapes by no human hand: 'All in a great half-circle they squatted, those dog-like mountains carven into monstrous watching statues ... It was only the flickering light of the clouds that made their mitred double heads to move ... ... There they squatted in a hellish half-circle ... sinister, wolf-like and double-headed' (*Dream-Quest*, p 179). Soon they notice to their horror – 'bringing to the lips of the ghouls a half-choked meep of cosmic fear' - that these gigantic beings have got to their feet and are paralleling their course. This striking image of Lovecraft's has a cabalistic origin: as Waite (1924, p 256) makes clear: 'Thaumiel, the doubles of God, said to be two-headed and so named, because they pretend to be equal to the Supreme Crown. This is properly the title of the averse Sephira corresponding to Kether.'

It also becomes clear that Kadath cannot be located on the Tree, since Leng was apparently located in the utmost Sephira of Kether. Kadath must then be identified with the next element, the Ain Soph Aur, 'the Limitless Light, the Radiant Darkness' in the words of Bias (1997, p xxii): but once again in this inverted Tree it is the opposite: 'a realm of eternal night', as Lovecraft takes pains to emphasise:

> 'At length a lone pallid light was seen on the skyline ahead, thereafter rising steadily as they approached, and having beneath it a black mass that blotted out the stars. Carter saw that it must be some beacon on a mountain, for only a mountain could rise so vast as seen from so prodigious a height in the air ... Higher and higher rose the light and the blackness beneath it, till half the northern sky was obscured by the rugged conical mass ...No mountain known of man was that which loomed before them ... Scornful and spectral climbed that bridge betwixt earth and heaven, black in eternal night, and crowned with a pshent of unknown stars ... Ghouls meeped in wonder as they saw it' (*Dream-Quest*, p 182).

The description plainly shows that Kadath is no earthly mountain, but is, like Mount Meru, the great mythical mountain in the north which represents the polar axis, here conflated with the Ain Soph Aur, on the edge of infinity: hence the increased power of the writing, striving to express what is inexpressible except in the language of symbolism.

Discussion

The above analysis of *The Dream-Quest* seems at first sight to indicate that Lovecraft was familiar with some of the symbolic structures of modern magic: the Tree of Life of the Cabalah, with the system of mapping the Tarot (specifically, the Rider-Waite pack) on to the Paths of the Tree, and with some of the associated symbolism: attributes such as colours, animals, plants, stones, artifacts, astrological signs, and numbers. In addition, he appears to have been cognisant with the system of gematria (i.e. the numerical values) of both Greek and Hebrew letters, and also with the *Qlippoth*, the demons of the Cabalah.

On the other hand, it must be admitted that such an interpretation is inevitably based on a selective reading of the text, choosing what fits and omitting from consideration what does not. Are we simply seeing pictures in the fire, shapes in the clouds, canals on Mars? It could be argued that the Tree of Life and its modern occult accretions form a poetic model of the universe which naturally includes everything, so it is not surprising if we find what we are looking for. Structuralist interpretations of this kind are now seen as problematic, in that many possible structures can be deduced from a reading of a text. Positing the existence of any one structure within some material can influence the interpretation and hence its outcome.

In response it could be argued that some of Lovecraft's most arresting images appear to have an esoteric origin: the Hanged Man / drowned sailor, and the mountainous two-headed Thaumiel, for instance. In addition to such isolated images, there appears to be a fair amount of consistency in the overall structure (which we have identified with the Tree and Tarot), as when Carter's ship sails east and turns sharply south, on to the Path of the Hanged Man. True, there is not always a total fit, but the story can be mapped onto the structure to quite a large extent – how large is a matter of opinion.

Some might object that the bleak mechanistic and materialistic view of the universe which Lovecraft espoused in his letters contradicts the theodicy, the providential cosmology implicit in the Tree of Life as a poetic structure of the universe. Our interpretation, however, postulates an inverse, Qliphothic version of the Tree, in which the universe can indeed be seen as one bereft of providence, order, meaning, love and hope - until Carter (and Lovecraft) are rescued by a return to their roots in New England - Carter in Boston, and Lovecraft (of course) in Providence.

Another objection to such a Cabbalistic interpretation is that it could be applied to any science fiction or fantasy novel. Perhaps we should take two other Quests for Dark Towers as the closest candidates for comparison: J.R.R.Tolkien's *The Lord of the Rings* and Stephen King's series *The Dark Tower* (I have not yet finished studying the final two volumes). The results are intriguing, but much less convincing than for *The Dream-Quest*. In Tolkien, for example, the Elven-kings have three rings, the Dwarf-lord seven; mortal men have nine, the Dark Lord one: twice ten, the same number as the sephiroth on a double Tree of Life, one normal and one infernal. King has a structure reminiscent of the Tree - a Beam that the companions follow towards the Dark Tower, which at one point crosses an Abyss, and he also has an idiosyncratic and partial version of the Tarot. Various locations can be tentatively mapped onto the Tree, especially the lower sephiroth, but with many question marks. Tolkien's city of Minas Tirith and King's City of Lud may be seen as the equivalents of Dylath-Leen on the sephira of Tiphereth, for example. Minas Tirith was originally Minas Anor, the Tower of the Sun, while Lud is at one point associated with the rose-pink colour of Tiphereth (on the King Scale!). It is difficult, however, to map either text on to the Tree very consistently or convincingly. This may be due to the complexity of these multi-volume epic-romances, with many journeys by different characters. It would seem, however, that neither author was following the same magical pattern that we suggest Lovecraft was; this not surprising, for why should a good Catholic like Tolkien or King, writing a generation or two later, be expected to do so? It might be better, in any case, to regard the mythopoetic structures that they do have as their own *cabbalas* or symbolic systems.

While many works of fantasy and science fiction can be analysed along different lines - psychoanalytical, apocalyptic, sociological, archetypal - they do not all yield to a Cabbalistic interpretation as well as *The Dream-Quest* does. Some do not seem at all fruitful, whatever the level of analysis: much fantasy appears to be literary whimsy only - not that there is anything necessarily wrong with that. An interesting comparison can be made with Brian Lumley, who seems to follow Lovecraft's geography of the Dreamlands pretty faithfully in his *Dreams* series, but appears to have no esoteric awareness or resonance: except for the following quotation, which suggests he might unwittingly have stumbled upon the possible Cabbalistic structure of *The Dream-Quest*: 'A tale of paths between the spheres, dim corridors leading to equally dim and conjectural lands of elder myth ...' (1978, p 10). Unless, of course, Mr Lumley knows more than he is letting on ... Another comparison could be with Lovecraft's mentor Poe, who displays a similar apparent contradiction, between the author of *Eureka* and the author of his fiction.

If we grant that *The Dream-Quest* may contain a possible Cabbalistic structure, more than other texts, the question arises as to why Lovecraft, if he knew what he was doing, never (to our knowledge) admitted to it, and instead usually maintained an attitude of scepticism and even ignorance towards such matters. This is a major objection to our hypothesis, and one that is perhaps ultimately unanswerable until some other evidence may be found to support or refute it - unless, of course, you agree with Kenneth Grant (2002, p xxix): 'It sometimes happens that non-Initiates are used by the Outer Ones as vehicles for the revelation of hidden knowledge in a manner inexplicable to those so chosen, which they cannot explain to themselves or others ... Such a situation was exemplified in the case of H.P.Lovecraft's persistent refusal to admit of any value attaching to his tales other than of a purely imaginative kind.' It might also be pointed out that Lovecraft, the anti-Semite who married a Jew, was quite capable of maintaining a double standard. In the meantime, some further rebuttals can be offered, as follows.

One is that an author can have a literary interest in using esoteric material without necessarily being a believer or a practitioner. It is undeniable that Lovecraft had such a literary interest, if nothing else, as displayed in *The Call of Cthulhu*, *The Case of Charles Dexter Ward*, and *Supernatural Horror in Literature*, to mention only a few. Part of the growing academic interest in the occult has been an increasing recognition of the number of modern authors who have used the esoteric as a source of inspiration and imagery - perhaps for the very reason that they do *not* 'believe' in it, but can use it freely and imaginatively. In this literary context, Lovecraft's apparent knowledge of the occult would not have been not unusual: parallels may be found with Arthur Machen and Algernon Blackwood, who had been members of the Outer Order of the Golden Dawn, and whom Lovecraft regarded as his masters in the art of 'weird' fiction. Another influence with an interest in the occult was Sax Rohmer, whose *Romance of Sorcery* (1914) may have been a source on the history of magic for Lovecraft, while *Batwing* (1921) could have influenced *The Call of Cthulhu*.

Such authors need not be practising occultists, however; the esoteric has been mentioned (by Materer, 1995) in connection with T.S.Eliot, Ezra Pound, H.D., Robert Duncan, Sylvia Plath, Ted Hughes, and James Merrill, among modernist poets. Modern novelists include John Cowper Powys (see Krissdottir, 1980); Malcom Lowry (see Epstein, 1969); Zola, Verne, Breton, Proust, Mann, Hesse, Joyce, Meyrink, Lindsay Clarke, Yourcenar, Eco and Butor (see Meakin, 1995).

One might also conjecture that Lovecraft, having used this material in *The Dream-Quest*, abandoned it as too constrictive, and thereafter developed his own 'mythos' in his fiction. A parallel might be drawn in this case with W.B.Yeats, a former member of the Golden Dawn, who likewise developed his own 'mythos', published as *A Vision* in 1925. Communicated via his wife's automatic writing, the sources said, 'We have come to give you metaphors for poetry', which Yeats used thenceforth. And, of course, a parallel to that is the channelling of *The*

Book of the Law to Crowley in 1904, following his wife's prior communication. (Did Mrs Lovecraft have a hand in *The Dream-Quest?* Perhaps it is not impossible that Sonia knew something of the Cabala or the Tarot). Interestingly, Crowley had, like Yeats, given up on Golden Dawn style magic before receiving *The Book of the Law*: 'All that he had attained, he abandoned. The intuitions of the Qabalah were cast behind him with a smile at his youthful folly; magic, if true, led nowhere' (Crowley, 1936). One might tentatively draw a parallel with Lovecraft: if our hypothesis is right he too might have said his farewell to the Golden Dawn style of magical symbolism in *The Dream-Quest*, and thereafter developed his own mythos in his fiction, as did Yeats in his poetry and Crowley in his magick. In that sense, if no other, Kenneth Grant (1972, p 114-7) would have been right to draw attention to the parallels between Crowley and Lovecraft.

(As noted above, Joshi's chronology (1980, p 37) argues against a water-tight distinction between the Dreamlands and the Mythos fictions; nevertheless, one clearly follows the other).

Lovecraft's letters shed some light on his attitude: for example, on October 9, 1925, Lovecraft had written to Clark Aston Smith asking for help, as he was "appallingly ignorant", in finding sources of material on magic. But this can be taken two ways: at that date, he was ignorant - but he was also interested. (Smith's reply no longer exists, but perhaps he came up trumps, as it were, by sending some unusual material that was later returned or lost - but this must remain mere conjecture). We have to bear in mind, however, that Lovecraft's published correspondence is only a small proportion of the total, and the *Selected Letters* were often abridged by August Derleth - some might say censored

(Gonce, 2003, p 85). Moreover, they lack many of Lovecraft's accompanying illustrations: Derleth himself, in his introduction to the first volume of the *Selected Letters* (1965, p xxii) states how 'sometimes he drew signs of cabalistic ritual or magic.' Needless to say, however, we cannot rely on the notional support of unpublished and perhaps non-existent letters by Lovecraft; but it is to be hoped that further research among any remaining unpublished papers may shed further light on this matter.

If we accept that Lovecraft had some knowledge of the esoteric, the question remains as to the source. Lovecraft is often said to have derived his esoteric knowledge from one book in particular, Lewis Spence's *Encyclopaedia of Occultism* (1920), which he owned. While Lovecraft was no doubt familiar with this work, a glance reveals it could not have supplied him with all the details mentioned above. While this knowledge can easily be gained today by a visit to almost any large bookshop, this was not so in the 1920s. Lovecraft could have learned some of it from only a few published sources, such as rare privately printed books, or the journal or correspondence course of an occult society. Lovecraft, however, read widely and omnivorously from his childhood onwards, with a great interest in many subjects, one of which the occult became; as a result it is difficult to be certain how much he read in a subject, and how much he knew. Lovecraft certainly improved his knowledge with time; in the 1930s he had several books on the occult in his library, and was able to advise fellow writers. (Gonce, 2003, p 12-15)

Hulse (1994, p 272, 280-1, 352-6) outlines the development of the Tree and the Tarot Paths as a combined symbolic structure. In 1856 Eliphas Levi made the first connection between the Cabalah and the

Tarot, followed by Papus in 1889. In Britain, S.L.MacGregor Mathers developed it in his *Book T* for the Order of the Golden Dawn in 1887. The attribution of the Tarot trumps to the Paths of the Tree was given to members in the Fourth Knowledge Lecture, as may be seen in Regardie (1986, p 71). The details of this were released by Aleister Crowley in his *Liber 777* in 1909, and his periodical *The Equinox* (1909-14), both privately printed. One V.N. (Victor Neuberg?) published the Golden Dawn system in *The Occult Review* of May 1910. In the same year A.E.Waite's *The Pictorial Key to the Tarot* (1910) described the Tarot, while his *The Holy Kabbalah* (1924, incorporating earlier works) described the Tree, and some of the Qliphoth, but neither mapped the Tarot onto the Tree. Waite also wrote on the relationship between the Cabalah, the Hebrew alphabet and the Tarot in his introduction to Knut Stenring's translation of the *Sepher Yetzirah* in 1923. In the United States, Harriette and Homer Curtiss revealed much symbology of the Tarot in relation to numbers, the Cabalah, the Hebrew alphabet, etc., in their *The Key to the Universe* (1919) and *The Key of Destiny* (1923).

It is therefore possible that Lovecraft may have seen something stemming from the British Golden Dawn tradition, or a parallel American one, which he was able to use in *The Dream-Quest*. This is assuming, of course, that the premise is granted that there is, within this text more than meets the eye at first sight, and that the eye of the beholder is not too biased.

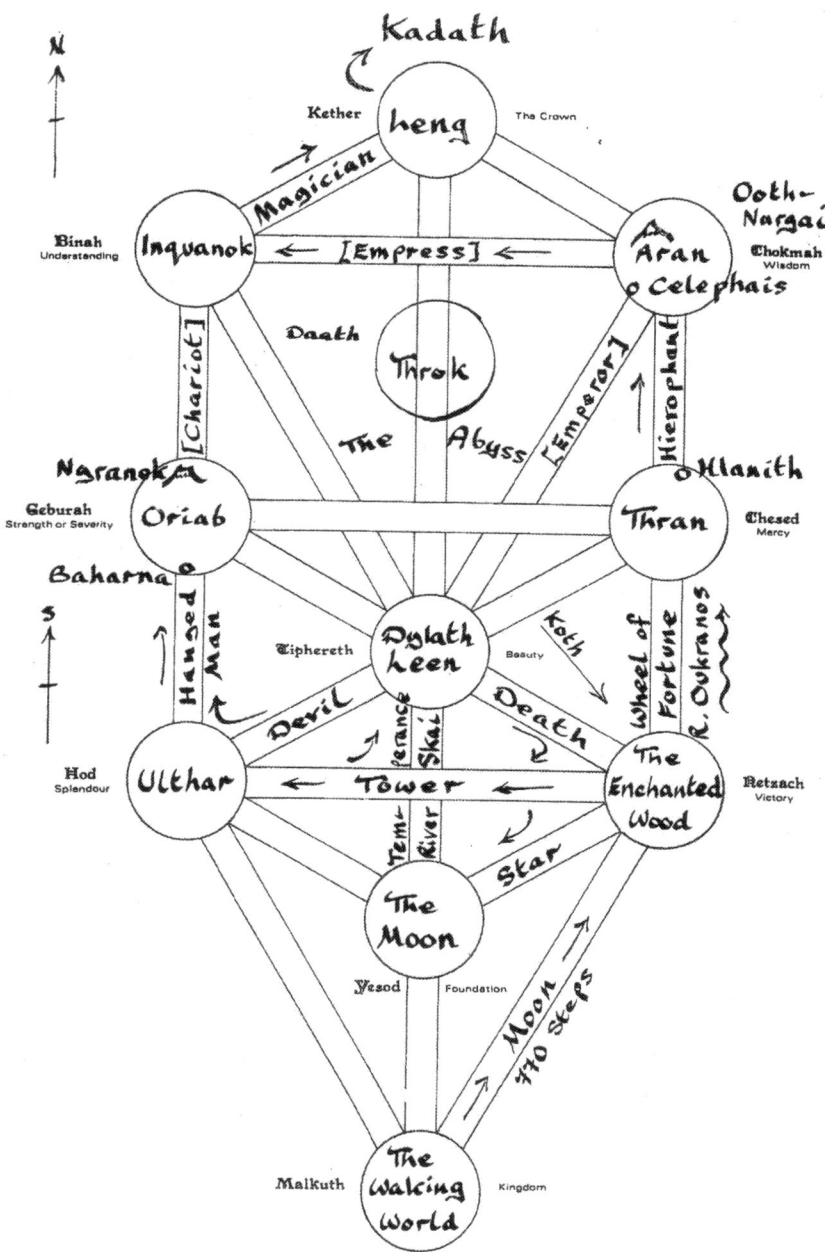

Notes on the illustration(s)

The blank chart of the Tree of Life, on which I have drawn my map, is supplied by the Sorcerer's Apprentice, 6-8 Burley Road, Leeds LS6 1QP, to whom are due many thanks for permission to reproduce it.

The illustrations of the Tarot cards are from the original 1910 line drawings that appeared in *The Pictorial Key to the Tarot* by Arthur Edward Waite, which is in the public domain.

References

Barry, Kieren, 1999, *The Greek Qabalah*, Weiser, York Beach Maine.

Bias, Clifford, 1997, *Qabalah, Tarot and the Western Mystery Tradition*, Weiser, York Beach Maine Burleson, D., 1983, *H.P.Lovecraft: A Critical Study*, Greenwood Press, Westport Conn.

Case, Paul Foster, 1947, *The Tarot*, Macoy, New York

Clute, John and John Grant, eds., 1997, *The Encyclopedia of Fantasy,* London, Orbit

Crowley, Aleister, 1912, *777 and other Qabalistic Writings*, reprinted 1998 by Weiser, York Beach Maine

Crowley, Aleister, 1936, *The Equinox of the Gods*, London

Curtiss, Harriette and Homer, 1919, *The Key to the Universe* and 1923, *The Key of Destiny*, reprinted 1983 by Newcastle, Hollywood California

Derleth, August, 1968, 'H.P.Lovecraft's Novels' in *At the Mountains of Madness and other novels of terror*, Panther, London

Denning, M. and O.Phillips, 1988, *The Sword and the Serpent*, Llewellyn, St.Paul

Epstein, Pearl, 1969, *The Private Labyrinth of Malcom Lowry: Under the Volcano and the Cabbala,* Holt, Rinehart & Winston, New York

Godwin, David, 1979, *Cabalistic Encyclopedia*, Llewellyn, St.Paul

Gonce, John and Daniel Harms, 2003, *The Necronomicon Files*, Weiser, York Beach Maine

Grant, Kenneth, 1972, *The Magical Revival*, Muller, London, and throughout his later 'Typhonian Trilogies' until *The Ninth Arch*, Starfire, London, 2002

Hulse, David, 1994, *The Key of It All, Book Two:The Western Mysteries*, Llewellyn, St. Paul

S.T. Joshi, 1980, 'A Chronology of Selected Works of H.P.Lovecraft', in *H.P.Lovecraft: Four Decades of Criticism*, ed. Joshi, Ohio University Press, Athens Ohio

Krissdotttir, Morine, 1980, *John Cowper Powys and the Magical Quest*, MacDonald, London

La Vey, Anton, 1972, *The Satanic Rituals*, Avon, New York (said to be written by Aquino)

Lovecraft, Howard Phillips, 1926, *The Dreamquest of Unknown Kadath*; edition cited is in *The Dream Cycle of H.P.Lovecraft*, Del Rey / Ballantine, New York 1995

Lovecraft, H.P., letter of 19 December 1926, in *Selected Letters II*, Arkham, Sauk City

Lovecraft, H.P., letter to Virgil Finlay, October 24, 1936, in *Selected Letters V*, Arkham

Lumley, Brian, 1978, *The Clock of Dreams*, Grafton, London

Materer, Timothy, 1995, *Modernist Alchemy: Poetry and the Occult*, Cornell University Press, Ithaca

Meakin, David, 1995, *Hermetic Fictions: Alchemy and Irony in the Modern Novel*, Keele University Press, Keele Staffordshire

Muller, W.H., 1996, *Polaris: The Gift of the White Stone*, Brotherhood of Life, Albuquerque

Regardie, Israel, 1986, *The Golden Dawn: A Complete Course in Practical Ceremonial Magic*, Llewellyn, St Paul

Spence, Lewis, 1920, *Encyclopaedia of Occultism*, Routledge, London

Sturzaker, James, 1971, *Kabbalistic Aphorisms*, TPH, London

Waite, A.E., 1910, *The Pictorial Key to the Tarot*, Rider, London

Waite, A.E., 1923, introduction to Knut Stenring, trans. *The Book of Formation or Sepher Yetzirah*, Rider, London

Waite, A.E., 1924, *The Holy Kabbalah*, reprinted by Oracle, Royston, 1996

Wetzel, George, 1980, 'The Cthulhu Mythos: A Study', in *H.P.Lovecraft: Four Decades of Criticism*, ed. Joshi, Ohio University Press, Athens Ohio

Yeats, W.B., 1925, *A Vision*, reprinted 1990 by Arrow Books, London

Zain, C.C. 1994, *Sacred Tarot*, Church of Light, Los Angeles: individual chapters originally copyrighted in 1921-1926 by Elbert Benjamine

Creative Revolution: Bergsonisms and Modern Magic

Dave Green

If intelligence now threatens to break up social cohesion at certain points – assuming society is to go on – there must be a counterpoise, at these points, to intelligence ... a virtuality of instinct ... will call up "imaginary" ones, which will hold their own against the representation of reality and will succeed, through the agency of intelligence itself, in counter-acting the work of intelligence. This would be the explanation of the myth-making faculty. (Bergson, 1977, 119)

A philosophy of the mystical

Alex Owen's *The Place of Enchantment* is an erudite exploration of the modern sociological currents which helped to shape the *fin-de-siècle* occult revival. Importantly, she places ambivalence and the ambiguous trajectories of the modern condition at the heart of late-Victorian society, and particularly, at the heart of its esoteric sensibilities. This is particularly true when it comes to understanding the philosophical underpinnings of this revival, moulded by the *Lebensphilosophie* of the Nietzscheanism and Bergsonism of the era. What interests me about

Owen's proposition is that whilst Nietzschean antinomianism has often been cited as an influence upon contemporary magic philosophy - especially when one thinks of Left Hand Path magics (see, for example, Sutcliffe, 1996) – in contrast, the influence of Henri Bergson has largely been ignored. If anything he becomes a mere footnote in the history of magic for being the brother of Moina Mathers, wife of MacGregor Mathers, and for failing to be convinced by the Matherses about the efficacy of Golden Dawn ritualism (Yeats, 1972, p 73). This neglect of Bergsonism within intellectual histories of magic is unjustified. Indeed, as Owen herself asserts 'If Nietzsche was claimed by occultists as a fellow traveller, it was Henri Bergson who came closest to articulating an "occult" philosophy' (Owen, 2004, p 135). In other words, whilst Nietzsche could be regarded as a mystical philosopher, Bergson could be thought as a philosopher of the mystical. Given this, this article seeks to expand upon Owen's analysis of the influence of Bergson's oeuvre, looking at the continuities and discontinuities of his philosophy on contemporary magic.[1] In particular, Bergson's philosophical propositions have, in recent years, been re-invented and revitalised by a range of philosophers, neuroscientists and complexity theorists, from Gilles Deleuze through to Daniel Dennett and Fritjof Capra. These new, often materialist, manifestations of Bergson – *The New Bergsonism* – have impacted upon contemporary magical theory, especially Chaos Magic. In the quest to understand these impacts, let us begin with Bergson himself.

Bergson: A brief philosophical biography

It is an irony that Bergson's work has exerted such an influence on modes of understanding *being* and *becoming*, such as occultism and neuroscience, when his own life was, according to Kolakowski, so 'uneventful' (Kolakowski, 2001, p vii). This assessment is perhaps harsh given that he was the most famous philosopher of his age. Bergson was born in Paris in 1859 and of middle-class Anglo-Polish Jewish extraction. He was educated at The École Normale - Emile Durkheim and Jean Jaurès were contemporaries - and, after teaching philosophy in several French universities, was in 1898 awarded a readership (*Maître de Conférence*) at the École, with a chair following at The Collège de France in 1900. Bergson is perhaps most widely known for his work on the philosophy of time, but his oeuvre spanned works on the Vitalist evolution of matter, laughter, freedom and subjectivity, and – importantly - the moral bases of religion and magic. In all of these endeavours he kept returning to the same issues – the creative processes that drive *being*, the antimonies of the intellect, and the personal and social need for intuitive insight. Whilst it was the flamboyance of these ideas that made Bergson one of the most significant cultural and intellectual icons of the early Twentieth Century – culminating in The Nobel Prize for Literature in 1927 – he was to fall victim to both the changing intellectual fashions of the time and religious bigotry:

Bergson's later works on religion, magic and morality were less well received than his earlier publications such as *Time and Free Will* (1889), *Matter and Memory* (1896), and *Creative Evolution* (1907). These lauded earlier works were famously subjected to criticism by proponents of the British school of Analytic Philosophy. Bertrand Russell's logical atomism, for example, had little sympathy for Bergson's championing of the role of intuition in either life or philosophy (see Russell, 1956). However, Bergson's most bitter academic critic was Julien Benda, the leader of the anti-Romantic movement of French philosophy. As Collinson states, Benda

> Regarded him [Bergson] as a supreme example of a general cultural and philosophical decline that had abandoned analytical and scientific thinking in favour of emotionalism, indeterminacy and a passive, feminine attitude. (Collinson, 1987, p 133).

Bergson's relationship with orthodox religion also became increasingly troubled. His work on evolution, coupled with his vehement anti-intellectualism,[2] caused his works to be prohibited by the Holy Office of the Roman Catholic Church in 1914. The reason for this prohibition, however, was arguably the political and intellectual sympathies that certain French Catholic modernists held for Bergson's work against the Catholic orthodoxy of the time (see Harris, 1976). Such an orthodoxy was epitomised by the Neo-Thomist Catholic philosopher Jacques Maritain who took particular delight in lambasting Bergson despite being initially influenced by his Neo-Vitalism. Ironically, Bergson, in spite of his Jewish heritage, became increasingly attracted to Catholicism, only resisting baptism because of the growing anti-Semitism he perceived within the Catholic Church of the 1930s. Again, in another ironic twist, it was own spiritual heritage that was ultimately to be the cause of his death. Following the German occupation of Paris, Bergson was required to register as a Jew. He died on 3rd January 1941 from pneumonia contracted from hours spent on the freezing streets of Paris awaiting registration.

Owen's depiction of Bergson makes play of the fact that, although he remained unimpressed by the magical philosophies of his sister and her husband, 'he was nonetheless involved with psychical research and deeply concerned with matters relating to spirit and consciousness' (Owen, 2004, p 135). She traces this concern through the impact of Bergson's ideas upon not just *fin-de-siècle* occultism, but also his legacy upon the artistic *avant-garde* of the era such as The Imagists and later Symbolists, and his influence on the later works of William James (Owen, 2004, pp 137-40). Bergson, however, should not just be viewed as someone whose ideas were adapted by others for various forms of spiritual inspiration, but as a theorist of magic in his own right. Bergson, despite his skepticism concerning The Golden Dawn, was extremely interested in magic, particularly the emergent anthropological material of the era on the concept of *mana* (see Bergson, 1977, pp 134-208). Thus, whilst Owen is correct to contend that Bergson's Vitalist philosophy has had a deep and lasting influence on esotericism, his later work, left undiscussed by Owen,[3] betrays a profoundly serious and innovative theorisation of magic. In order to understand Bergson's theory of magic in his later works on spirituality, one needs an appreciation of his more famous earlier works. I wish to begin this with a discussion of Bergson's *Vitalism*.

Vitalism

Arguably, it is Bergson's commitment to *Vitalism* which proved to be his lasting influence upon fin-de-siècle occultism. Whilst Bergson's genius was his ability to connect Vitalist philosophy to the scientific theories of the day, he was in fact drawing upon an enduring philosophical tradition going back at least as far as Aristotle. Aristotle argued that 'life' can never be satisfactorily explained in purely material terms. Whilst such a notion has obviously become the foundation of various forms of religious and occult philosophies throughout the ages, it once again became popularised by the anti-Kantian philosophical sentiments of late nineteenth century Europe. In existentialist critiques of the perceived scientific reductionism of the age, philosophers such as Nietzsche, Dilthey, and Bergson promulgated Vitalism as a bulwark against the encroaching materialism of the age (see, for example, Schnädelbach, 1984). Whilst Nietzsche's Vitalism leans towards the willed impulse towards self-mastery and power, Dilthey's to hermeneutics, and Bergson's to the creative evolution of being, all three share common ideas: That

> Life, and reality in so far as it is living, consists in movement and becoming, rather than in static being. Reality is organic, not mechanical: biology, and often history, are more central than physics. Life is known empirically or by intuition, rather than by concepts and logical inference. Life is objective and transcends the knowing subject. Vitalism stresses the diversity of life and tends towards pluralism, and occasionally relativism, rather than monism. (Inwood, 1995, p 901)

As Owen states, 'Bergson's notion of an *élan vital*, a vital force or impulse that permeates the universe and everything in it, bore a distinct relationship to animistic occultism' (Owen, 2004, p 135). In what ways is this the case? In simple terms, Bergson, despite being heavily influenced by the evolutionary theories of Charles Darwin and Herbert Spencer, rejected materialist and mechanist explanations of reality, life and being, along with notions that individual senses of purpose control the functioning of each and every organism. In their place he posited the existence of a collective life-force or vital spirit – the *élan vital* – which powers organic evolution. In doing so, Bergson eschewed teleology by arguing that the élan 'is a creative and originating force which produces endless variations of forms against which it then has to contend in order to create further variations' (Collinson, 1987, p 132). In this sense, Bergson, following Spinoza, is often accused of pantheism, identifying a creator God with the élan vital. Indeed, in *Creative Evolution*, Bergson consciously identifies God with the élan:

> Thus defined, God has nothing of the ready-made, he is uninterrupted life, action, freedom. And the creation, so conceived, is not a mystery; we experience it in ourselves when we act freely (cited in Kolakowski, 2001 p 61).

Bergson's last major work *Two Sources of Morality and Religion*, first published in 1932, however, was in many respects a more nuanced spiritual articulation of his earlier works on the nature of matter and the evolutionary mechanism of the *élan vital*. As Kolakowski observes

> In *Matter and Memory* he attempted to show that modern neurophysiological research did not affect the notion of the mind's independence from the organism. The goal of *Creative Evolution* was to prove that the theory of transformism, far from justifiying a purely naturalistic concept of man and the universe, provided more reasons for perceiving the Great Mind behind the physical machinery. The task of *Two Sources* was to demonstrate that sociological investigations of religious phenomena and their social functions are not only compatible

with, but indeed, support, a view of religious life as a form of communication with the original élan which penetrates the world and coincides with the spirit of the Creator (Kolakowski, 2001, p 72-3).

In such instances, Bergson appears to construct divinity as *panentheistic*.[4] Indeed, his later conceptions of the élan bear similarities to Dennis Carpenter's characterisation of Paganisms as panentheistic (see Carpenter, 1996). As Carpenter argues, for many Pagans divinity permeates and animates matter, is communed with and quested on the individual level, yet simultaneously, is transcendent. In this sense, one can begin to make significant parallels between the Pagan notion of spirit and the élan.

Indeed, Bergson came to argue that not only was the élan responsible for the evolution of different forms of matter, but - despite lacking a *telos* – was also progressive. One form of this progress, for Bergson, is the development of religion, magic and morality. Whilst, I will outline Bergson's perspective on magic in a later section, it is worth noting here that these phenomena developed out of a meeting of the human mind with the élan. Bergson argued that it is in the altered states of consciousness of the mystic in which the most effective meeting of the élan and the mind can occur (see Goodchild, 1996, p 27). Crucially, Bergson's philosophy is based around an anti-intellectualism which valorises intuition over reason. This is not to say that the intellect does not have important functions for the survival of humanity but, rather, it is only through intuition that the creative and authentic being of the élan can be grasped.[5]

Thus, for Bergson, the élan not only underpins magical experience but his conception of magic arises out of a cluster of concepts familiar to occultists: A basis in the alteration of consciousness – specifically for Bergson in an intuitive consciousness - which facilitates the meeting of the macrocosm (the élan as spiritual force) with the microcosm (the magical self, specifically the mind). Not only that, but this encounter with the élan is, in a sense, an encounter with authentic being and this authenticity is subject to a specific form of authentic temporality – the durée.

Time and authenticity

This concept of time is of fundamental importance to Bergson's work. In making a distinction between the scientific timekeeping of clocks, which exhibit a precise and regular periodicity, and *pure time* or *durée* (duration), the way in which time is phenomenologically apprehended by the self, Bergson is also making existential distinctions between inauthentic and authentic forms of selfhood (see Collinson, 1987).[6] Importantly, Bergson's duration is built around a similar anti-intellectualism which characterises the élan. That is, it is the intellect which conspires with clock time to give reality an order which is, in fact, illusory.[7] For Bergson, philosophy based around this illusory temporal order creates an inauthentic philosophy of being. Rather, for Bergson, time is linked to Heraclitan flux, ephemerality and becoming. As he contends:

> [T]he interval of the *durée* exists only for us, and because of the mutual penetration of our conscious states; outside us one would find nothing but space, and thus simultaneities, of

which one may not even say that they objectively succeed each other. (Bergson, *Time and Free Will*, cited in Kolakowski, 2001, p 16)

Time, therefore, is the basis of Bergson's existentialism. As Collinson states of Bergson, 'Freedom belongs with our direct, non-spatial experience of reality ... only when one's action derives from the totality of one's being' (Collinson, 1987, p 131). As Bergson himself states in Time and Free Will, 'We are free when our acts emanate from the whole of our personality, when they express it and when they have this kind of indefinable resemblance to it that we sometimes see between a work and the artist' (cited in Kolakowski, 2001, p 129). In this way, freedom and authentic action are intrinsically linked to will and intent. Thus, one begins to see interesting parallels between the intentionality which underpins Bergson's authentic self and that of the magical self, even to the extent in which will - as the totality of being, rather than intellect - becomes the basis of freedom.

Not only is will linked to authentic forms of temporality, but such a commitment to *durée* underpins magical ritual. One sees this most strikingly within Paganisms, where the temporality of ritual actively contributes to the creation of magical identity: Firstly, the temporality of ritual – the context in which Pagan identities and community are forged (for example, Pike, 2001) – conforms to *durée* rather than *temps*. Secondly, developing Bergsonist thinking, theorists contrast premodern notions of time embedded in the cyclical rhythms of nature with the mechanical rhythms of modern temporality (Adam, 1995:, pp 23-4, 29-30). There is the implicitation that the rise of modernity obliterated 'natural time', with the irreversible, eschatological notions of time expounded by Christianity acting as catalyst for the eventual dominance of Newtonian clock-time (Perkins, 2001). This temporal sequestration from nature - especially from its constant life and death scenarios of being 'red in tooth and claw' - parallels the inauthentic sequestration of late modern existence from the uncertainties surrounding death (Becker, 1973; Ariès, 1974; Kearl, 1989). Pagan ritualism, however, is often based upon a meditative contrast between vitality of life and the frailty of mortality with the effect that the sensuousness of life, rather than its sanitization, is valorised (see Green, 2002). This acts as an exhortation to many Pagans to re-immerse themselves in the temporal flux of nature through forms of ritualization. In other words, ritual urges one to exist in terms of lived duration, rather than clock time.

Bergson on Magic

Bergson's emphasis on intuition rather intellect, and d*urée* rather than *temps*, not only lays the foundations for his ontology, but, as Owen argues, 'had clear implications for early twentieth century occultism' (Owen, 2004, p 136). If one examines Owen's characterisation of Bergson's thought one sees that his appeal to occultism was broad-based:

> Firstly, Bergson, paralleling Jung, placed emphasis, through the lens of the élan, on the holistic unfolding of spirit within individual selves. As Owen argues, 'Bergson argued for the importance, intensity of inner experience, and proposed the interrelationship not only of inner and outer realities but also of body and spirit. In a striking parallel with occult thought, he argued that matter and spirit are not opposites but part of a whole' (*Ibid.*).

Secondly, his emphasis upon the centrality of individual consciousness in temporal constructions of the authentic self, coupled with the notion that the élan functions, for Bergson, as a form of spiritual supra-consciousness, appealed to occultists well versed in the role that alteration of consciousness plays in magical practices.

> Thirdly, and most importantly, was Bergson's notion of the illumination of the intellect through intuition. In other words, it is through intuitive insight – the non-rational – that 'a phenomenal world invested and animated with spirit' can be apprehended (*Ibid.*).

Importantly, these same foundations are to prove important to his theorization of magic. In particular, it is this latter assertion that intuition and the intellect sit at opposite poles of the spectrum of human consciousness – that which F.T.C Moore terms the *antimonies of intelligence* (Moore, 1996) – which lies, for Bergson, at the heart of magic.

Bergson's theory of magic has been largely overshadowed by the polarised debates of the intellectualist and symbolist anthropologists of the era concerning the rational status of magic. On the one hand, Lévy-Bruhl was asserting that 'primitive' pre-logical thought was incompatible with scientific Western civilised discourse, whilst, on the other, intellectualists, such as Tylor, placed emphasis on the evolutionary basis of science in pseudo-scientific pre-modern magic.[8] Against this backdrop of the linkages between magic and rationality, Bergson pursued an altogether different approach. It is Bergson's contention that magic arises from the inadequacies of human the intellect. As Moore explains:

> [W]hen we look at societies which are themselves composed of individual organisms, we find, according to Bergson, two patterns, the *hymen-opteran*, built upon instinct, lacking any short-term or inbuilt ability to change behaviour, subordinating the individual organism to the group, as in the case of bees and ants, and the *human*, built upon intelligence , able to adapt, and leaving a great margin for independent individual action. Bergson argues that in several ways, religion and magic should be seen as nature's way of coping with various problems arising from the second (human) mode of social organisation. (Moore, 1996, p 126).

As with his concept of durée, Bergson argues that these problems arise from the intellectual segmentation of our experiences, particularly actions endowed with purposive or instrumental rationality. One tends to impute certainty to such instrumental behaviour in marked opposition to expressive behaviours which possess affective dimensions. However, a liminal space exists between these two types of behaviours in which any new form of action has uncertain consequences. As Moore explains:

> While there are plenty of cases where we are confident in our ability to do something towards achieving a goal (such as opening a window to let air in), and plenty where we are confident that we have no such ability (people don't usually think that they can do anything which will help to bring about a fine day tomorrow), there are plenty more where we are not sure. (Moore, 1999, pp 140-1)

Thus, for Bergson it is when we as humans reach for new goals – when attainment and outcome are uncertain - that magic comes into play:[9] 'Thus the description of actions *in this margin* between what we believe and to be in our power and what we do not believe to be within our power will ... turn out to have the form or structure of magical descriptions, since the agent is not in possession of any specific belief which makes the instrumental link between the action and its goal' (Moore, 1999, p 141). Magic, in this sense, underpins creative action and, in a neat reversal of Kant, it is magic which appears to be a prime catalyst for human progress.[10] As Bergson himself put it, we see 'superstition arising from the will to success' (cited in Moore, 1999, p 141).[11]

Furthermore, magic for Bergson is part of human cognitive structure and evolution, but is also, following Durkheim and Mauss, a fundamentally social generator of meaning: One has already seen how the *durée* of Pagan ritual involves an existential re-embedding of practitioners both in the rhythms of nature, but also in a meditation on, and a meditative form, of mortality. For Bergson, one important quality of human intelligence which distinguishes it from animal intelligence is the knowledge that one day we will all die. Bergson argues that the social mechanisms of magic and religion provide the meaning which overcomes the potential for apathy which this knowledge may bring. That is, magic is not the exotic activity that the anthropologists of the era would have us believe. Rather, for Bergson, it is not only part of our human make-up – akin to the cognitive locus of spirituality one finds in the works of, for example, Sperber (1975), Lawson and McCauley (1990;

also Lawson, 1993), and Boyer (1993) - but is also a fundamental and relevant facet of human being and society. As Kolakowski concludes

> Far from being an inferior kind of science, magic is an aspect of natural religion, a part of the instinctive barrier which life erects in order to prevent our intelligence from enfeebling or dissolving men's will to assert themselves in a hostile environment. The growth of knowledge and technical skills gradually reduces, though never abolishes, the margin of uncertainty in our practical efforts, thereby correspondingly reducing our need to discover conscious intentions behind all the events and to cope with the world by magical means. Without magic the intelligence of primitive man would have paralysed his practical efforts and killed progress.
> (Kolakowski, 2001, p 80)

But does this reduction of magical to a materialist cognitive mechanism, albeit with social meaning, rob it of its 'magic'? To answer this question one needs to look at theorists who have elaborated classical Bergsonist thought:

Deleuze on Bergson

Thus, Bergson not only sees magic as innate to existence, but also reclaimed it from its intellectualist status of Skorupskian pseudo-science. One of the most potent legacies of Aleister Crowley for contemporary magicians has been his insistence on the illumination of magic through an encounter with science. Crowley consciously inverted the common conceit of magic being a pre-science by contending that science could be harnessed by magicians in the service of magic. The rise of Chaos

Magic, in particular, coupled with an explosion of interest in popular science – has demonstrated ways in which complexity theory – especially quantum and chaos theories – can be used not only as a heuristic of magic, but also as a cornerstone for a materialist magical paradigm.[12] Importantly, what is often unacknowledged is the debt that the origins of such a paradigm owes to Bergsonist philosophy:

Sean Watson, in an important article on the philosophical overlaps between theories of complexity and the recent shifts of focus in some branches of contemporary neuroscience and philosophies of consciousness, argues that theories of self-organisation are 'really just part of a more general trend in the conceptualization of human consciousness …. "the new Bergsonism".' (Watson, 1998, p 6). Much of this new Bergsonism takes its cue from the work of French post-structuralist philosopher Gilles Deleuze: His early works comprise a number of reworkings of famous philosophers of the past, most notably Hume, Spinoza, Nietzsche and Bergson. Concepts taken from these philosophers then went on to form the foundation of Deleuze's later *philosophy of desire*, particularly his co-authored work with Felix Guattari critiquing Capitalist and Oedipal relations. These re-readings are also fundamental to the rise of Neo-Bergsonist philosophy:

Deleuze re-read Hume to provide a monistic semiology of desire, and from Spinoza he took the notion of immanence which he then applied to embodied forms of desire. For purposes of this article, however, I wish to focus upon Deleuze's Nietzsche and his Bergson - interestingly the same two philosophers proposed by Owen as most important to fin-de-siècle occult thought. From Nietzsche Deleuze took the notion of will and reinserted it in his own idiosyncratic philosophy of desire, in particular to understand the way that individuals seek to impose power over others, especially over their bodies (Deleuze, 1983, pp 39-42, 49-52).

Deleuze's reading of Nietzsche not only concentrates on his vitalistic will to power - the dominion over others - but, as Goodchild argues, on the negative will to power (Deleuze, 1983, p 166). That is, the ways in which people accept the dominant norms and values of the cultures into which they are socialised. This acceptance of cultural hegemony – the Nietzschean herd mentality – therefore becomes a block to becoming. If, from a Bergsonist perspective, magic is linked to dynamic action and progress, then habits formed by the negative will to power create a stasis of being. As Bergson himself states, 'His [Human's] instinctive resistance to innovations is a proof. The inertia of humanity has never yielded, save under the impulsion of genius' (Bergson, 1977, p 171). Indeed, one sees this notion strongly in Chaos Magic where habit is constructed as inhibiting human potential. Dave Lee, for example, contends that 'Magicians are generally aware that , in order to get results ... you have to do things that you don't initially like – you have to break out of your 'comfort zone', in order to change ... We prefer to repeat comfortable and familiar thoughts, even if they make us unhappy, rather than strike out into new thought patterns which would make us feel batter; we tend to repeat familiar actions which have become ineffective rather than adopt new and more powerful strategies.' (Lee, 1997, p 121)

One has seen that, in classical Bergsonist thought, magic is one such strategy which accompanies a Nietzschean will to change. Importantly, the Nietzsche of Deleuze, rather like the Nietzsche of much of occultism, is not the racist Nietzsche read through the lens of German

National Socialism or of magic based on white supremacy or separatism (for example, Gardell, 2003; Goodrick-Clarke, 2003), but rather points 'to a different kind of mode of existence, beyond historical humanity' (Goodchild, 1996, p 32). That is, to a *transhuman* or *posthuman* order of being. For Deleuze, the will to power becomes bound to desire, and desire, like magic, is a force which wishes to create rather than habituate. I will discuss some of the implications of this for magical practice and thinking below, but what of Deleuze's Bergson?

Deleuze's reading of Bergson centres on the concept of duration and notions of *real, lived experience* rather than the *possibility of experience* forwarded by Kant. That is, the *actual* rather than the *virtual*. By grounding philosophy in this way Deleuze's Bergsonism seeks to engage 'the whole of the subject in his or her passions' (Goodchild, 1996, p 24). That is, rather like Deleuze's Nietzsche, his Bergson becomes part of his philosophy of desire, with the élan as a monism of desire (see Deleuze 1991, pp 91-113). As Matt Lee argues in his excellent article offering a Deleuzo-Guattarian perspective on Spare's Sorceries of Zos and Chaos Magic:

> One of the driving forces of the 'post-structuralist' movement in philosophy was a 'theoretical anti-humanism'. This anti-humanism placed itself in opposition to any thought that centred on Man as the primary analytical category. Deleuze's particular contribution focussed on developing concepts of 'immanence' and 'difference' which put forward a univocal ontology – that is, which put forward a unified being, a thought of life that has no 'outside' or 'duality' but which contains within itself its own means of development. This

univocal universe is full of flux and becoming, a constantly shifting ocean of change. The role of Bergson in Deleuze's thought is to give him the means to make this 'univocal ontology' move and evolve. (Lee, 2003, p 103)[13]

The New Bergsonism

Indeed, Deleuze is very much a philosopher of actualizing movement through the flux of the virtual (see Marks, 1998). This *movement of being*, and Neo-Bergsonist thought in general, can be summarised through five general propositions - anti-Cartesian monism, connectionism, anti-representationalism, selectionism, and duration (Watson, 1998; also Deleuze, 1991):

At its most simple level, **anti-Cartesian monism** refers to a lack of separation between mind and body. As Watson states, 'There is only matter and its energetic movement ... Consciousness is entirely reducible to the complex movement of matter' (Watson, 1998, p 6). Linked to this monism, is a monism of matter which sees no separation between the *inner* and *outer*. That is, As Deleuze states 'there cannot be a difference in kind but only a difference in degree between the faculty of the brain and the function of the core, between the perception of matter and matter itself' (cited in Watson, 1998, p 6). Deleuze and Guattari, for example, have conceptualised this monism as 'the plane of immanence' (Deleuze and Guattari, 1994). Such a plane reveals that 'the relationship between consciousness, brain and material world is one of absolute continuity and connectedness' (Watson, 1998, p 6). Given this connectedness there is an underlying doctrine of **connectionism**.[14] As Watson states:

> In the traditional Cartesian model, in which an 'occult' mind gains experience of a separate material world via the senses and consequent perceptions, there is usually an intermediate term. The intermediate term is 'representation'. The world is somehow re-presented to the mind, or to consciousness, as though there were a homunculus hidden inside our heads looking at images projected onto a screen and listening to sounds from hidden internal speakers. (Watson, 1998, p 6)

In other words, the self or brain is part of the same monistic reality – the same plane of immanence without the need for the mediating power of representation. Neo-Bergsonism therefore rests upon **anti-representationalism**. This reality, however, is experienced purely as a result of how the brain is wired as a result of experience. Indeed, for Deleuze, the brain becomes a complicating factor in our experience of reality. As Deleuze contends

> The brain does not manufacture representations, but only complicates the relationship between a received movement (excitation) and an executed movement (response). Between the two, it establishes an interval (écart), whether it divides up the received movement infinitely or prolongs it in a plurality of possible reactions. (Deleuze, 1991, p 24)

The corollary of this is the brain acts as a buffer zone between excitation and response within which will becomes exercised. Such will occurs as a result of **selectionism** – a resolution of the virtual and the actual. In these senses, the virtual refers to the infinite complexity of the world as it really is prior to processing by the brain – 'a world in its totality, as it really is, beyond what can be experienced' (Watson, 1998, p 7) - and how this world is actualized in experience.[15] Importantly, therefore, these terms imply a nested form of monism rather than a dualism. As Watson explains:

> [W]e must, of course, guard against any Kantianism – in which the former is the 'world in itself' and the latter simply 'phenomenal experience' going on in a place somewhere removed from the real world 'in itself'. Similarly, we must guard against any Cartesianism in which the 'virtual' is the material world outside, and the 'actual' is a mysterious, immaterial, 'representation' of that world for the 'eyes' of an equally mysterious, immaterial, 'cogito' within. Both the 'virtual' and the 'actual' are as real and solid and material as one another. The latter is effectively a subset of the former; a subtraction from the total, the total which Deleuze sometimes refers to as 'the Absolute'. (*Ibid.*)

Importantly for New Bergsonist thinkers, such as Deleuze and Guattari and Brian Massumi, the actual refers to conscious experience. They also recognise that one is also affected by one's environment at a subliminal or unconscious level. Unconsciously we are both complex organisms and are affected by the complexity of our environments. The brain acts to select (or filter) this complexity both to make it intelligible – the 'blooming, buzzing confusion' of William James - and to prevent sensory overload (Massumi, 1992, 1996). The Neo-Bergsonist brain, therefore, becomes part of web like structure of experience and consciousness rather than its pure locus. Thus, there is a clear link between this decentredness of consciousness and the decentred subjectivities of post-structuralist theory of, for example, Deleuze, Derrida and Foucault. That is, a scientific anti-humanism underpins the theoretical anti-humanism.

Finally, by developing Bergson's notion of durée – **duration** - Neo-Bergsonist thinkers locate experience within his particularly existentialist philosophy of time (see Watson, 1998, pp 9-10). That is, following Bergson, Neo-Bergsonist thinkers see the unfolding of the self as being intimately bound with lived duration. Given that durée implied a freedom of being at odds with rationalised forms of temporality, what can Neo-Bergsonism reveal about contemporary magical practices? In order to answer let us examine an important subset of Neo-Bergsonist thought – complexity theory.

Complexity, chaos and magic

A number of Chaos Magicians have stressed emphasis upon complexity theory in their particular understanding of the operations of magic. Peter Carroll and Jaq Hawkins, for example, both emphasise the role that the Austin Osman Spare has played in the formulation of Chaos Magic. However, his contribution is not just that of occult aesthete and trance visionary but as an avatar of the science of chaos (Carroll, n.d.; Hawkins, 1996). As Carroll himself observes:

> Crowley certainly helped put the boot in against monotheism but the process was already well advanced. Science, which had basically evolved out of renaissance magic, had more or less finished monotheism as a serious parasite on advanced cultures ... However it is Spare's work that appears more austere and scientific when compared to some of Crowley's

> more baroque symbolic extravagances ... Spare's work forms the bridge between an older style of magic brought to fruition by Crowley (which derived most of its appeal, power and liberating potential from its religious style of anti-religion) and the new magic. The new approach is characterised by a kind of scientific *anti-science*. This is increasingly becoming known as Chaos Magic. (Carroll, n.d.)

Whilst I have written on this topic before - for example, Green (2001a) – it is only recently that it is occurred to me that Chaos Magic is framed by Neo-Bergsonism. Certainly, both are concerned with actualising in experience the flux of being and becoming. Hawkins, for example, uses complexity theory to demonstrate how the flux of the virtual actually contains subtle forms of ordering, analogous to Jung's synchronous ordering, but also to the spiralling ordering of energies at sacred sites and the ubiquity of labyrinth designs across cultures (Hawkins, 1996, pp 58-63). For Hawkins, magic concerns the recognition of patterns and the creation of new forms of existential patterning. This occurs principally through a cognitive commitment to non-linearity – operationalised by Hawkins as imaginative creation - and is rooted in Spare's concept of *free belief* and his process of sigilization. Whilst these relationships remain theoretically underdeveloped by Hawkins, the Neo-Bergsonist complexity theory as developed by Fritjof Capra - via Varela and Maturana's work on *autopoetic systems* and Prigogine's work on *dissipative structures* - can act as an important heuristic (Capra, 1996; also Szendrei, 1989):

Autopoetic systems are organic structures such as the human organism which are self-regulating, self-repairing, and hence, self-creating. They self-produce through a system of complex feedback loops – a simple example being homeostasis - both within the organism and in tandem with the environment. Autopoetic systems are able to create such links with the environment through a process called *structural coupling* (Capra, 1996). Capra argues that structural coupling is effected by the creation of temporary structures of cognition by the body – an ephemeral co-ordination of the decentred networks of brain and nervous system – to produce an extended link into one's environment. Given this, the organic structure of the body therefore is also web-like – Deleuze and Guattari term this human organism as open system *the body without organs* – as well as connected to the web of decentred consciousness outlined above. Importantly such coupling happens not only at the biological level, but also at the social level through interactions of selves, bodies and language creating new autopoetic networks which transcend individual selves (Massumi, 1992).[16]

What we have here therefore is a Neo-Bergsonist model of human selfhood and society which begins to chart the multiplicity of mind-body-environment interactions which underpin magical practices. The relationship between Chaos Magic, Neo-Bergsonist philosophy and autopoesis can be made more concrete through the examination of Dave Lee's use of quantum theory in his *immanentist* magical paradigm. Like Neo-Bergsonist thinkers Lee advocates both an anti-Cartesian monism and a connectionism in which the environment, brain and will are intrinsically linked. Lee does this with reference to Dana Zohar's use of quantum theory, more specifically the Bose-Einstein Condensate (BEC). As Lee states

> The theory makes the connection between a widespread type of quantum structure called a *condensed phase* and the known properties of nervous tissue. A condensed phase is a system within which all the units making it up do the same thing at the same time – the system has achieved alignment or *phase coherence.*[17] (Lee, 1997: 90)

Lee's (and Zohar's) use of the theory contends that this coherence is a coherence between the brain and the environment, with one being able to affect the other. For Chaoists, the BEC predicts 'a similarity between the behaviour of fundamental wave/particles and that of brains - because one is rooted in the other' (Lee, 1997, p 92). That is the condensed phase is akin to Capra's notion of the temporary structures of cognition which facilitate the structural coupling of body and environment and abolish any notions of *inner* and *outer*. This is the foundation for a materialist theory of magic wherein altered states of consciousness are akin to condensed phases which can bring about macrocosmic change.

Thus, the insight that Neo-Bergsonism underpins this 'new magic' is important for two major reasons: Firstly, it helps one to understand its materialist basis. What is crucial here is that one stays true to Bergson's original panentheistic conception of matter as pervaded by spirit, with the élan transcendent.[18] Secondly, it helps to locate it in its correct intellectual context in the history of ideas. In other words, that the 'new magic' does not form a radical break with fin-de-siècle occultism but, rather, both are influenced by Bergsonist thought in its various guises.

Sorcery and The Rhizome

Importantly, the Neo-Bergsonist magical consciousness gives rise to the sorts of multiplicity of the self and becoming which, as stated above, have been presaged by the post-structuralist decentring of subjectivity (see Lee, 1997, pp 131-3). The works of Deleuze and Guattari are arguably the closest that philosophy has come to conceptualising this flux and multiplicity of being. In many respects the arguments presented in this section of this article complement Matt Lee's excellent article on Deleuze and Guattari and ways in which their conceptual commitment to immanent Vitalism and desire can be used as a heuristic of anomalous sorceries (see Lee, 2003). Lee's article concentrates on the relationship between their notion of becoming and the anomalous magic of Spare's Sorceries of Zos. In particular, there is an implicit connection between *Kia* and the élan. Whilst Richard Sutcliffe (1996, p 129) has noted the Neo-Nietzschean influence of Deleuze and Guattari on Chaoism, the influence of Bergson has, once again, escaped detection.

Deleuze and Guattari set out to make their philosophy a transformative experience in itself (see Green, 2001b). Their book *A Thousand Plateaus* (Deleuze and Guattari, 1988), for example, uses juxtaposition and pastiche to affect the reader on multiple levels simultaneously. Indeed, it is a central strategy of Deleuzo-Guattarian thought to work on the affective and semiotic, as well as intellectual, places. Indeed, following Bergson's privileging of intuition over the intellect, their *oeuvre* resists branching hierarchies of knowledge so beloved of the Enlightenment – particularly those branching taxonomies of the natural and human sciences which they term *arborescent* (Deleuze and Guattari, 1988, pp 293-4; also Moore, 1996, pp 105-114). Arborescent taxonomies of knowledge are products of Weberian processes of rationalization which imprison the modern intellect just as the modern self is imprisoned by the *iron cage* of bureaucracy or - more pertinently to Deleuzean thought - Oedipus. In contra-distinction, Deleuze and Guattari glorify *nomad*, rhizomatic thought. This seeks to break the strictures of hierarchical cognition through an engagement with difference, becoming and flux, rather like the Chaoist notion of ideospheric knowledge (see Hine, n.d., p 2). The very restlessness of the rhizome both resists categorisation and creates new forms of knowledge – intellectual, but also sensual, super-sensory, and embodied forms of knowing – through the blurring of boundaries and use of *bricolage* (see Magliocco, 1996). In this way, rhizomatic consciousness underpins much of Pagan magical thinking and practice, but strikes a particular chord with Chaos Magic. Brian Massumi could be describing the Chaoist attitude to magical working when stating that

> "Nomad thought" does not lodge itself in the edifice of an ordered interiority; it moves freely in an element of exteriority. It does not repose on identity; it rides on difference ... Rather than reflecting the world, they are immersed in a changing state of things. A concept is a brick. It can be used to build the courthouse of reason. Or it can be thrown through the window. (Massumi, 1992, p 5)

It is at this point of breakthrough that the nomad becomes the schizo. Deleuze and Guattari use the notion of the schizo (and their concept of *schizoanalysis*) in order to demonstrate how immersion in the semiotic – for them, the realm prior to Oedipal symbolisation and socialization - can disrupt the symbolic order, and thus the social order. In particular, they look to schizophrenics such as the Surrealist playwright and performer Antonin Artaud, children, indigenous peoples and magicians – *sorcerors* - for models of the pre-symbolic (Deleuze and Guattari, 1984). Crucially, they do not glorify schizophrenic psychosis as a way of being, but rather conceptualize it as a mode of becoming. Indeed, it is a magical mode of becoming. As Colebrook explains:

> They celebrate the 'schizo' against paranoid 'man'. Their 'schizo' is not a psychological type (not a schizophrenic), but a way of thinking a life not governed by any fixed norm or image of self – a self in flux and becoming, rather than a self that has submitted to law. (Colebrook, 2002, p 5).

Indeed, the 'self that has submitted to law' is not just Oedipalised, but is egoistic. In contrast, it is the self in flux which lies at the heart of Chaos Magic. In such an 'outlaw self' - put through a Neo-Bergsonist lens - ego and habit become an ossified cluster of arborescent cognitions which can be ruptured by schizoid, magical becoming. As Guattari observes:

> Schizoanalysis obviously does not consist of miming schizophrenia, but in crossing, like it the barriers of non-sense which prohibit access to a-signifying nuclei of subjectivation, the only way to shift petrified systems of modelisation. It implies an optimal enlargement of pragmatic entrances into Unconscious formations. (Guattari, 1995, p 68)

Here one can return to Spare as godfather of the 'new magic'. Spare's death posture was one such entrance into these 'unconscious formations'. The loss of ego experienced during the posture is analogous to the loss of the fixity of identity in the schizo mode of becoming. Indeed, Spare's description of the ego-loss experienced during the posture is a brilliantly apt description of magical becoming in a macrocosm composed of flux, complexity, and multiplicity – 'The Ego is swept up as a leaf in a fierce gale' (cited in Drury, 2000, p 131).

The Two Bergsonisms

Bergsonism in its twin manifestations are valuable heuristics of magical practice. Given this, by way of a brief conclusion, I wish to re-emphasise the four major propositions presented here:

Firstly, scholars of magic have unjustly neglected Bergson's theory of magic. Owen has done a wonderful job of rehabilitating Bergson by charting his influence upon the fin-de-siècle occult revival. This in itself, however, tends to obscure both Bergson's later work on magic and spirit and also his continuing, albeit mediated, influence upon contemporary magical practices.

Secondly, linked to this first proposition, Bergson's theory of magic overcomes some of the stuckness of symbolist versus intellectualist debates which still serve to *orientalise* magic throughout the human sciences. Bergson potentially gives one a theory of magic as dynamic, relational and linked to the spiritual unfolding of self and humanity. Given this, one can only agree with Owen that Bergson came closer than other philosophers of his age in articulating an occult philosophy.

Thirdly, this location of 'the new magic' in its correct Neo-Bergsonist context not only brings new insights into its operation, but also helps to locate it both intellectually and sociologically. In Chaoism, for example, there is a tendency to play up its postmodern elements without examining its modernist heart in Crowley's psychologization of magic and scientific illuminism and the grand narratives of fin-de-siècle occultism. Thus, although not without their problems, Bergsonisms provide innovative ways of dissecting contemporary magical practices and traditions as regards their relationship to spiritual – material modes of being and becoming, rather than around a proscrustean modern-postmodern dichotomy. Such a heuristic also has the advantage of recognising that contemporary Pagan magics share a common philosophical and intellectual heritage – of modernity and Bergson – whilst also recognising that this might be articulated in nuanced ways. For example, Golden Dawn magic is very much linked to the classical Bergsonist thinking of the élan, whilst Chaos Magic and Spare's Sorceries of Zos are much more connected to Neo-Bergsonism.

Finally, just as Neo-Bergsonism provides important new ways of thinking about the self as multiple and decentred, it also provides a new understanding of how magic might operate within a connectionist, immanentist paradigm without the need for the enslavement of the spiritual by the material. Indeed, by raiding the conceptual toolbag of Deleuze and Guattari, one can see how decentred consciousness can be harnessed to achieve magical illumination and personal breakthrough: Massumi could be talking of Chaoist modes of becoming when stating that 'Schizophrenia is a breakaway into the unstable equilibrium of continuing self-invention' (Massumi, 1992, p 92).

Notes
1   During the course of this article Bergson will be subjected to a number of multi-disciplinary and unconventional treatments These might be

seen as contentious from the viewpoint of mainstream philosophical readings of his work. This is due to three major factors: Firstly, the familiar flamboyant Bergson is the early Bergson of *Time and Free Will*, *Matter and Memory* and *Creative Evolution* and not the more introverted Bergson of his later works on religion and morality upon which this article concentrates; secondly, although his works are subjected to philosophical analyses by the likes of Moore, Kolakowski and Deleuze in this article, they are also read through the lenses of cultural history (Owen) and sociology (my own discipline – I must admit to having only a rudimentary grounding in philosophy), all with different emphases; finally, Bergson's theory of magic is perhaps the least known of all his *oeuvre* which again opens it up to more non-traditional readings of his ideas, particularly an engagement with early evolutionary theories of magic from anthropology.

2   Although a number of authors place stress upon Bergson's *anti-intellectualism* it has to be stated that they do not mean an attack on intellectual endeavour, but rather a privileging of *disinterested* intuition over *practical* intellect. Indeed I am indebted to a personal communication on this point from Dr Matt Lee of Sussex University on this point who emphasises that, in an epistemological sense Bergson is honest in his own form of intellectualism which notes the limits of the human intellect and looks for a more intimate alternative grounded in intuition.

3   Admittedly this is not the focus of her excellent study.

4   Panentheism, a term first coined by Karl Krause in 1828, is distinguishable from pantheism in the sense that although the divine is held to be co-existent with matter, it also transcends it. This doctrine has a long history traceable to early Hasidic Judaism, through the religious philosophy of Hegel before finding more recent expression in the works of prominent Christian theologians Charles Hartshorne and Matthew Fox. Diané Collinson, for example, discusses letters penned to French theologian Joseph de Tonquédec in which Bergson 'maintained that he regarded God as a free creator, the generator of life and matter but distinct from them' (Collinson, 1987, p 132). Perhaps Bergson's panentheism stance stems partly from his own ambiguous relationship to Catholicism as a personal faith and politicised ideology.

5   See note 2 above.

6   This question of authenticity is a property of Bergson's later work, particularly *The Two Sources*. Indeed, it is contentious and virtually unthinkable in the context of his earlier work given the hostility of Heidegger to Bergson's philosophy of time.

7   As Bergson states, "*Time is invention or it is nothing at all.*" (Bergson, 1911, p 341).

8   Having said this, Bergson still does, at times, privilege science over magic, which sits uneasily with his appeal to intuition over intelligence (see Bergson, 1977).

9   In this sense, Bergson's ideas concerning the limitations of the intellect find an interesting parallel in *The Malinowski Thesis* that magic compensates for the inadequacies of indigenous technologies (see, for example, Tambiah, 1990, pp 22, 71-3).

10 Indeed, this would go some way to explaining the particular relationship between the occult and the *avant-garde*.

11 Curiously, Bergson (1977) often discusses magic along with institutionalised forms of religion as being static forms of spirituality. However, the dynamic character accorded to magic by Bergson in the development of creative human action seems at odds with such stasis. I would therefore see (contemporary) magic, alongside mysticism, as dynamic in contra-distinction to the stasis of institutionalised religions.

12 Some of these overlaps and interfaces are developed in much more detail by Szendrei, 1989).

13 It has to be noted here that although Bergson's Vitalism gave movement to Deleuze's thought, Deleuzean thinking also seeks to empty this Vitalism of its transcendent element. This anti-transcendentalism is a crucial difference between Bergson himself and Deleuze's reading of Bergson.

14 Connectionism or inter-connectedness is a staple element of esoteric philosophy (see, for example, Faivre, 1994, pp 10-15).

15 Magic, therefore, implies some sort of extra-ordinary actualization of the virtual.

16 This idea of social inter-connection, however, was never forwarded by Varela and Maturana, for example, who limit their work to the biological sciences.

17 Capra terms this process *phase locking*.

18 A common misconception about chaos magic is that it is a materialist magic devoid of transcendent spiritual content – a myth exposed by Woodman (1998). A panentheistic, Neo-Bergsonist view of matter acts as a corrective to this perception.

References

Adam, B., 1995, *Timewatch: The Social Analysis of Time*, Polity, Cambridge

Ariès, P., 1974, *Western Attitudes Toward Death from the Middle Ages to the Present*, Marion Boyars, London

Becker, H., 1973, *The Denial of Death*, Free Press, New York

Bergson, H., 1911 [1907], *Creative Evolution*, Henry Holt & Company, New York

1977 [1935], *The Two Sources of Morality and Religion*, The University of Notre Dame Press, Notre Dame, IND.

1991 [1896], *Matter and Memory*, Zone Books, New York

Boyer, P. (ed.), 1993, *Cognitive Aspects of Religious Symbolism*, Cambridge University Press, Cambridge

Capra, F., 1996, *The Web of Life*, Harper Collins, London

Carpenter, D.D., 1996, 'Emergent Nature Spirituality: An examination of the Major Spiritual Contours of the Contemporary Pagan Worldview, in J.R. Lewis (ed.), *Magical Religion and Modern Witchcraft*, State University of New York Press, Albany, NY, 35-72.

Carroll, P., n.d, *The Magic of Chaos*, [On-line],

http://www.chaosmatrix.org/library/chaos/texts/mach.html

Collinson, D., 1987, *Fifty Major Philosophers*, Routledge, London

Colebrook, C., 2002, *Gilles Deleuze*, Routledge, London

Deleuze, G., 1983 [1962], *Nietzsche and Philosophy*, Athlone, London

    1991 [1966], *Bergsonism*, Zone Books, New York

Deleuze, G. and Guattari, F., 1984 [1972], *Anti-Oedipus*, Athlone London

    1988 [1980], *A Thousand Plateaus*, Athlone, London

    1994, *What is Philosophy?* Verso, London

Drury, N., 2000, *The History of Magic in the Modern Age: A quest for personal transformation*, Carroll & Graf, New York

Faivre, A., 1994, *Access to Western Esotericism*, SUNY Press, Albany, NY

Gardell, M., 2003, *Gods of the Blood: The Pagan Revival and White Separatism*, Duke University Press, Durham, NC

Goodchild, P., 1996, *Deleuze & Guattari: An Introduction to the Politics of Desire*, Sage, London

Goodrick-Clarke, N., 2003, *Black Sun,* New York University Press

Green, D., 2001a, 'Modernity Magickal Cosmologies and Science: A New Cauldron for a New Age?', *Pomegranate: a New Journal of Neo-Pagan Thought*, 15, 22-35

    2001b, 'Tree to Rhizome? Pagan spirituality, science and resistance in the new millennium', in U. King (ed.) *Spirituality and Society in the New Millennium*, Sussex Academic Press, Brighton, 206-219

    2002, 'Death, Nature and Uncertain Spaces: Commentary from a sociology of paganism', *Omega: Journal of Death and Dying*, 44 (2), 127-149

Guattari, F., 1995, *Chaosmosis: An Ethico-Aesthetic Paradigm*, Indiana University Press, Bloomington, IND.

Harris, G., 1976, 'Bergson and Catholic Thought', *Month*, December, 414-7

Hawkins, J.D., 1996, *Understanding Chaos Magic*, Capall Bann, Chieveley

Hine, P., n.d., *Pandemonaeon Magicks,* [On-line], http://www.chaosmatrix.org/library/chaos/texts/pandmag.html

Inwood, M, 1995, 'Vitalism', in T. Honderich (ed.), *The Oxford Companion to Philosophy*, Oxford University Press, Oxford, 901-2

Kearl, M.C., 1989, *Endings: a Sociology of Death and Dying*, Oxford University Press, Oxford

Kolakowski, L., 2001 [1985], *Bergson*, St. Augustin's Press, South Bend, IND.

Lawson, E.T., 1993, 'Cognitive categories, cultural forms and ritual structures', in P. Boyer (ed.), *Cognitive Aspects of Religious Symbolism,* Cambridge University Press, Cambridge, 188-205

Lawson, E.T. and McCauley R.N., 1990, *Rethinking Religion: Connecting Cognition and Culture*, Cambridge University Press, Cambridge

Lee, D., 1997, *Chaotopia! Magick & Ecstacy in the PandaemonAeon*, Attractor, Leeds

Lee, M., 2003, '"Memories of a Sorcerer": Notes on Gilles-Deleuze-Felix Guattari, Austin Osman Spare and Anomalous Sorceries', *Journal for the Academic Study of Magic*, 1, 102-130

Magliocco, S., 1996, 'Ritual is my Chosen Art Form', in J.R. Lewis (ed.), *Magical Religion and Modern Witchcraft*, State University of New York Press, Albany, NY., 93-120

Marks, D., 1998, *Gilles Deleuze: Vitalism and Multiplicity*, Pluto Press, London

Massumi, B., 1992, *A User's Guide to Capitalism and Schizophrenia: Deviations from Deleuze and Guattari*, MIT Press, Boston

1996, 'The Autonomy of Affect', in P. Patton (ed.), *Deleuze: A Critical Reader*, Blackwell, Oxford.

Moore, F.C.T., 1996, *Bergson: Thinking Backwards*, CambridgeUniversity Press, Cambridge

1999, 'Magic', in J. Mullarkey (ed.), *The New Bergson*, Manchester University Press, Manchester, 135-145

Owen, A., 2004, *The Place of Enchantment*, Chicago University Press, Chicago, ILL.

Perkins, M., 2001, *The Reform of Time: Magic and Modernity*, Pluto Press, London

Pike, S.M., 2001, *Earthly Bodies, Magical Selves*, University of California Press, Berkeley

Russell, B.A.W., 1956, *Logic and Knowledge*, Allen & Unwin, London

Schnädelbach, H, 1984, *Philosophy in Germany 1831-1933*, Cambridge University Press, Cambridge

Sperber, D., 1975, *Rethinking Symbolism*, Cambridge University Press, Cambridge

Sutcliffe, R., 1996, 'Left-Hand Path Ritual Magick: An Historical and Philosophical Overview', in G. Harvey and C. Hardman (eds.), *Paganism Today*, Thorsons, London, 109-37

Szendrei, E.V., 1989, 'Bergson, Prigogine and the Rediscovery of Time', *Process Studies*, 18, (3), 181-193

Tambiah, S.J., 1990, *Magic, Science, Religion and the Scope of Rationality*, Cambridge University Press, Cambridge

Watson, S., 1998, 'The New Bergsonism: Discipline, Subjectivity and Freedom', *Radical Philosophy*, 92, 7-16

Woodman, J., 1998, 'A Means to an End? The Role of Altered States of Consciousness in Chaos Magic', paper delivered to the *Shamanism in Contemporary Society* conference at the Department of Religious Studies, University of Newcastle-Upon-Tyne, 24th June, 1998.

Yeats, W.B., 1972, *Memoirs*, Macmillan, London

Becoming a Sorcerer: Jean-Pierre Bekolo's *Quartier Mozart* and the Magic of Deleuzian and Guattarian Becoming

Susan Gorman

'I have a problem. I'm not how you see me,' declares miserably Mon Type, the main character in the film *Quartier Mozart* to his girlfriend, Samedi. She asks him what exactly he means. 'I'm not a man,' he replies with a look of desperation in his eyes. He is instead, the viewer knows, the adolescent girl, Chef du Quartier, who has been made into a man through the help of the sorceress, Maman Thékla.

Chef du Quartier in *Quartier Mozart* has changed genders. Gilles Deleuze and Félix Guattari in their 1987 seminal text *A Thousand Plateaus: Capitalism and Schizophrenia* theorize a process of becoming that emphasizes the 'becoming-woman', a minoritarian becoming that epitomizes the progression. In their attempts to hypothesize such change more practically, they refer specifically to magic. Jean-Pierre Bekolo changes the terms of process of becoming and sets it inside a neighborhood (the *quartier*) of a Cameroonian village in order to explore gender and sexual politics.

Quartier Mozart was produced and directed by Cameroonian filmmaker Bekolo in 1992. When it was shown at Cannes that same year, it won the Prix Afrique en Creation for the best film coming out of Africa that year. The story follows the transformation of Chef du Quartier, an adolescent girl, into the man, Mon Type, in the Mozart neighborhood. The growing relationship that develops between Mon Type and Samedi, the daughter of the local police chief, Chien Mechant, is the focus of the film. The entire neighborhood seems interested in this relationship and the secondary stories mostly revolve around it. Chien Mechant takes a second wife and throws Samedi's mother out of his house when she is angry at the unexpected second marriage. This event allows Samedi freedom of movement as her mother is no longer home to supervise her movements and so she is able to spend time with Mon Type. The young men who hang out in the neighborhood bar are intensely interested in whether or not Mon Type can convince Samedi to have sex with him. The women who congregate around the well at the center of the village are deeply interested in all the events happening in the village and are frequently shown gossiping about Chien Mechant's family saga as it unfolds.

The film's narrative is framed by two mirroring series of shots. After having the main characters of the film introduce themselves to the camera, Bekolo shows the young girl Chef du Quartier interacting with the other main characters of the film. They each exchange a single line with Chef du Quartier, offering a bit of insight into their characters and her character as they do so. The film ends with a repetition of this scene and differs only in the dialogue exchanged. Perhaps the most interesting exchange occurs between Chef du Quartier and Atango, a young man who later becomes a friend to Mon Type. At the beginning of the film, Chef du Quartier is pointed out by the narrator as 'She's the one they call Chief of the Neighborhood, arrogant like a girl who has never known a man.' This comment highlights Chef du Quartier youth and immaturity. She has not had sex, and this seems to be both what makes her arrogant.

This remark clearly sets up a relationship dynamic between men and women. A woman can be arrogant when she has not yet come into close contact with men. Once she does enter into a relationship or marriage, then her role as woman necessitates her being humble. At the end of the film, instead of marking her youth again, Atango states, 'That girl there, she has grown up.' Somehow, over the course of the film, she has grown up. The only event that has occurred during this film that could have affected her in this way is her becoming of Mon Type, her 'becoming-man'. The argument for this film that I wish to pursue is that, in opposition to that which Deleuze and Guattari claim concerning the impossibility of the becoming-man and the necessity of becoming-woman for the process of maturation, Chef du Quartier grows up through a process made possible by magic in which she instead becomes-man.

In order to further this argument, I examine how Chef du Quartier becomes Mon Type. Chef du Quartier has two highly interesting conversations with Maman Thékla, the village sorceress. The first concerns Maman Thékla's earlier becomings-man:

MTh: I assure you that I traveled like that. It was me, a man.

CduQ: A real man!

MTh: I knew many different kinds of women - Japanese, English, American.

This verbal exchange first introduces the idea of becoming-man. Maman Thékla has already become-man and known many different women. She has had the same affect as a man in having sex with these foreign women and therefore, in a Deleuzian and Guattarian schema, did in fact become-man. An affect is an impulse produced in oneself or another figure. If a figure has the same affects as a woman, it has become-woman. It is important however to make sure that there is no privileging of what one has become over that which one started as. Deleuze and Guattari (1987, p 305) write that 'becoming is always double; that which one becomes becomes no less than the one that becomes.'

Chef du Quartier is very impressed by this sorceress's achievement in turning herself into a man. She then asks:

CduQ: Maman Thékla, what did you like more? Being a man or a woman?

MTh: Being a woman in the body of a man.

Maman Thékla's comment sends both women into gales of laughter and also forms the premise of the film. Both Chef du Quartier and Maman Thékla become-men before the film concludes Chef du Quartier, as already mentioned, becomes the young man Mon Type; Maman Thékla becomes Panka, a man who is given the odd ability to cause men's penises to disappear by shaking their hands. Her/His ability prompts Chien Mechant to hire Panka as a guard for his house and thus provides a narratological means for the sorceress in male form to survey the fledgling relationship of Mon Type and Samedi.

Chef du Quartier's actual becoming of Mon Type occurs off-camera. The viewer instead sees a car, in which the magical becoming is presumably taking place, mystically back-lit. Mon Type emerges from the car as the voice-over narration states, 'She has become a man.' Directly following that scene, Mon Type is shown taking some clothing off a clothesline and sews the clothes to fit himself. In this first scene of Mon Type actually doing something, he has not yet entirely become-man since he still has the affect of a woman in performing a task gendered female. Since Deleuzian and Guattarian becomings are judged according to their affects, this sewing scene shows that although Chef du Quartier is now within Mon Type's body, she/he must be judged according to the feminine affect and is thus only in the beginning stages of the process of becoming-man. Switching gendered bodies alone does not constitute becoming.

It is possible to trace the trajectory of Chef du Quartier's becoming-man in this film through Mon Type's affects. He is depicted in different scenes learning how to become-man. After initial confusion concerning Mon Type's place in the neighborhood (he is initially believed to be a mercenary and is posited as an Outsider), he is shown trying to blend in with other young men of the neighborhood. He immediately befriends Atango and two of his friends, one of whom owns a small bar where they all pass their time. Once it is decided that Mon Type is attracted to Samedi, Atango tells Mon Type the rules of the game, the rules of etiquette, whereby he may pursue Samedi and attempt to have sex with her. Atango tells Mon Type how to read the signals of what Samedi wears. If she wears pants, Atango says, it will not go well; however, if she wears a skirt, then success is a foregone conclusion. During this scene, Mon Type learns how to read a woman's behavior according to the mind of a man. This ability to think as a man will greatly help his process of becoming man.

Mon Type's ability to become-man is also aided by Samedi's behavior. When the two characters stand by goalposts talking to each other during their first rendezvous, Samedi tells Mon Type what he should say and how he should act if he wants to succeed with her. She states that a man must love her if he is to sleep with her. She is, however, skeptical of his too-quick profession of love and Mon Type does not succeed in having sex with Samedi that night. In terms of Mon Type/Chef du Quartier's becoming-man, the character is again learning how to produce the affects of a man. He/she begins to understand the code of conduct that may produce the hoped for effects. The magic can only work in providing the external changes necessary to change from a woman to a man; the internal changes necessary for becoming must be learned and take much longer.

Just how well Mon Type learns how to become-man is evident in a conversation he holds with Samedi the next day. Mon Type has by this point allowed Atango to spread the rumor that he has had sex with Samedi, which flies quickly around the small neighborhood. When Chien Mechant hears that Samedi has been seen with a man (he does not hear that they have supposedly slept together), he tells Samedi that he wants to meet Mon Type. Samedi searches him out to inform him of her father's wishes. When he denies his relationship with her and states that he will not go to meet her father, she complains, 'Don't start those things that boys do to girls.' This statement is when Mon Type (Chief du Quartier) turns the corner from producing 'woman-affects' to producing the affects of a man. With that statement, Bekolo has called attention to how Mon Type's affects are to be read. He has begun, apparently, acting as a man.

Mon Type continues their conversation and confesses that he is not what he seems to be; he confesses that he is not a man. Samedi counters this statement by angrily saying, 'When you were touching me yesterday, you forgot that.' She argues that his identity is based upon his actions, his affects. This answer is an effective argument for Deleuze and Guattari's idea of becoming who posit affect as the more critical element in a becoming; however, it is not effective for Mon Type who says that he thinks that he and Samedi shouldn't continue their relationship anymore.

Once the two young characters later reunite and tell each other that they are in love, Bekolo shows a scene in which Mon Type and Samedi decide to have sex. He never shows if they actually follow through, however. Directly following this scene, Panka and Mon Type meet in a cab that Panka is driving. After having recognized each other as Chef du Quartier and Maman Thékla, Panka asks, 'And now? You've become a real man now?' This question would mark sex as the ultimate defining affect of the becoming-man. Importantly, this question also marks the last scene in which Chef du Quartier is shown as Mon Type.

From this scene in the cab, Bekolo immediately dissolves into a scene in which Chef du Quartier and Maman Thékla sit around a fire. This scene choice mirrors the one at the beginning of the film when Chef du Quartier asks Maman Thékla whether she would prefer to be a man or a woman. Now Chef du Quartier tells Maman Thékla and the viewers what she has learned through her process of becoming-man. She sums up her experience by saying, 'In any case, with what I saw there, before a boy goes out with me, he has to first prove to me that he loves me. And real love!' For a girl who in the beginning of the film had not yet 'known man', Chef du Quartier now knows what it is to become-man. She demonstrates a sophisticated and nuanced understanding of both genders. She understands the sexual politics of the neighborhood and will not be duped by men. She has grown up. I assert that through her process of becoming-man, Chef du Quartier has become a more knowledgeable woman.

The becoming-man of Chef du Quartier complicates Deleuze and Guattari's conception of the becoming in another interesting way. Crucial in the becoming-woman is its universalizing and universalizable feature. Deleuze and Guattari (1987) claim, 'it is not the girl who becomes a woman; it is becoming-woman that produces the universal girl' (p 277). Through her becoming, Chef du Quartier, a specific girl, has become Mon Type, a generic man. Even his name, *Mon Type*, literally 'my guy' in French, gives no specifics about who he is. It is a generalized name perfect for the 'universal man'.

Through the negotiation between the multiplicity of women and the multiplicity of men, this becoming of Mon Type, the generalized man, has taken place. He begins his role in the community as an Outsider, a catalyst for becoming, as was mentioned earlier. After this position as outsider, he develops affects in order to become-man, all of which occurred through the initial help of sorcery. Chef du Quartier's becoming-man seems to fit precisely Deleuze and Guattari's envisioning except for one major flaw: Deleuze and Guattari exclude the possibility of the becoming-man because man is not minoritarian. How then can this process of becoming make sense according to Deleuze and Guattari's writing?

The exclusion of the possibility of becoming-man is based upon the traditional patriarchal power that men hold in society. It is this power, this order, that makes men molar and therefore unable to facilitate or sustain a becoming. However, what if in this case it is not men who have more power? If this power relation were inverted, then there should be a possibility for the becoming-man. The reversal of power relations would render men molecular (in Deleuzian language). However, does the film sustain such an inversion?

The very fact that an adolescent girl could be named *Chef du Quartier* plays with the power structure within this neighborhood. If a young girl can be the *chef*, then power must be displaced. If Chef du Quartier really were the head of the neighborhood, then everyone within it would have less power than she has, a fact that would open up the possibility for her becoming-anyone else.

The other powerful figure shown in the film is Maman Thékla. Her sorcery gives her power. For Deleuze and Guattari, the sorcerer is a figure who haunts the boundaries. He or she can move easily between spaces and is granted a certain amount of power through that ability. Deleuze and Guattari (1987) accentuate the association of the sorcerer with borderlines (p 246). This association then underscores the facility of movement that is necessary for a becoming. The sorcerer can enable the becoming because of his position that facilitates alliance making (*Ibid.*). Since (s)he lives on the fringes, (s)he is perfectly situated in a position through which to make local connections among other figures, which is critical to the process of becoming. In this particular film, Maman Thékla is the one who has already become-man; therefore, there must have been a way in which a woman could become-man in this society. This power inversion - and the power given to her by her position as sorceress - must have been already in existence.

Chien Mechant seems to have power in this movie: he is the head of police and the head of his family. However, he mostly appears to be a comic figure. When he cannot control his first wife and imagines that she is mad at him, he has to have her thrown out of his house rather than deal with her. He cannot control his daughter Samedi. He is continually kept unaware of political events in the neighborhood and is shown numerous times listening to promotion results, desperately hoping that his friend will be promoted so that he can gain power and position by association. His violent reactions and his unrepressed rage could be expressions of anger at the lack of any real power he has in his neighborhood and family. If he is the most powerful male figure in this neighborhood, then perhaps women really do have more power.

Maman Thékla's becoming of Panka opens up interesting questions concerning village power dynamics in *Quartier Mozart*. Panka has the ability to make men's penises disappear simply by shaking their hands. He(She) makes Atango's penis disappear, much to Atango's dismay. Chien Mechant fears Panka's ability although he does eventually shake his hand with no result. Maman Thékla's sorcery can emasculate. If the male power structure were solidly secure, it should not be so easily undone by a powerful woman. Sorcery, that which is not known to the supposedly dominant power structure, could undermine the whole village. This woman's wielding of her magical power threatens but ultimately helps the village. Having a Chef du Quartier who understands both the female and the male and can negotiate both gender positions could only be a positive factor in the village; this new understanding could not happen without the powerful intervention of the sorceress Maman Thékla who initiates the events of the film.

Panka's ability to remove penises also raises the question of whether this facility forces the becoming-woman on these men. It also calls into question the role of desire in becoming-woman. Does one have to *want* to become in order to do so, or will it happen anyway? To revisit the question of desire in becoming, it is interesting to examine Massumi's elaboration on Deleuzian and Guattarian thought in his 1992 *User's Guide to Capitalism and Schizophrenia: Deviations from Deleuze and Guattari* and his depiction of a connection between desire and becoming. He claims that becoming is a process caught between two kinds of desire - molar and supermolecular (p 94). Becoming impels, without necessarily having the agent's agreement. He asserts:

> Although the indeterminacy of the supermolecular state [of becoming] invites the use of such words as 'choice' and 'freedom', it is not a question of a consciously willed personal decision. Becoming is directional rather than intentional. The direction it moves in may appear 'unmotivated', 'irrational', or 'arbitrary' from the point of view of molarity; but becoming is

no more deserving of these epithets than molarity itself. Both are modes of desire. (p 95)

According to Massumi's reading of Deleuze and Guattari, it does not matter if a person wants to or agrees to become in order for the process to take place. Personal choice and desire are not important.

So, can Panka's involvement in the disappearance of penises be seen as the forcing of a process of becoming-woman on these men? Sorcery, for Deleuze and Guattari, plays an important role in becoming. Panka is still the sorcerer Maman Thékla; is she simply using her sorcery in this way to facilitate becomings? It is unclear whether Panka's sorcery ever wears off on Atango, for instance. Perhaps Atango's process of becoming has not yet been completed, as it has been for Mon Type. Mon Type acts in such a way as to produce masculine affects; however, we never see Atango producing feminine affects. Perhaps it is after he proceeds along his path of becoming-woman until he produces feminine affects that the sorcery will wear off. Despite the ultimate lack of resolution concerning some of these questions of Maman Thékla/Panka's sorcery, this problematizing of the becoming process prompted by the character of Panka is intriguing.

In their final conversation, Chef du Quartier and Maman Thékla, having transformed back into women, raise a last point about becoming in this film. Seated around the fire, they say

MTh: You do witchcraft now?

CduQ: Who, me? I'm not a sorcerer.

MTh: You already are, you already are.

CduQ: You're the sorcerer.

As is evident from this conversation, Chef du Quartier has become-sorcerer. Through her transformation into the body of a man, through her becoming-man, she has created sorcerer-affects. This fact further harkens back to Massumi's point concerning desire and becoming. One does not have to desire to become; indeed one does not even need to be aware of becoming in order for it to take place.

In *Quartier Mozart*, there are becomings-man, becomings-woman and becoming-sorcerer. Although this film does not always precisely fit Deleuze and Guattari's projection of the becoming, it certainly lends an appealing, concrete way of viewing the complicated idea.

What does this film mean for the becoming-woman? How can the reading of Deleuze and Guattari's theory of becoming and *Quartier Mozart* intersect productively? Deleuze and Guattari's presentation of the becoming is highly abstract. Trying to find practical applications for theory in this film highlights how the process of becoming can be comprehended. Perhaps the becoming-woman theory does not always work perfectly for this film, yet even where it breaks down is useful.

Combining the becoming-woman with *Quartier Mozart* suggests that it is possible to conceive of a becoming-man, a possibility that Deleuze and Guattari closed off. There must be an inversion of male/female power structures within a particular society in order to allow for this possibility of becoming-man, but it does exist. *Quartier Mozart* opens up new possibilities in understanding the becoming and offers concrete dramatization of it, even though it is couched in this fantastic magical transformation.

This film problematizes how greatly desire figures into the becoming. In *Quartier Mozart*, desire is not necessary in the facilitation of the becoming. Panka forces men into a becoming-woman. They do not have to agree to a becoming or even be aware that such a process will take place.

The sexual politics played with in *Quartier Mozart* are brought to the forefront by both the becoming-man and becoming-woman. What could be read as a magical folktale situated within a small neighborhood is now rendered highly political. Instead of having to choose between reading the film as a folktale about sorcery or an allegory about Cameroonian village politics, Deleuze and Guattari give a model for reading both interpretations together. It is not necessary to choose between sorcery and *reality* since both have equal sway within the Deleuzian and Guattarian model of becoming.

I am very interested by the fact that Deleuze and Guattari's transitional process of becoming has taken on such importance in a post-colonial context. Perhaps it is in part because of the liminality of the post-colonial African setting that these becomings are able to occur.

Because of the status of Cameroon as a former colony, this space is inherently criss-crossed with striated lines of different kinds of authority, whether they be colonial, traditional, magical, gender-related, family-related, police, etc. Different kinds of authority are at war in this setting and could possibly be an easy space for such transitional, rhizomatic movement. When there is no clear-cut authority figure, when different ideologies and different models of behavior exist simultaneously, perhaps all movement is a line of flight. The process of becoming recognizes these inconsistencies in power dynamics and brings them to the forefront. The post-colonial space could be a critical, magical plane for the becoming, as is demonstrated in this film.

References

Bekolo, Jean-Pierre [Producer and Director], 1992, *Quartier Mozart*, California Newsreel, San Francisco.

Deleuze, Gilles and Guattari, Félix, 1987, *A Thousand Plateaus*, trans. Brian Massumi, University of Minnesota Press, Minneapolis.

Massumi, Brian, 1992, *A User's Guide to Capitalism and Schizophrenia: Deviations from Deleuze and Guattari*, The MIT Press, Cambridge, MA.

Living the Mystery: Sacred Drama Today

K. A. Laity

For many, the words "ritual" or "sacred" drama conjure up notions of ancient Egyptian or Greek mysteries, or at the very least, medieval miracle plays. There is, of course, a long and venerable history for this kind of drama, but it is one which may lead many modern rationalists to doubt its applicability in the twenty-first century. However, a growing body of work in this particular genre does exist. While Broadway lumbers through retreads of previously successful works and off-Broadway celebrates the often incestuously self-referential intellectual exercises, a grass-roots dramatic effort has sprung up in various spots around the world. It seeks to renew the connection with the divine, with the spiritual. People following earth-based religions are at the forefront of this movement, portraying the lives of their goddesses and gods and the journey of the soul. This paper will examine the people who create this new sacred drama, what goals they seek to accomplish with it, and the nature of the rituals they create.

The group I want to look at can be described under the greater umbrella of "earth-based religions," for the majority of them have this shared starting point, holding the earth as sacred. The more common designation "pagans" or occasionally, "neo-pagans" speaks to the centuries-long hegemony of the Christian church; pagan of course coming from the Italian for *pagani*, the country dwellers. Similarly, some use the designation "heathen" which comes from the Anglo-Saxon word for the heath dwellers. Nonetheless, most modern pagans will be found in the suburbs and cities of this country, for although their beliefs often derive from the ancient traditions of agrarian societies, they are very much of the modern world. As Prudence Jones and Caitlín Matthews (1990) write in *Voices from the Circle: The Heritage of Western Paganism*, it 'draws upon the past' but 'it is designed for living in the present' (p 13). While it is not my intent to discuss the rich rainbow of modern pagan groups, from the Church of All Worlds to the Dianic women's temples to the revived Druids, I do want to give a clear picture of this group as widely varied, and more importantly for my purpose today, as a subaltern group within the hegemonic Christian culture of the United States. While I realize it is problematic to speak of any group in an industrialized, neo-colonial nation as "subaltern," I think the case can be made for this particular population, even more so in the last four years (and the recent national election). Let me answer the question Gayatri Chakravorty Spivak (1990, p 223) asks of a young Marxist author proposing science fiction as 'the Third World fiction of the industrial nations.' In *Poststructuralism, Marginality, Postcoloniality and Value*, she asks 'How is the claim to marginality being negotiated here?' I am negotiating the claim because of the clear hegemonic power of Western Christianity in the United States. While pagan religions continue to make inroads into American culture with, for example, the U.S. military's recognition of one branch, Wicca, as a valid and supported religion, and sociological studies identifying the nature-based faiths as the fastest growing religion group in the country, rank hostility against this population remains the norm. Public discourse has broadened in recent years to include the third of the major Abrahamic religions, but we see little acknowledgement in the American media of any religion outside that cluster of interrelated faiths, save for the occasional coverage of a colorful festival, usually offered as a kind of quaint picture or a curiosity. These marginal groups wield little power in the current political climate despite national (and international) efforts at organization and activism. The overall hegemony of an administration that aligns itself with the most conservative facets of Christianity assures that pagan groups will remain marginalized and unvoiced. In a nation where the Secretary of Education Ron Paige talking to the Baptist Press (2003) proclaims the superiority of a Christian education, we can be sure that pagans and other under-represented religions will remain marginal. Even outside the United States, pagan groups receive little recognition and even less support from the more conventional hierarchies. Yet even in less overtly controlling cultures, pagans of today (as opposed to indigenous, non-Abrahamic cultures) remain on the margins of their industrial cultures.

Of course, to use the words of Emory M. Roe (1994, p 113) from *Against Power*, the reality is that we have today a 'politics of complexity' and not a simple hegemonic power. Barbara Hernstein Smith (1990, p 71) argues too, in her critique of Hirsch's *Cultural Literacy*, that "there is, however, no single comprehensive [American] macroculture in which all or even most of the citizens of this nation actually participate." Yet it is this very complexity that requires subaltern groups to struggle to maintain a presence - and some power, if only to exist - through performance. A critique of power must be from a marginal position, yet it remains possible to declare a public response to the dominant power through performance. While many members of the pagan minority simply refuse to engage, remaining in what they call "the broom closet", others struggle daily to bring attention and acknowledgement to their faith(s).

Pagan groups must always negotiate a dialogue with the dominant powers, sometimes through public declaration of their beliefs - whether it be "Goddess Powered!" bumper stickers on their cars or a sabbat celebration in public area with press attention - but often through subtler means apparent only to those who share their beliefs. Such closeting remains necessary in a society where pagans face job loss and family devastation through perception of their faith as "devil-worshipping" or "cult" behavior. There are genuine risks to those who profess these beliefs, including literal demonizing of their ideology.

While many pagans continue to practice as solitaries, their ritual observations remain performance. This is essential to the nature of pagan worship. Because they do not often have a set place of worship - indeed any grove or living room will do - pagans create their own sacred space. This creation comes through performance of ritual. Public rituals, of course, embrace the element of performance and proclaim their subaltern beliefs to all who will observe. More importantly, the ritual provides numerous benefits to the members-and possibly, observers-through its devotion to examining and reiterating real experience. As Richard Schechner (1986) argues in *Between Theater and Anthropology* 'Restored behavior is a living behavior treated as a film director treats a strip of film... Restored behavior is used in all kinds of performances from shamanism and exorcism to trance, from ritual to aesthetic dance and theater, from initiation rites to social dramas, from psychoanalysis to psychodrama and transactional analysis. In fact, restored behavior is the main characteristic of performance' (pp 35-36). The utilization of restored behavior in ritual allows the players to both imitate and transcend mundane experience.

Just as the Passion play reiterates the tenets of Christianity, pagan seasonal rituals reinscribe the presence of deity and magic in any given location through sacred drama. As Kathy Jones (1996, p 3) argues in her collection of mystery plays of the goddess,

> The simple repetition of patriarchal religious myths and value systems ... does not hold my interest ... By sacred drama I mean drama that is inspired, written, directed and performed in service to the creative informing energies of the universe. Its purpose is to communicate with and to give expression to the divine as far as we humans are able.

The necessarily performative aspects of the dialogue with the divine also result in a greater cohesion for the community group, often a challenge in a population that prides itself on individuality and the uniqueness of each one's spiritual path. Paul B. Rucker (1999, p 6) writes that 'as a community, we shape our reality most directly through ritual.' Rucker describes ritual as 'a simultaneous experience that is physical, emotional, and spiritual at once. Such communion denotes an ideal theatrical experience as well, so that in the convergence of theater and ritual we find today's sacred theater.' (*Ibid.*) Thus ritual, inherently theater, binds performers and audience as one. While this may initially seem a kind of "reversion" to some observers, a return to the "primitive," these rituals are intimately connected to the present. As Victor Turner argues (1982, p 110), 'the performative genres of complex, industrial societies…have their deep roots in the enduring human social drama, particularly in its redressive phase, the drama that has its *direct* source in social structural conflict, but behind which perhaps is an endemic evolutionary restlessness; for we seem to be a species that becomes easily bored with even its most advantageous cultural adaptations.' The innate social dramas of societies change little over time: how to live, how to worship, how to survive, how to do what is right concern people in societies both ancient and modern. The modern pagan rituals use old legends (and new) to continue to address the on-going issues of today's 24/7, internet-fuelled culture. In Turner's argument, these rituals - public or private – 'keep us alive, give us problems to solve, postpone ennui, guarantee at least the flow of our adrenaline, and provoke us into new, ingenious cultural formulations of our human condition and occasionally into attempts to ameliorate, even beautify it' (1982, p 111). Modern pagan rituals accomplish many of the same goals as those of their forebears did, but they do it with full knowledge of their place in today's society.

Past rituals included both aretalogies and recreations of significant events or mysteries. An aretalogy of the goddess Isis lists her many accomplishments to show her as the source of all power and happiness. Among the qualities to be announced are: 'I am she who findeth fruit for men', as well as 'I brought together woman and man' and 'I revealed mysteries unto men' (Meyer, 1987, p 173). While many of the characteristics were not meant for emulation but for adoration, many others provide the order and sense of the world, the compass of right and wrong: 'I taught (men) to honor images of the gods', and 'I broke down the government of tyrants' as well as 'I made an end to murder' and 'I established penalties for those who practice injustice' (p 173). The performance of these mighty deeds-whether live or in this case, as carved before a temple-inspires awe as well as offering a firm guidance to shared beliefs of the community. Similarly, the ancient mystery plays offered the same sense of established order, but with the added invigoration of dramatic action and emotion. In the sacred drama *The Triumph of Horus over His Enemies* (Blackman and Fairman, 1943, p 15) one can see the same figure of Isis engaged in the dramatic fight between her son Horus and their enemy Set, urging 'Be of good courage, Horus my son. Lo, thou hast him fast holden, yon enemy of thy father. Be not wearied.' While the recitation of deeds may be more straightforward in disseminating information, the dramatic reenacting of pivotal mythic moments no doubt provided greater and more vivid reactions. Imagine the reaction to the dismemberment of the enemy on stage, composed of clay or bread (Blackman and Fairman, 1942, p 34).

The major change between today's pagan performances and those of the past is that the latter were publicly sanctioned, government regulated productions, expressions of shared belief that most of the public would recognize. Whether medieval mystery plays, where the entire community played a role, or the Greek mysteries of Dionysos, where adepts shared the god's bounty, publicly sanctioned dramas acted chiefly to reinforce the shared beliefs of the society and to shape those beliefs into orthodoxy. Pagan rituals today are at the very least subversive to the hegemonic authorities in content, but often in performance as well. Witness the Portland Reclaiming group's Magickal Activism Cluster (2002), who perform ritual explicitly as protest. On their website this Reclaiming group lists such activities as: 'mummers plays that bring the sacred dimension into view, public ritual in the midst of more mainstream political actions, [and] humorous street theatre.' Most public performances by pagans, if not overtly political, at least strive for recognition and legitimacy of their alterity.

Of course the majority of sacred dramas are primarily celebratory. Some examples will show the breadth in the kind of performed rituals you can find across the country - indeed the world - today. Kathy Jones (1996) lives in Glastonbury, England. Several of the sacred dramas she has worked with involve older pantheons such as those of the Greeks and the Celts, but always they are revised within a modern context. In reviewing the transformation of one persistent myth, that of the goddess's descent to the underworld, Jones noticed how the Greek version of the myth, the story of Persephone, removed all the agency and choice from the goddess that had been the hallmarks of the earlier Sumerian version of the story featuring the goddess Inanna. Jones says, 'I began to see the ways in which universal myths are altered over time reflecting changes in the collective unconscious and external society' (p 22). Making this realization gave her the freedom to alter the myth further, and for several years Jones and her group, Ariadne Productions, offered a series of sacred dramas exploring their connection with the divine.

Among the offerings was *The Sacred Marriage*, a play that enacted the ritual of Beltane, also known as May Eve, one of the traditional fertility days of the agrarian calendar. As written by Jones, the drama encompasses both the mundane world of a bickering couple and the explicitly mythological lives of gods and goddesses. Eventually the two strands intertwine as the characters reveal the mythic in the mundane, the gods in the flesh. In one exchange the all too real humans break through the elevated rhetoric of the mythic folk, first speaking as Blodeuwedd and Llew Law Gyffes, then as Maia and Loui:

BLODEUWEDD: At this season of the year

When all Her nature springs

I greet you in the bowering place

On Beltane's springtime eve.

LLEW: I greet you by the sacred fire

I greet you on the mountain

I greet you, lady of my heart

Beside the holy fountain.

MAIA: You always had to try and outdo me.

LOUI: But this is how I really feel.

God and goddess, man and woman embrace and heal the rifts that had separated them, at least for a while. One truth that becomes clear through Jones' narrative is that these rifts reappear and must be readdressed. Relationships require effort - especially relationships with gods. Just as the play brings together real people in ritual performance, it also unites the sacred and the mundane within movement and voice, and should produce total engagement on the part of both participants and observers. In an interview with the author, R. A. Carey (2002b) expressed it this way: 'If it's done right, there should be no spectators in Sacred Drama.'

Jones explicitly writes that inclusion into the performance of the Samhain Healing Rite *The Spinning Wheel of Ana* which she describes as 'a present day shamanic healing rite for individual participants, for audiences and for the wider community of which we are all a part. This healing rite is based on the re-membered Sacred Wheel of Ana, Spinner of the Thread of Life and Weaver of the Worlds, as revealed in our own British ancestral myths and legends' (1996, p 169). Jones' drama provides both restored behavior and restored mythology, offering both a healing of the past and a movement toward new discoveries, as she notes 'one of our purposes in Ariadne Productions is to remember and celebrate the ancient lost traditions of many lands. Our aim however is not merely to reassemble the forgotten past, it is to help create the future world in which the reality of equality between men and women, between the goddess and the god, is brought into being' (p 166). Ancient tools produce modern results. It is essential to draw the audience into the spectacle if true change will be enacted.

Thus, even when a group enacts sacred drama to inform or educate the public, they generally offer the possibility of drawing the audience into the proceedings. When The Witches Gathering (2002) put on their production of *The Ritual of the Resurrection of Osiris*, they invited nominal audience members to become a part of the proceedings, first by explaining the drama's arc, then by demarcating sacred space, and finally by asking them to 'Enter now the sacred space and write the name of the one whose soul you would honor this night. And make yourself ready to be purified to enter' (p 2). This offers the possibility of abstaining if any member of the audience remains discomfited, but also leaves an openness to honour whomever the spectator may be thinking of that night. Making that connection proves essential - there is no sacred without it.

Connecting the sacred and the mundane always figures as the heart of truly sacred drama. In the dramatic narrative of *The Resurrection of Osiris*, the human nature of the gods receives emphasis, but on a grander scale, where the love and hate magnify into forces of creation and destruction. The lesson remains that connection-the god in the human, the sacred in the mundane. To be effective, sacred drama must become a living presence. Conrad Bishop (1999) argues in *Stage Blood & Celebration* that 'there's a profound difference between *depicting* a ritual and *living* a ritual' (p 9). Effective sacred dramas provide this experience, a living embodiment of the divine. As Piero Ferruci describes it, when 'ritual is performed well, external representation becomes an internal reality, consciousness expands, and a purely private experience is shared by all' (quoted. in Rucker, 1999, p 6).

Most pagan groups utilize this form of ritual on a regular basis, but a few actually focus on the specific form of drama for most rituals. One of these groups is the Fellowship of Isis. Sacred drama forms the heart of the training of their adepts. In their available on-line training they stress enacting the kind of sacred dramas performed in ancient Egyptian culture but updated for modern concerns. Co-founder Olivia Robertson (2003) in her collection of rituals *Dea: Rites and Mysteries of the Goddess* writes that 'Any Rite which invokes Deity or Deities through a Mystery Religion-that which deals with the Unknown-has effect throughout all levels and on the earth itself. Throughout the ages people of varying cultures have learned to communicate with those from other spheres: we need all the knowledge, understanding and good feeling we can obtain, in order that we may live here in peace with each other and with all creatures; and obtain happiness and wisdom in the spheres beyond "death."' For the Fellowship of Isis it is imperative for spiritual growth and for the earth that adepts master the performance of sacred drama.

In part, this focus on dramatic performance grows out the pagan community's desire for and recognition of the sacred always immanent within the mundane, finding the carnivalesque in apparently ordinary life. In an essay in *PanGaia*, R. A. Carey (2002a, p 29) writes about her first encounter with *The Rocky Horror Picture Show*: 'I do not expect to find myself in the middle of a Mystery Play.' Yet she does, and under further analysis Carey decides that 'The Mystery Play is working on three levels: On the stage, the costumed performers are the priests and priestesses acting out the Technicolor myth flickering behind them, and we, the Rocky Horror communicants, shout out our liturgical responses... we hold up our brave little flashlights, throw divinatory playing cards, and celebrate the Sacred Marriage of Frank and Rocky, and Rocky and Brad, and Janet and Rocky and Frank. We are ecstatic' (p 29).

It becomes a way to read the spectacle of the world. A sporting event with its chants and rituals and its endless loops of restored behavior functions as a performance in tribute of Mars. The endless parade of American Idols reenacts the work of the sacred muses as the unskilled, untutored try to recover the mystery of inspiration. Every public ritual-from protest to parades-enact the sacred mysteries to a well-trained observer. For modern pagans, the most important aspect of this may be that, informed and trained, they can alter their alterity through performance and move from the perceived margins to the safety of the broadening mainstream.

References

Baptist Press, 11-4-2003, *Transcript: Interview with the Secretary of Education*, [on-line], http://www.bpnews.net/bpnews.asp?ID=15707

Bishop, C., 1999, 'Stage Blood & Celebration', *Green Egg*, 31 (127), 8-10

Blackman, A. M., and Fairman, 1942, 'The Myth of Horus at Edfu-II: C. The Triumph of Horus Over His Enemies: A Sacred Drama', *Journal of Egyptian Archaeology*, 28, 32-38

Blackman, A. M., and Fairman, 1943, 'The Myth of Horus at Edfu-II: C. The Triumph of Horus Over His Enemies: A Sacred Drama (continued)', *Journal of Egyptian Archaeology*, 29, 2-36

Carey, R. A., 2002a, 'Hot Patootie, Bless My Soul', *PanGaia*, 32, 29-30

Carey, R. A., 2002b, *Re: Surrey*, [email communication], 12-12-2002

Jones, K, 1996, *On Finding Treasure: Mystery Plays of the Goddess*, Ariadne, Glastonbury

Jones, P., and Matthews, C., 1990, *Voices from the Circle: The Heritage of Western Paganism*, Aquarian, Wellingborough

Meyer, M. W., ed., 1987, *The Ancient Mysteries: A Sourcebook*, New York, Harper San Francisco

Portland Reclaiming, Accessed 12-3-2003 *Magickal Activism*, [On-line], http://www.portlandreclaiming.org/

Roe, E., 1994, 'Against Power, for the Politics of Complexity', *Transition*, 64, 113-169

Rucker, P. B., 1999, 'Making Spectacles of Ourselves: Theater and Modern Pagan Ritual. Part One of Three: The Politics of Enchantment', *Green Egg*, 31, (127), 5-7, 49.

Schechner, R., 1986, *Between Theater and Anthropology*, University of Pennsylvania Press, Philadelphia

Robertson, O., Accessed 24-2-2003, *Dea: Rites and Mysteries of the Goddes*, Fellowship of Isis, [On-line], http://www.fellowshipofisis.com/liturgy.html

Smith, B. H., 1990, 'Cult-Lit: Hirsch, Literacy, and the "National Culture"', *South Atlantic Quarterly*, 89, (1), 69-88

Spivak, G. C., 1990, 'Poststructuralism, Marginality, Postcoloniality and Value' in P. Collier and H. Geyer-Ryan (eds.), *Literary theory Today*, Cornell UP, Ithaca, 219-244

The Witches Gathering, 26-10-2002, *Ritual of the Resurrection of Osiris*, [performance script]

Turner, V., 1982, *From Ritual to Theatre: The Human Seriousness of Play*, Performing Arts Journal Publications, New York.

Book Reviews

Nicholas Rogers, 2002, *Halloween: from Pagan Ritual to Party Night*, **Oxford University Press, Oxford and New York. 172 pages, ISBN 0195168968 Paperback £9.99**

Single-subject histories on the likes of salt, codfish and even the colour red have become a fashionable lately, and Nicholas Rogers' book is a fine specimen of the genre. This little book traces the history of the celebration of October 31 from *Samhain*, the year cycle rite observed by the pagan Celts in Britain, to the many ways it is marked in North America at the time of the new millennium. His central thesis, supported by myriad examples and illustrations, is that Halloween has always been a liminal time, a boundary between autumn and winter, this world and the other world, life and death.

Drawing from the theory of anthropologist Victor Turner, he argues that liminal times are also periods of ritual inversion in which the obverse of cultural values, however they are construed, are temporarily allowed to emerge into public consciousness and celebrated before being relegated once again to the cultural closet. Whether these oppositional symbols are spiritual otherworlds, as they were for the ancient Celts, or consist instead of what is disavowed by the dominant cultural paradigm, Halloween provides a framework during which they can be publicly explored and performed. This central feature of Halloween, more than any individual rite or symbol, constitutes the core of the holiday that has endured for over a thousand years.

Rogers begins by examining the practices of the ancient Celts, for whom Samhain was a year cycle rite that marked the passage from autumn into winter, a time out of time when the boundaries between the world of humans and that of otherworldly creatures – be they ancestors, deities or other kinds of spirits – were thought to be thin, and the 'reverse world' was allowed to briefly overlap with the everyday world. Carrying this metaphor forward into history, Rogers shows how Halloween's supernatural connotations continued in medieval and early modern festivities associated with All Saints' and All Souls' Days, from which we get many of the rituals still associated with the holiday today, including jack-o'-lanterns, pranking behaviour and petty vandalism. He traces the migration of these customs to the New World with two groups of immigrants: English Catholics and liberal Protestants (the Puritans disdained the observance as too Popish), and the Irish.

Rogers really shines in describing the growth of Halloween in New World soil. He addresses the development of trick-or-treating in the 20th century not only as a form of social inversion in which children demand candy from strangers, in a reversal of the usual cautions, but as a rite that prepared children to become consumers of sweets and other paraphernalia associated with the holiday, such as costumes and decorations. But the dangers of the otherworld could not be tamed by conspicuous consumption; they re-emerged in the 1960s and 70s as fear of contaminated treats – the infamous razor blade in the apple. The very symbol of harvest home, the fruit of the Celtic otherworld, the Isle of Apples, was transformed into an instrument of danger – not, this time, from otherworldly beings, but from other human beings.

Human beings similarly were the source of other Halloween dangers, such as the arson and vandalism of 'Devil's Night' in Detroit and other North American cities. Meantime, Hollywood horror films picked up

Halloween's association with the supernatural, darkness, death and decay, often weaving in themes associated with contemporary legends and rumour panics. The resulting mix blurred the lines between reality and the imaginary in a way that was new in the history of Halloween, emphasizing gory hyperrealism over the spiritual or supernatural frights that predominated in earlier centuries. At the same time that parents began to be afraid of allowing children to trick-or-treat on Halloween for fear of candy contamination and crime, Halloween emerged as a party night for adults, when those who had enjoyed costuming and rites of reversal as children wanted to experience them in a new, grown-up context. It reached its apotheosis in street parades of large North American cities such as Toronto, New York and Los Angeles, where it has become an occasion for gay, lesbian, bisexual and transgendered communities to publicly celebrate identities usually relegated to the margins of society by the dominant culture. As in much of Halloween behavior, this is done through play, humor and parody, hallmarks of symbolic inversion at the core of Halloween.

Rogers also treats the holiday's globalization: both the spread throughout North America of the analogous Mexican holiday El Día de los Muertos on the heels of Latino immigration, and the global diffusion of the commercialized Halloween to Europe and other markets. He provocatively asks whether the transformation of the holiday into a mass-marketed occasion for conspicuous consumption will eventually trump its subversive qualities, or whether individuals' creativity and sense of play will ultimately reclaim Halloween as a site of contestation.

Regardless of the cultural changes this holiday undergoes, Halloween seems to attract to it the oppositional and the carnivalesque. No wonder, then, that is has become a popular target for the invectives of conservative Christian ministers and their congregations, who label it "Satanic" and call for its suppression. But the suppression of culturally contested symbols never successfully eliminates the ideas behind them. In fact, as Turner and French cultural historian Michel Foucault argue, these oppositional images are fertile ground for cultural renewal, and provide alternative ways of envisioning reality: they are cultural countersites where social mores and pretensions can be mocked, parodied, and lampooned with impunity, and an alternative universe can temporarily be imagined.

Rogers does not address at any length the reclamation of Halloween by Neopagan groups in Europe and North America – a pity, because this trend fits well with his overarching theoretical approach. And he seems ignorant of the considerable work done on the holiday by American folklorists. Still, this excellent book will appeal to a wide range of readers. It reads fluidly and easily, is theoretically well-informed without being jargon-ridden or using theory as a bludgeon, and could easily be adopted for use in large undergraduate courses on cultural history, folkloristics and anthropology.

Sabina Magliocco

Robert Muchembled, 2003, *A History of the Devil from the Middle Ages to the Present*, Polity Press, Cambridge. 349 pages. ISBN 0745628168   Paperback £17.99

First published in French in 2000, it is useful to have a well translated English edition of Muchembled's *History of the Devil*. Muchembled is an influential historian of early modern popular culture whose books and articles on the witch trials are required reading for scholars of the subject. It is perhaps not surprising, then, that the strongest section of this book concerns the period up until the nineteenth century. When Muchembled moves on to the modern period the discussion is less comprehensive and contains several errors.

The book is structured chronologically, beginning with the fleshing out of the character and traits of the Devil by medieval theologians. The abstract conception of the fallen angel was turned into a potent physical reality, with Satan becoming the personification of all evil. As the story moves into the fifteenth century Muchembled describes the growing fear of heresy, a sign that Satan was increasing his work across Christendom. The rise of the witch trials and the development of the concept of witches being part of a satanic conspiracy are handled particularly well.

There then follows two excellent chapters on 'The Devil and the Body' and 'Satanic Literature and Tragic Culture'. The former considers the nature of the Devil and sexuality in early modern thought, and also putrefaction, smell and the sense of evil. The chapter on early modern literature looks at the distinctive *Teufelsbücher* ('Devil Books') written mostly by German Lutheran pastors as a vehicle for denouncing the sins of the age and the dangers of resorting to magic. It also examines the role of the Devil as represented in French tragedies.

Moving on to the late seventeenth and eighteenth centuries, Muchembled provides an account of how the great fear of the Devil, inspired by a strong millenarian impulse in intellectual though, weakened under the influence of new developments in science and philosophy. This section is too brief, however, and could have engaged more with the ardent religious debates at the time about divine and satanic intervention in human affairs. However, he is certainly right to stress that the Devil remained a strong influence on the cultural imagination of the Enlightenment.

Muchembled has little substantive to say about the Devil in nineteenth-century society, focusing on artistic representation and neglecting to discuss the theory of demonopathy developed by French alienists and the continued outbreaks of demonic possession, such as that in Morzine in the 1860s. The final section on the twentieth century is uneven. There is an interesting discussion on the conception and preoccupation with 'evil' in modern American culture, but an insufficient consideration of the fear of ritual satanic child abuse in the 1980s and 1990s.

The very brief discussion of Aleister Crowley, is – as a discussion with JSM editor Dave Evans has verified – 'riddled with clumsy errors of simple fact.' I have no idea, for example, where Muchembled got the idea that Crowley died in America. Despite this cluster of errors, and some unevenness in coverage, overall this book is a lively, informative and sometimes provocative contribution to the study of the Devil in European society.

Owen Davies

The Pomegranate (Journal)

This is not so much a review as a 'welcome back' for another academic journal in this minority interest field. When the JSM started out in 2003 the Pomegranate was in the midst of a publishing hiatus, and there were various dark rumours abounding in academia that it may never return. It is a great pleasure to see those rumours to be entirely false, and have it emerge unscathed, and perhaps stronger than ever. While the JSM shares some editorial board personnel with the Pomegranate we are working in rather different academic areas, and so we have no business-related reservations buried within our sheer academic delight in welcoming it back into print, since it is likely that buyers of one will also be buyers of the other, as we are complementary, not competitors.

As well as the current issue, a compact disc containing all of the 18 hefty back issues of this fine Journal, in printable PDF format, can be ordered from the publishers for around $20 (depending on your location, additional shipping rates may apply), and this is quite exceptional value for money. The print version of 'The Pom', as it is fondly known, is considerably more expensive if rated purely in 'pennies per page', but it provides a treasure house of varied and fascinating quality academic material, and is heartily endorsed here.

For more information see **http://www.equinoxpub.com/journals/main.asp?jref=51**

Dave Evans

James R. Lewis, ed., 2003, The Oxford Handbook of New Religious Movements, Oxford University Press, Oxford and New York. 560 pages, ISBN: 0-19-514986-6 Hardcover £52

Alex Owen, 2004, *The Place of Enchantment: British Occultism and the Culture of the Modern*, **University of Chicago Press, Chicago. 384 pages, ISBN: 0-226-64201-1 Hardcover £16**

I shall not give away my trade secrets as a reviewer, but I often begin a book half way through. This is a problem if the second half is dreadful, the first half not good enough to save it.

That's the trouble with the first of these two publications. Regular punters, lured by the OUP label, will expect a fine reference text for their New Age bookshelves. What awaits them is a dusty traversal of the literature written by specialists for specialists, sunk by a prose style that empties the material of all interest.

The best chapter, on new religious movements (NRMs) in Asia prints some useful information but seldom rises above the level of a laundry list. As Ronald Hutton has consistently shown, it is possible to explain complex concepts in scholarly English graced with wit and humour. Academics who claim otherwise are overspecialized and have not read very widely.

Since the Handbook's authors apologize for sloppy writing (it 'can make the analysis and discussion quite ponderous and difficult for the less specialized reader'), so will I. What are *detraditionalized*, *deinguistified*, and (arrrggg!) *de-exoticized* doing in there? Watch out also for a veritable plague of *locuses*. And try this on for size:

> '[Sentiment] cannot reside in the role system of a bureaucracy; it must be enacted and embodied in authentic sociality (...) Where Habermas privileges discourse oriented toward mutual

understanding as the foundation of rational community, Maffesoli privileges participation in a defining sentiment that is only articulated and refined through language as the foundation for a community (...) Neo-Pagan organizations (...) must resist the temptation to borrow existing structures and reflexively invent themselves according to the imperatives provided by the legitimating ideology of the Neo-Paganism itself.'

This book contrives to be choppily edited and boringly homogeneous all at the same time. There is a special place in Hell reserved for editors who let this sort of thing slip through. Good points come in a sprinkling (you expect just a few in the course of 500 pages). We are introduced to the concepts of 'lready, but not yet'(aliens have landed, but they have not yet stepped forward). If nothing else, NRMs are skilled at excuse-making when their prophecies do not pan out.

The movements mentioned range from 'feel good' organizations like Transcendental Meditation to high-commitment groups like Scientology. Some background is given: 'Early efforts at social control of controversial new religions in the US involved issues of controversial protection, with attempts (…) to define newer religions legislatively as a consumer good or service subject to regulation… such efforts usually foundered (…) over issues of religious freedom or freedom of association.'

A pity, then, that the authors should have so little feel for the American scene. We read that 'There is little argument that the US, Canada, and the UK are increasingly secular...' (really?). James Dobson is mentioned for his child care texts (*Dare to Discipline*, etc.) but not the campaign against acceptance of homosexuality for which he is nationally known. In their more lucid moments, the contributors stress that treating NRMs with objectivity is not political correctness run wild, but an aid to understanding. If we know little about cults, we know less about deprogrammers and should not automatically side with them. Family members bent on deprogramming brainwashed relatives have their own agendas (luring black sheep back into the fold of marriage and 9-5 jobs). And cultists who exit organizations voluntarily are often willing to chalk their cult membership up to experience.

A further nugget of gold: 'brainwashing' and 'deprogramming' are journalistic concepts bereft of scientific meaning. At last the authors are on to something! It's all very well to talk about cult members being in a 'trance state' but what if their mental function is otherwise normal? I asked myself, how did cultist Charles Manson differ, neurologically speaking, from the solitary Unabomber (and what, if anything, does that tell us?). Meaningful explanations for cult affiliation/disaffiliation— and better mental models for cult member behavior—are needed. This book doesn't provide them. Maybe it can't. This is a wretched format for the subject. And one reference to PhD dissertation politics is one too many.

It's better to read about what actually happened inside these cults. I want to be right there in the room when the Jonestown children sipped the Kool-Aid, when Sharon Tate was stabbed. Much insight can be gained through personal description. A friend of Marshall Herff Applewhite (chief of the Heaven's Gate community) remembered him as a popular young teacher at the University of Alabama School of Music: 'Nobody thought him perfect, however. There was always something suspect about him. He smiled too much. In that time and place, other, more sinister things were seen as wrong with him even though there barely existed a language with which to discuss them.' (*The Beginning of the Journey* by David Daniel, Newsweek, April 14, 1997). Observe how a gifted writer sets the scene in a few swift strokes!

In contrast, personal touches abound in *The Place of Enchantment* by Alex Owen. All our friends are there, from WB Yeats to Aleister Crowley. We learn how much the occult mattered to the pre-WWI elite (from Lewis Carroll, to Gladstone, Ruskin, and Lord Tennyson). Physicists jumped aboard, including Marie Curie. Notions of human identity and consciousness were in ferment; and while practitioners of medical psychology were keen to cleanse their field of the taint of association with the occult, the spirit world was Freud's secret passion.

The occult was 'intrinsic to the making of the modern.' Our host deftly portrays the cross-currents in this era of spiritual revolution, whose pioneers sought to create what they thought of as a better—or Socialist—new world. Amidst all this social engineering, nobody knew for sure whether "magic" was an egalitarian or elitist force. Of course there would be tears before, during, or after bedtime, with branches of spiritualism/messianic beliefs splitting off into eugenics, phrenology, and worse. Many Edwardian spiritualists foresaw a ghastly global Armageddon, and they weren't wrong. WWI crushed but also revalidated communication with the dead, making it less of a parlour trick and more a matter of private urgency and despair.

Owen is not averse to academic jargon and Chapter 8, in particular, feels dictated. But overall the signal-to-noise ratio is high. The following paragraph cuts to the heart of the subject: 'Perhaps, after all, what is so recognizably familiar about the fin de siècle is not so much its disenchantment as the evident unresolved tension between the spiritual and secular that surely marks the modern period. I have pursued this theme (...) by exploring the ways in which occultism at the turn of the century was deeply engaged in the reconciliation of secular imperatives and spiritual desire through a renegotiation of the idea of self. Advanced occult theory and magical practice represented a reworking of the concept and experience of self that underscored the self's contingency while anchoring it in the coherent and spiritualized realm of human consciousness. (...) I am also proposing that the occult constituted a crucial enactment of the ambiguities of the modern.'

Granted, this is jargon, but there are insights in there. I found the following very succinct: 'Magic (...) was based on the belief that an Adept can use a series of revered and ancient techniques in conjunction with a knowledge of correspondences in order to converse with those worlds beyond our own and gain control over the invisible forces of the universe.'

Owen doesn't just bandy about big words, but offers lucid definitions. We discover who late Victorian spiritualists were, what their self-perceptions and feuds entailed, what they did and how. Exercises in ritual magic ranged from astral journeys to the planets, to putting a hex on vivisectionists, all the way through to 'magick'. This was sex magic – 'Pain, blood, sexual fluids, and excrement became the trademarks of Crowley's "repulsive rituals"', as Owen is careful to explain.

Mind-altering substances were available in prodigious quantities—including hash and mescaline (sampled by Yeats and Maude Gonne). One experimenter overdosed on chloroform and suffocated. If you cherish little touches like this—as I do—you will enjoy this book.

Members of the Golden Dawn and other magical orders embraced bizarre hierarchies, titles, and pretentious Latin *noms de plume* (*Deo Date, Omnia Vincam*). Practitioners took this all in earnest. Magic was not fluff but a serious task, involving real effects on the exterior and interior world achieved through the disciplined application of the imagination.

As Owen explains, magic blurred distinctions between real/unreal, inner/outer, and subjective/objective—*but it was always absolutely real*. And in contrast to religion, with its pie in the sky, the tangible effects of magic were demonstrations of proof to enthusiasts. There was something comforting about it all. As they plied their parlor tricks in Chelsea and Knightsbridge, Edwardian occultists were in less obvious peril than camp inmates across the Atlantic—Waco, Jonestown, Heaven's Gate—a century later. Crowley bestrode both worlds and marks a kind of midpoint between them. He specialized in the systematic destruction of the ego and his followers in the 1920s were severely punished if they used the word "I".

Owen treats the subjects mostly with the kind of respect and restraint favoured in *The Oxford Handbook of NRMs*. As reviewer I feel no such constraints. To take one example, a lack of irony was prevalent among spiritualists: Crowley (he of the 'pain, blood, sexual fluids, and excrement') insisted his wife's alcoholism was responsible for their divorce. This was hardly a race of supermen. In a flash of insight, *The*

Oxford Handbook earlier noted that 'When disclosed, the "higher knowledge" that is revealed often turns out to be something that to the outsider is either quite banal or incomprehensible.' And in Owen's account, Yeats, Gonne, and the rest are recognizable as mortals who, though smart and innovative, are neither as imaginative nor as perceptive as they fancied themselves to be. Were these people feeling their way toward a pre-Einsteinian glimpse of relativity or quantum physics, as modern-day admirers might claim? Alas, no. The activities of the Golden Dawn are to science as the canals of Mars are to astronomy or Dan Brown to Christianity.

Sorry to be so brutal. I'm a recovering skeptic, but these books show me how much of a square and a reductionist I remain. Both have lengthy bibliographies, but Owen belongs on your bookshelves if you have the space.

Neil L. Inglis

Sabina Magliocco, 2004, *Witching Culture,* **University of Pennsylvania Press, Philadephia. 268 pages, ISBN 0-8122-1879-5, Paperback £14.00**

Before reading this, I knew of Sabina's work from her excellent chapter on the use of *bricolage* among Pagans in James Lewis' (1996) book *Magical Religion and Modern Witchcraft* and her more recent work on Pagan artwork *Neo-Pagan Sacred Art and Altars: Making Things Whole* published in 2002 by the University Press of Mississippi. Given this, I was expecting much from this new book – I was not disappointed. *Witching Culture* may be the latest in a line of ethnographies of Paganisms in North America, but what differentiates Magliocco's offering from the others is a theoretical freshness rooted in her imaginative application of folklore studies.

She begins with an introductory chapter which elucidates this innovative use of theory culled from folklore studies and anthropology. In particular, there is a concise but valuable discussion of *emic* and *etic* terminology and the insider/outsider debate. Although such debates have gained critical currency within Pagan studies of late – see for example, Jenny Blain's et al (2004) *Researching Paganisms* published by Alta Mira - Magliocco persuasively argues that these, in themselves, are essentialising categories:

> 'They [these debates] remind me of the well-meaning people who would ask me, when I was a child, whether I was really more American or Italian. This question would always stump me, because it was perfectly obvious to me that I was both, and that being part of one culture did not exclude belonging to the other ... My answer to readers who want to know whether I am "really" an insider or an outsider to the Pagan community is that I am neither and both – that how I look at things depends very much upon context, but contains both anthropological *and* Pagan perspectives at the same time' (p 15).

Indeed, the success of this ethnography is Magliocco's ability to blend seamlessly the world of the passionate practitioner with that of the rigorous academic.

The book is divided into three main parts: The first tackles the so-called 'Roots and Branches' of Paganisms. Magliocco is not content to give her readers a conventional and rehearsed history of Paganisms. Rather, she weaves a satisfying web of her own experiences in a Bay Area coven, with the emergence of folklore and anthropology as disciplines, and an exploration of how the seeds of Paganisms were sown by the mystical disavowal of the Enlightenment. She then moves on to examine the ways in which the *imagined communities* of Paganisms are constituted. In doing so, she charts how the idiosyncrasies of Pagan humour and spiritual distinctions within the Pagan community help to create magical identities. She illuminates these processes via snapshots of North American traditions of witchcraft such as Reclaiming and NROOGD alongside those of covens of her personal acquaintance such as the Berkeley-based Gardnerian Coven Trismegiston of Anna Korn and Don Frew.

The second part focuses upon the experience of magico-religious phenomena within Pagan witchcraft. In doing this she explains the role of magic within Pagan witchcraft drawing upon a blend of perspectives from within the Pagan and anthropological communities. Whilst this provides a good summary and retread of relevant the debates - spiced up with engaged scholarship from within Paganisms - I think that this particular section could have been more theoretically ambitious in her otherwise innovative study. Having said this, her discussion of ritual is certainly innovative. Using a conceit taken from her earlier book on Pagan sacred art and altars, Magliocco rightly sees Pagan ritualism as an art form. In doing so, she is able to analyse ritual through a folkloric lens which is rightly sensitive to aesthetics, creativity and performance.

The section finishes with a discussion of the ecstatic states which underpin Pagan ritual performance. This includes a brief, but informative, history of ecstasy arguing that The Enlightenment's commitment to rationality not only exalted reason but also acted to exclude ecstatic states. She parallels this notion with Foucault's construction of madness as the enemy of reason - in his book of 1961 *Madness and Civilisation* - and the attendant pathologisation of altered states of consciousness which entails. In contra-distinction, Magliocco sees Pagan witchcraft as creating 'a cultural context that normalises and privileges ecstasy' (p 181). Such a privileging of ecstatic experience is viewed, in part, as a counter-cultural strategy.

Indeed, in the third part of the book Magliocco does turn her attention to the ways in which Paganisms are Romanticised forms of 'oppositional culture'. Rooted in an exploration of Gramscian *hegemony*, she examines the role of Pagan story telling, myth making and songs as aesthetic forms of protest against mainstream cultural forms founded upon Enlightenment values.

Whilst this point is well made and innovatively wrought, I think that Magliocco, at times, has a tendency to oversimplify the relationship between Enlightenment thought and Paganisms given that Paganisms themselves are rooted in certain Enlightenment *values* – such as tolerance and the liberation of the individual - if not its *dogmas*. Indeed, in the last chapter of the book the Enlightenment's commitment to synthesis is demonstrated in Pagan uses of *bricolage* and 'cultural borrowing'. In a development of her article in the James Lewis collection, Magliocco explores relationships between Pagan practices, race, culture and authenticity. It is to her credit that she does not shy away from the intricacies of this undertaking, rooting questions of authenticity within the complexities of the new global order, especially the ability of magical traditions to transgress the boundaries of nation states. In one of the most evocative passages of the entire book, Magliocco concludes:

> 'In the end, what moves us may not be a matter of blood or power at all, but of spiritual and emotional longing. The art of magic allows our imagination to transcend the boundaries of blood and geography, to experience, at least in part, other cultures and time periods and fell empathy with other living beings. In the words of Ruth Barrett, "The heart is the only nation."' (p 237)

In sum, academic books about Paganisms, through a commitment to theoretical conservatism, can make the fascinating and numinous seem dull and quotidien. Magliocco's book, on the other hand, manages to preserve the sacred aesthetics of Pagan practices whilst demonstrating scholarly imagination and theoretical ambition. This volume ranks among the very best of ethnographies of contemporary Paganisms. Highly recommended.

Dave Green

Nevill Drury, 2003, *Magic and Witchcraft: From Shamanism to the Technopagans*, Thames & Hudson Ltd, London. 240 pages including 205 illustrations, 61 in colour, ISBN 0-500-51140-3 Hardback £14

Paganism is held to be the fastest growing religion in Britain (and elsewhere in the West) and there is a fast-growing plethora of books on such subjects as magic, shamanism, witchcraft and druidry which cater to an audience hungry for esoteric knowledge. One of the most recent of these is Nevill Drury's *Magic and Witchcraft: From Shamanism to the Technopagans*, titled perhaps to capture the interest of Pagans, and Wiccans in particular. In offering a detailed overview of ancient practices and techniques, and more recent manifestations, Drury's work makes a welcome contribution to the study of magic.

Magic and Witchcraft is far-reaching in its scope, with chapters starting with shamanism and proceeding through such areas as ancient magic (principally Greco-Roman), gnosticism and Kabbalah, medieval witchcraft and hermeticism, to the Victorian era and present day. This is 'magic' and 'witchcraft' broadly cast and as such it is significant for engaging with both ancient and contemporary forms of magic in a single volume, where other works are either Pagan tradition-specific (e.g. Thorsson, 1984; Farrar & Farrar, 1990) or do not conflate the archaic and the (post)modern (e.g. Thomas, 1991; Dickie, 2002).

Overviews of this sort inevitably risk simplifying and dealing too slightly with a vast and diverse range of examples. The sub-title and logical unfolding of the chapters hint that chronologically shamanism is archaic and that the 'technopagans' (a term not defined) are the inheritors of this tradition. The consistent representation of shamanism and animism in literature of this sort as essentially prehistoric and primitive is misleading, reifying Eliade's much-criticised characterisation of shamanism as 'archaic techniques of ecstasy' (e.g. Wallis, 2004).

Continuing this metanarrative, such phrases as 'the world's oldest spiritual tradition' (rear cover flap), 'From the earliest animist concepts' (p 6), and a 'hunter-gatherer tradition' (p 10), do not resonate well with current approaches to shamanisms which contest 'shamanism' singular and embrace the plurality and vitality of shamanisms, past and present.

The revival of shamanisms in areas subjected to colonialism, and the engagement between indigenous shamans and neo-shamans, mark fascinating areas for study. Yet despite stunning photographs of contemporary Tuvan shamans (cover, pp 2-3, 11) there is no discussion of the nationalistic revival of shamanisms here and elsewhere in Siberia in the post-Soviet era, nor is there discussion of instances where Siberian shamans have drawn on Harner's core-shamanic practices in order to re-construct and revitalise their own traditions (Wallis, 2003). Essentially, Drury's short (twenty pages or so) chapter offers nothing new on shamanisms that might be found elsewhere (e.g., Joan Halifax's equally beautifully illustrated coffee table book 'Shaman', 1982), and neglects recent critical examination of the topic (e.g., Harvey, 2002).

Afro-Caribbean traditions of 'possession' are dismissed as 'having not substantially shaped the Western magical tradition' (p 8), the latter being the focus of the book. Indeed, discussion of shamanism at all, given a focus on Western magic, seems incongruous with the rest of the book. This situation might have been remedied with discussion of shamanisms in the West, such as recent analyses of Palaeolithic cave art (e.g., Dowson, 1998); instead, Drury's brief comment (p 12) relies on outdated literature on hunting magic. Discussion of 'Celtic' or 'Germanic' shamanisms might also have linked shamanism to the West: despite recent interpretative approaches to the former, we are only offered an image of The Gundestrup Cauldron (p 13), and despite the use made of Afro-Caribbean possession techniques in contemporary Heathen shamanistic practices, Drury has already omitted possession as irrelevant (e.g., Wallis, 2003).

When dealing with contemporary Paganisms, Wicca is privileged above other Pagan pathways such as Druidry and Heathenry. There is an engaging discussion of the history of Wicca (chapter 10), but only one mention each for Druidry and 'Odinism'. Given that Wicca is the most prominent of Pagan traditions, such overemphasis may be appropriate, yet the term *wicce/wicca* itself is Old English and the plethora of sources on Anglo-Saxon witchcraft and magic (e.g., Storms, 1948; Griffiths, 1996; Pollington, 2000) – all arguably part of the Western magical traditions – are neglected by Drury.

A book of this nature can not cover everything and the chapters on more recent magical practices in the West are fascinating, especially the chapters on Satanism, the Golden Dawn and Crowley, which are necessary, erudite and do much to deconstruct some negative stereotypes. In addition, Drury's broad scope does not reduce the Western magical traditions to Crowley and the Golden Dawn.

An unfortunate omission none the less, is Chaos magic(k) which is not mentioned at all, along with the artist and occultist Austin Osman Spare (apart from a mention [pp 154, 231] and an illustration [p 156]). Spare's contribution to the history of occultism over the last century, and to the practices of Chaos Magic(k) in particular, is hugely significant – any volume on the history of magic is incomplete without discussion of the Zos-Kia Cultus and Chaos.

In the final analysis, I am pleased to have this book on my shelf. Following in the tradition of Thames & Hudson's related volumes (e.g., Green, 1997), *Magic and Witchcraft* is sumptuously illustrated, with stunning photographs of contemporary Central Asian shamanic rites, darkly bewitching Satanists, and *skyclad* Wiccan rites of the late twentieth century. Short chapters introducing such topics as Alchemy and Freemasonry are useful as starting points for future reading, and there is a useful list of chapter notes and a bibliography at the end of the book.

I have commented favourably on Drury's embracing the analysis of both ancient and recent instances of magic and witchcraft in the West, in a single volume. This is a point I would like to have seen taken further, drawing greater attention to the diversity of indigenous witchcraft and modern Pagan magic.

None the less, this is a salient reminder for scholars and practitioners, that magic and witchcraft are not one thing: all too often the books available indicate the simple equation witchcraft + magic = wicca.

Robert J Wallis

References

Dickie, M.W., 2002, *Magic and Magicians in the Greco-Roman World*, Routledge, London

Dowson, T.A., 1998, 'Rock Art: handmaiden to studies of cognitive evolution', in: C. Renfrew & C. Scarre, eds., *Cognition and Material Culture: The Archaeology of Symbolic Storage*, McDonald Institute Monographs, Cambridge, 67-76

Farrar, J. and Farrar, S., 1990, *Spells and How They Work*, Robert Hale, London

Green, M., 1997, *Exploring the World of the Druids*, Thames and Hudson, London

Griffiths, B., 1996, *Aspects of Anglo-Saxon Magic*, Anglo-Saxon Books, Frithgarth, Norfolk

Halifax, J., 1982, *Shaman: The Wounded Healer*, Thames and Hudson, London

Harvey, G., 2002, *Shamanism: A Reader*, Routledge, London

Pollington, S., 2000, *Leechcraft: Early English Charms, Plantlore and Healing*, Anglo-Saxon Books, Hockwold-cum-Wilton, Norfolk

Storms, G., 1948, *Anglo-Saxon Magic*, Martinus Nijhoff, The Hague

Thomas, K., 1991, *Religion and the Decline of Magic: Studies in Popular Beliefs in Sixteenth and Seventeenth-Century England*, Penguin, London

Thorsson, E., 1984, *Futhark. A Handbook of Rune Magic*, Samuel Weiser, York Beach, ME

Wallis, R.J., 2003, *Shamans/Neo-Shamans: Ecstasy, Alternative Archaeologies and Contemporary Pagans*, Routledge, London

Wallis, R.J., 2004, Book reviews of M. Stutley 2003. 'Shamanism: An Introduction'.

London: Routledge, and J. Fries 2002 [1993]. 'Helrunar: A Manual of Freestyle Magic', *Journal of the Society for the Academic Study of Magic*, 2, 340-357

Joscelyn Godwin, 1997, *Music, Mysticism and Magic*, Arkana, London. 349 pages, ISBN 0-14-0190406 Paperback £8.99

Joscelyn Godwin, one of the foremost researchers in the study of speculative music (the area of musical studies that investigates the connections between music and the wider cosmos), has prepared this compilation of 78 extracts from 61 different authors, ranging from Plato in the fifth century B.C.E. to Karlheinz Stockhausen, a contemporary music composer currently living and working in Germany.

In his Preface, Godwin tells us that 'This book documents the perennial wisdom associated with music, especially regarding the human being who is the potential worker of magic and the subject of mysticism' (p ix).

The selections include texts by occultists, mystics, philosophers (including 'occult philosophers'), writers and musicians. To name but a few, extracts on music from the Greek Hermetica, from Boethius' *De Institutione Musica*, from Agrippa's *De Occulta Philosophia*, from *De Vita Coelitus Comparanda* by Marsilio Ficino, and from *Harmonices Mundi* by Johannes Kepler. The personalities represented include the philosophers Plotinus, Simplicius, Dionysius and Schopenhauer; the romantic poets Chateaubriand, Novalis, Heinreich von Kleist, E.T.A. Hoffmann and George Sand; the composers Beethoven (through the pen of his friend Bettina Brentano), Robert Schumann, Richard Wagener and Karlheinz Stockhausen; the occultists Robert Fludd, Rudolf Steiner and G.I. Gurdjieff, as well as mystics such as Luis de León, Richard Rolle and Jalalu'ddin Rumi. There is also a whole section dedicated entirely to

Judaic and Islamic sources from the first to the thirteenth centuries C.E., which are comparatively less know in the West.

Each extract is prefaced by a short introduction by Godwin (sometimes not longer than two paragraphs), explaining the historical and ideological context surrounding the author, aspects of their lives and their most important work, and also, when most necessary, introducing the more obscure authors to the reader potentially unfamiliar with them. Full references are given before each passage for all of the sources used, in case the reader might be interested in following the passage further, or approaching it in its wider literary context.

Godwin's contribution is not limited to these introductory paragraphs, and his own referencing, connections, clarification and thoughts on the passages are expanded in 39 pages of notes at the end of the book, followed by a six-page listing of all of the works cited in his introductory and chapter notes, as well as the sources from where the passages were extracted.

For those interested in the subject of Music and Magic (in all its ramifications: music in magic, magic in music, magic of music, music of magic, etc.) who wish to have a general, historical overview of the subject, and would prefer to read smaller passages before following up the potentially enormous bibliography on the subject, this book proves to be of great aid.

Johann F.W. Hasler.

Robert A. Segal, 2004, *Myth: A Very Short Introduction,* **Oxford University Press, Oxford and New York. 163 pages, ISBN 0192803476 Paperback £6.99.**

This is a concise and very well written compendium of the theories of myth from the late nineteenth century to the present, and is suitable for undergraduates, postgraduates and anyone else who already has a basic knowledge of the subject. As the author says in the introduction 'there is no study of myth as myth' (p 2), but there are multiple approaches to it, united by the three main questions about its origin, its function (how it is used), and its subject matter. To illustrate the applications of the various theories Segal chooses the very complex myth of the preternaturally beautiful Adonis, in which several themes are displayed, from incest to death.

He starts with the problematic relationship between science and myth, presenting the various views that the latter is the primitive counterpart to science (Taylor, Frazer); that it embodies a mystical communion of primitive man and nature (Lévi-Bruhl); or that it is a means of reconciliation with uncontrollable natural events (Malinowski). The second chapter is about philosophy and myth, discussing, among others, Cassirer's idea of myth as a form of knowledge by its own, and Camus' existentialist interpretation of the myth of Sisyphus. Chapter 3 develops the symbolical interpretation of religious myth by Bultmann and Jonas, and Mircea Eliade's idea of its regenerative power.

The following chapter deals with the myth-ritualistic theories, from the pioneer William Robertson Smith to the application of them by J.G. Frazer. The reader is next guided around the links between literature and myth, with insight in to the works of Jessie Weston, Northrop Frye and Lord Raglan. It is in chapter 6, on psychology, that Segal produces his most analytical and comprehensive discussion, with an introduction to the theories of Freud, Rank, Jung, Campbell and a brief nod to the contemporary American folklorist Alan Dundes. Through Jung's child archetypes Segal provides the first full interpretation of the Adonis myth as a failure to succeed in being a complete individual.

Chapter 7 is on myth and structure, dealing with the theories of Lévi-Strauss, Propp, Dumezil and Detienne, while in chapter 8 Segal turns to myth and society, and explains the failure of Adonis as a citizen, lacking not only self-development, but even an accepted 'pedigree', being the son of an incest. In this last chapter Segal focuses on René Girard's theories (previously hinted in chapter 4), for whom the hero can be read even as the scapegoat (the Oedipus myth), and myth and ritual become 'ways not of coping with nature but with human nature – with human aggression' (p 129). Finally Segal shows how myth is still operating today, through cinema (we could add television as well), demonstrating how it can live in modern times without challenging science, so that nowadays myth is not only the preserve of scholars, but is a fertile reality of everyday life.

Francesca Matteoni

Pamela J. Stewart & Andrew Strathern, 2004, *Witchcraft, Sorcery, Rumours, and Gossip*, Cambridge University Press, Cambridge. 244 pages, ISBN: 0521808685 Hardback £40.00 ISBN: 052100473X Paperback £14.99.

Pamela Stewart and Andrew Strathern have offered an interesting, sometimes important, but nonetheless problematic anthropological assessment of the role of gossip and rumour in the construction of witchcraft accusations and other moral panics. As their starting point, the authors take the position that localised rumour and gossip are 'not trivial or epiphenomenal but central and fundamental' to understanding large-scale historical processes. It is through informal social channels, they argue, that we can better understand the dynamics and processes involved in the spread of witchcraft accusations and other moral panics. Taking a lead from the earlier ground-breaking work of Jean and John Comaroff, and Peter Geschiere, the book also examines how contemporary witchcraft and sorcery beliefs have emerged as responses to the moral ambiguities incumbent upon the encounter with modern capitalist ideology. In this respect, the authors also emphasis the role of witchcraft beliefs, moral panics, and conspiracy theories as both sources of empowerment and protest, and as state-legitimised incitements to mob violence against unwanted 'outsiders'.

The first chapter of the book present a thoughtful and pointed theoretical summary of key sociological and anthropological approaches to witchcraft and scapegoating. This material is skilfully assimilated into the authors' theoretical claims about the centrality of rumour and gossip in the second chapter; these claims are then systematically tested over four chapters which constitute the illustrative and ethnographic core of the book, taking in witchcraft movements and moral panics in African, Indian, New Guinean, and Euro-American contexts.

The aim of this wide-ranging and comparative cross-cultural review is to demonstrate seemingly pan-human propensities in both the process of rumour-mongering, and in terms of the form and manifestation of social concerns which cluster about the category of 'witchcraft'. With media-heightened fears surrounding asylum seekers, and the current spate of politically-motivated Islamophobia, the subject matter of the book, it would seem, is both timely and important.

But herein lies the problem: despite the universalising thrust of Stewart and Strathern's argument, the authors fail to enter into a sustained discussion of recent Euro-American moral panics (such as the allegations of Satanic ritual abuse, and the gamut of conspiracy theories that place blame for various social and economic ills on the Jews, Eastern Europeans, or even baby-eating interdimensional reptoids). Even though one chapter is dedicated to Western exemplars of witchcraft accusations, the authors fall back on the familiar and well-trodden terrain of the witch hunts of early modern Europe and the Salem witch trials. Given that its theoretical aims rest on both contemporary ethnographic as well as historical sources, the book recapitulates an unconscious (but sadly widespread) tendency within anthropology to relegate witchcraft beliefs to the domain of a 'primitive' non-Western other.

While at various points throughout the text, passing reference is made to what Jeffrey Victor has termed 'the Satanic Panic', a lack of sustained analysis of Euro-American Satanism scares tends to reaffirm the notion that witchcraft accusations and other kinds of moral panic - especially where couched in terms of the supernatural powers of evil - are only of interest where they populate the cultural imagination of 'exotic' peoples. This is especially the case where the authors make direct comparisons between the early modern European witch hunts and contemporary African witchcraft movements. Here, the analysis could be seen to buttress the assumption of an historical disparity between Western and non-Western modes of thought ('our' superstitious past is 'their' intellectual present); as such, the authors' comparative approach is sometimes in danger of communicating (especially to the non-specialist reader) outdated social evolutionist suppositions.

This is clearly not Stewart or Strathern's intention, but their failure to promptly address the problem means that they also inadvertently fail to emphasise the cultural salience of moral panics in presumably 'rationalised' and 'modern' Euro-American societies. As a consequence, it would be easy to mistake the authors' all-too brief treatment of ritual abuse allegations as an obfuscation of the 'irrationalities' that suffuse Continental, British, and North American modernities. Thus - and despite Stewart and Strathern's claim that the Satanism scares of the 1980s-1990s 'reminds us again of the universality and contemporaneity of the phenomena discussed in this book' - the material contained therein does fall somewhat short of expectations.

Another point of contention lies in the fact that the authors do not really seem to acknowledge the role of contemporary media and communications technology in facilitating the spread of rumour. In this regard, Stewart and Strathern place far too much reliance on the position that the widespread and rapid transmission of rumours is a consequence of their collective construction in concrete and embodied (rather than virtual) social networks. Granted, some of the groups in question (New Guinean horticulturalists) may not have ready on-line access; even so, the failure to fully recognise the centrality of these channels of communication in the substantiation of rumour infers an all-too familiar Western suppositions concerning the intellectual 'backwardness' made evident by moral panics and witchcraft movements in non-Western contexts.

Despite the problems that dog the authors' approach, the book does provide a valuable and reasonably solid anthropological overview of witchcraft accusations which will prove useful to students undertaking initial steps towards a study of the subject. The book also offers a substantial contribution to studies of witchcraft and moral panics by placing the micropolitics of localised jealousies, interpersonal discontents, and human aggression at the forefront of macrosocial and historical processes.

Even so, the book also tacitly - but unintentionally - reiterates an all-too comfortable hierarchical evaluation of the superiority of Western individualism over the presumably irrational mob-rule of 'traditional' and 'collectivised' societies; as such, the reader should be wary of imputing too much significance to the largely non-Western nature of the ethnographic material contained within the book: racism, ethnic conflict, and other forms of violence targeted at socially marginal groups which permeate Euro-American society are as much a product of 'irrational' and manipulable fears of 'modern' Westerners as they are of non-Western peoples.

Justin Woodman

Henry Cornelius Agrippa of Nettesheim, 2004, *Three Books of Occult Philosophy*, **Translated by James Freake, edited and annotated by Donald Tyson, St. Paul, Minnesota. 938 pages +**

LXXII **pages of preliminary notes written or compiled by the editor, ISBN 0-87542-832-0 Paperback £20.04 US$ 39.95.**

The more academically-inclined reader might be put off by the fact that that this re-edition of one of the core books of western esotericism is prepared and annotated by Donald Tyson, one of the most active and prolific contemporary authors in *practical* magic, and a confessed magician himself, whose titles include, among many others, the likes of *The Magician's Workbook, Ritual Magic: What It Is & How to Do It, How to Make and Use a Magic Mirror* and *Familiar Spirits: a Practical Guide for Witches and Magicians*. This initial scepticism might be further reinforced by the fact that the book, like all of Tyson's books, is published by Llewellyn Publications, one of the most prominent publishers in the English language of very popular and best selling titles in the subjects of New Age, Wicca, Astrology, paganism and all matters occult, whose catalogue is both overwhelmingly vast and varied in terms of the different degrees of academic rigour, ranging from magical and New Age bestsellers printed by the tens of thousands to a number of titles of surprising scholarly depth, insight and sometimes even difficulty. I am pleased to say that, quite deservingly given the importance of the original source, this book falls into this latter category.

The book is typeset on two columns per page throughout, yet it is still slightly under one thousand pages long. Of these, 708 pages correspond to the actual core text by Agrippa, translated from the Latin original into English by James Freake for the London edition of 1651. The reader will be relieved to know that the text has been modernized for this edition, both in spelling and punctuation, though not in style, which has the advantage of making the material easily readable while keeping some of the original flavour of the first English edition.

The remaining 230 pages are by Tyson. Of them, seventy-two are placed before Agrippa's text, in the form of a colourful 37 page-long biography of the author, followed by a preliminary study about the text itself, with the complete history of its several versions and the vicissitudes it went through before and after the publication of its final version in 1533. The remaining 158 pages by the editor are placed after Agrippa's text, in the form of eight informative appendixes, on *The Emerald Tablet, The Soul of the World, The Elements, The Humors* [sic], *Magic Squares, The Sephiroth, Practical Kabbalah* and *Geomancy*. They prove, along with the biographical and geographical glossaries (termed by Tyson *'dictionaries'*) of extreme usefulness in the oftentimes daunting task of keeping up with Agrippa's peculiar lateral thinking and fondness for unreferenced citations and name dropping. Furthermore, each one of the short 65 chapters by Agrippa has a selection of endnotes by the editor, shedding even more light on the author's often un-attributed and obscure references and connections to classical and contemporary works.

Apart from these notes and appendixes, the editorial work of Donald Tyson on the actual text seems to be quite thorough, and he acknowledges he has intervened the work more than just superficially: '[…] so many errors that have been handed down the Western occult tradition for centuries are here corrected for the first time' (p xiv). 'It was necessary to reconstruct and redraw, or at least amend, *every one of the tables and illustrations, often with no guide*, since the errors in the English edition were transcribed from their Latin model' (p xiii, italics mine).

These corrections and amendments, as well as other of Tyson's interpretations, are clearly marked and acknowledged in the end of chapter notes wherever they occur within the text, often scrupulously supported with citations of modern scholarly works that clarify some obscure or confusing passages of the original text. Yet the purist historian might feel a little uneasy that the original text has been touched at all, let alone, as is this case, *corrected*.

The reasons for such heavy editorial work are understood, as I see it, once we consider that the book is primarily aimed at, as it openly declares in its first page, 'to all occultists and magicians', and only *secondarily* ('Likewise'), as 'a necessary reference tool', to 'all scholarly students of the Renaissance, Neoplatonism, and Western Kabbalah, the history of ideas and sciences […], and the occult tradition'. If Tyson has annotated and corrected Agrippa's text when he felt it necessary, as he honestly acknowledges, it is because he, being a practicing magician, believes that the Hermetic tradition is a *living* tradition, and thus in constant development, and he wishes to contribute to the further development of this tradition. In this sense it does not aspire to transmit a historically exact record of a document written 475 years ago, but to give a modern reading of one of the most revered sources of the Hermetic Tradition, and therefore, it is part of its homage to update it and annotate it with the more current and updated understanding of the material treated.

It is a book by a hermetic magician, who considers his tradition to be alive and kicking, and not by a historian who considers it a finished chapter of history: The approach to a living and developing field of knowledge is, as it might be easily concluded, totally different to that given to a dead and fossilised remnant of the past. To those readers preferring a more historically conservative approach, who happen to be fluent enough in Renaissance Latin and can spend the £143 it costs in the market – or can manage to find a copy in one of their local libraries- I would rather recommend the 1992 Brill edition edited by Vittoria Perrone Compagni.

Overall he book appears as a long awaited and very welcome reprint of this rare and fundamental text, aimed mainly at the hermetic enthusiast and rigorous practitioner, for, as Tyson shows through example, it is not a contradiction in terms to be *rigorous* and a practitioner of magic at the same time, albeit *rigour* might not always be measured by the academic with the same ruler that the magician would use: It is, after all, a matter of paradigm, or, should we say, of *ontology*. As long as the reader has this always in mind, and is able to shift and adapt his or her critique of the editorial material accordingly, the book is of great value, and an important addition to the library of any enthusiast of the period or the subject matter – for whatever reason. Furthermore, it is available at a very affordable price, considering the obscurity of the material, its arguably low appeal to many modern readers, and the sheer volume of ink and paper it has taken to produce.

Johann F.W. Hasler

Henrietta L. Moore and Todd Sanders, 2001, *Magical Interpretations, Material Realities: Modernity, Witchcraft and the Occult in Postcolonial Africa,* **Routledge, London. 272 pages, ISBN 0415258677 Paperback £19.99.**

This collection of anthropological essays edited by two of the London School of Economics' academics is an eminently worthwhile addition to the library of any scholar of magic. Though those who are familiar with contemporary western esotericism, magic(k), witchcraft, occultism or alternative spirituality may find the initial pages of the editors' introductory chapter both debateable factually and problematic politically (the words 'cults' and 'gullible' are particularly questionable), I would reassure the would-be reader that here is but a small flaw in an otherwise most rewarding text.

The editors' introduction proceeds to tackle head-on the thorny issue of what, exactly, is 'witchcraft' (or indeed 'sorcery' or 'magic')? There is indeed little agreement in the anthropological literature, and whether Moore and Sanders' use of the word 'occult' and related terms (after Geschiere) is any less slippery or any less imbued with ethnocentric and negative connotations remains to be seen.

However, perennial problems of definition and labelling aside, most would heartily agree with Moore and Sanders' main proposition that occultism and modernity are not mutually exclusive opposites and (after a handy history of past anthropological approaches to witchcraft) the rest of the introduction and the following ten essays set out to explore how, precisely, this may be so. For, if witchcraft and modernity are not simply juxtaposed, in what sense(s) are they engaged with one another? Are they inter-related in that witchcraft, real or imagined, resists modernity? Or might witchcraft and/or perceptions thereof be somehow caused by modernity? Or are such binary approaches now outmoded? Might the two not be much more subtly intermeshed? Might even modernity and the occult not be so different after all? Is not modernity too replete with myth and enchantment all of its own?

As is the way with so much contemporary social anthropology, both the editors and the contributors to this book resist simplistic generalizations in addressing manifold permutations of these and similar questions. Rather than offering brash propositions of cause and effect or explanatory analyses of the very general, they tend instead towards more descriptive treatments of specific situations. Thus a wide variety of contemporary African manifestations of nexuses between witchcrafts or occultisms and modernities are illustrated by a wide diversity of data, and this material is in general presented with great politico-economic sensitivity and ethnographic richness. Voices, faces, ideas and images will linger long with the reader, and just some of these are: reports of the shrinking penises of Cameroonian men and of the vulture men, magical gangsters and teen witches of Nigeria; the newly updated Ghanaian gods who read the papers and watch the football and the would-be entrepreneurs who try to financially exploit their shrines and talismans; the relation between the International Monetary Fund and the symbolism of the (all too sickeningly real) trade in human skins in Tanzania; the awful mass 'necklacing' of alleged witches in the new South Africa; and the youthful sorcerers of Cameroon whose magical attacks on symbols of the nation's development resulted in what to the best of my knowledge is the only ritual or divinatory procedure in the whole of human culture to be centred around group vomiting.

Two pieces worth specific mention are a splendid mixture of anthropology and history (with regard to narratives of cannibalism) typical of Rosalind Shaw and a piece analysing the all too often overlooked interface of magic and humour (in and around Malawian witchcraft accusations) by Rijk van Dijk. Ultimately then, what one has here is an at once accessible and outstanding collection of essays by some of anthropology's leading Africanists which cannot be recommended too highly.

William Redwood

Greg Humphries and Julian Vayne, 2004, *Now That's What I call Chaos Magic,* **Mandrake of Oxford, Oxford. 192 pages, ISBN 1869928741 Paperback £13.99**

Ramsey Dukes, 2005, *The Little Book of Demons: The Positive Advantages of the Personification of Life's Problems,* **Aeon, London. 100 pages, ISBN 1904658091 Paperback £9.99**

Jaq D. Hawkins, 2002, *Chaos Monkey,* **Capall Bann Publishing. 190 pages, ISBN 186163188X Paperback £10.95**

As we announced in JSM2, included in our remit of 'academic' is the selective coverage of well-written and *significant* books by practitioners as well as by those studying the subject academically. This will not mean that we wish to see or review every last magical practitioner book published, however, but as was highlighted by one of our editorial board, "we simply would not be doing our job properly if we ignored what the magicians themselves were writing about their own subject", and there is a considerable grey area between what is purely academic and what is practitioner-prose, in any case. This is a valid point that Johann Hassler also raises in his review of the Donald Tyson edited book, above. Therefore I am delighted to present a combined examination of several recent books by those who are nominally chaos magicians, although that itself is a slippery label, as can be seen by the sheer variety of material reviewed here.

Julian Vayne was one of the star speakers at our 2003 conference in Bristol, and it is a great pleasure to see this book in print, having read a typescript version of it some 2 years ago. He and his co-author Greg Humphries are modern and extremely innovative and intelligent magical practitioners who have a deep grounding in the philosophies and theories underlying modern magic, and wider society/culture. To read the various metaphorical tangents to which they take their magic, and the methodological justifications behind their work is a multi-level and rewarding experience for academic and magician alike.

Any reader will be literally enchanted, as this book can be read simply (but it is not a simplistic book) as a narrative novel, as it has a timeline running through the events. The magical practitioner reading this material will find much to admire, much to agree with, and much to adapt for their own uses. The academic researcher given this book will mine many a useful quote and concept, and find much material that provides ready source material for discussion and analysis. I would liken the scope of this relatively slim (but by no means lightweight) book to something by Marx, in that different readers will find different areas of one or more of beauty, synthesis and utility, as one volume of Marx would differently delight the historian, the political theorist, the philosopher etc with the source material it provides. Quite excellent, highly recommended; and future output from these authors is eagerly anticipated.

In similar vein to Julian and Greg above, the magician and philosopher Ramsey Dukes, under his actual name of Lionel Snell was a well-received article contributor to JSM2, with a piece on Magical philosophy as compared to Art, Religion and Science. This latest book is also written by Dukes-Snell in his role as occult philosopher, and concentrates on greatly expanding and analysing an earlier brief essay in one of his own books where he discussed the phenomena of 'ghost in the machine', whereby personification of inanimate objects can have a magical and useful effect in daily life. Dukes' thesis is that by acknowledging troubles or negative factors in life as literally 'demons' one can work with them, negotiate with them and use them, rather than be under their thrall; which is a considerably different focus from that found in mediaeval demonological tracts. It is hugely entertaining for a philosophy book, but provides a recondite and robust magical philosophy at the same time, every page being thought-provoking, and since it is a practical, or at least 'thought-experiment' book it is being marketed as a variation on the 'self help' genre. If you enjoyed his article in JSM2 (or his other books) this is essential reading.

Despite the free-for-all and egalitarian attitude expressed by many chaos magic philosophies, there seem still only a few significant, or at least visibly significant *women* writing on the subject in a practical, coherent or useful fashion. 'Jaq Hawkins' (another pseudonymous author) is one of the exceptions, and her most recent book, *Chaos Monkey*, can be seen as a companion volume to that of Dukes (although the two writers have no close links, to my knowledge), in that it deals with the personification of magical matters, in this case having the Chaos current as an animal, and one that 'behaves' in an animal fashion, which is a slightly different tack to Dukes and Humphries and Vayne.

If you have the money and the inclination, buy all three. If strapped for cash get Vayne and Humphries and borrow the other two, but all are pretty much essential reading for the academic wishing to study modern chaos magic, or anyone working practically in that field. For those who are both academic and practitioner, as I am, they are vital source materials for both strands of activity.

Dave Evans

Neil Whitehead and Robin Wright, eds., 2004, *In Darkness and Secrecy: The Anthropology of Assault Sorcery and Witchcraft in Amazonia*, Duke University Press. 256 pages, ISBN 0-8223-3345-7 Paperback. $22.95, £17.50

Readers of this journal hardly need to be made aware that 'shamanism' is a loaded and highly contested word. In addition to the range of neoshamanisms which currently proliferate in the popular religious landscape, the usefulness of the term 'shaman' as a universal descriptor of a variety of beliefs and practices is not entirely clear. In both the preceding cases discourses concerning geographic origins and cultural 'authenticity' are central to understanding how we can most effectively discuss a variety of seemingly similar practices in disparate parts of the world which exist in often radically different cultural contexts.

Latin America and Amazonian indigenous cultures have a rich legacy in the abundant scholarly and popular literature of shamanisms, yet *In Darkness and Secrecy* aims to fill a lacunae in the topic. In this collection

Whitehead and Wright have assembled a collection of fourteen essays which address the position of 'Dark Shamanism' and assault sorcery in the worldviews of the diverse indigenous groups of Amazonia. The definition of dark shamanism is not tightly defined by the authors or editors, but in short, it deals with a range of practices and social behaviors which involves the perception that one person is doing another person harm through supernatural means. In this collection, shamanism emerges as a more morally ambiguous concept. Those who can contact and manipulate supernatural powers are understood to be able to do so for either good or for harm.

In the introduction Whitehead and Wright explain that the majority of writing on shamanic practices from this region focus on the more positive applications such as healing and native medicines. Another focus of scholarship is the interaction and appropriation of these techniques, especially those from Latin America, within the broader category of neoshamanisms. The editors suggest that there is a double-edged sword to these scholarly foci. On the one hand it draws attention to the value and potential contributions that indigenous knowledge and cosmologies of Amazonia bring to the rest of the world.

However, this focus ignores an important part of the Amazonian worldview, namely that cosmic forces can just as readily be harnessed for ill as well as healing or enlightenment. The editors also suggest that for anthropologists to reveal too much about the darker aspect of native cosmologies may bring negative attention to indigenous peoples, who already struggle to overcome poorly informed perceptions of their religious practices. Too much explication of the cultural complexes surrounding assault sorcery may also jeopardize the often tenuous relationships that these groups have with support agencies and government authorities. With these concerns in mind, Whitehead and White go forth to present a more comprehensive, and nuanced understanding of the range of influence of shamanism within different segments of Amazonian cultures.

The essays focus on the practice and interpretation of 'dark shamanism' among a variety of tribes in the Amazonian basin, including Venezuela, Peru, Guyana and Brazil. The diversity of cultures and belief systems is staggering, and the essays demonstrate the ways in which notions of assault sorcery engage with a number of contexts, including colonialism, invasion and missionary activity. The essays in this collection broadly fall into two categories: dark shamanism as a variety of techniques in a wider catalogue of magical practices, and dark shamanism as a response to social tensions, both internal and externally located.

A minority of the essays focus on magical techniques and cosmology, but those that do are fascinating reading and raise interesting questions. Wilbert's detailing of the position and training of Warao dark shamans of northern Venezuela reveals an amazingly complex and stunning cosmology in which the different types of shamans operate. Fausto asks why those who have an interest in Amazonian shamanism have downplayed or downright ignored the two of its most central themes, blood and tobacco, in favor of seemingly more enlightening substances such as hallucinogens.

Most of the chapters, however, explore the familiar cycle of accusation and retribution for illness, misfortune and deaths, which are attributed to assault sorcery. These essays reveal both similarities and vast differences in how assault sorcery is used almost universally among these cultures to explain illness, social fractures and to identify the marginal members of society. Vidal and Whitehead address the fascinating intersection of assault sorcery accusations with contemporary politics and millennial prophecy in Guyana and the ways in which prophets and politicians have been discredited due to allegations of dark shamanism.

In a very different context, Pollock explores how sorcery accusations are used among the Kulina of Brazil to demarcate varying levels of kinship affiliations and social conduct. Through these essays dark shamanism is revealed as a foundation of Amazonian cultures, an adaptive strategy which explains the root of misfortune, but also which also serves as a social corrective.

Some of the more distressing aspects of this collection concern the processes of accusation and retribution for accused acts of assault sorcery. Santos-Granero account of accusations of child sorcery among Arawak speaking groups in Peru is quite chilling. He describes how accusations of child sorcery arise during times of externally motivated cultural stress, and the children who are accused are insiders with links to external forces of change. Reading of the torture and executions of children is very difficult, but the importance of the data and its analysis is abundantly clear.

There may appear to be some ambiguity in this work about how the term 'shamanism' is used, but it is actually quite context sensitive. Some, however, may find the usage here to be too imprecise. In many ways the cultural complexes here are more in line with Evans Pritchard's use of either witchcraft or sorcery in the African context. However, this collection demonstrates that the phenomenon of Shamanism in the Amazonian worldview embraces a wider continuum of cause and effect and moral retribution involving a notion of vital energies than is often explored in the literature. In this sense, the healing shaman cannot exist without the shaman who also harms.

Amy Hale

Michael D. Bailey, 2003, *Historical Dictionary of Witchcraft: Historical Dictionaries of Religions, Philosophies, and Movements, No. 47*, Scarecrow Press, Lanham, MD and Oxford. 248 pages, ISBN 0-8108-4860-0 Hardcover $60, £46

Michael Bailey's research for *Battling Demons: Witchcraft, Heresy, and Reform in the Late Middle Ages* (Penn State University Press, 2002) was extensive and thorough. His analysis focused primarily on the figure of Johannes Nider, the reformist theologian who proved central to 15th century notions of witchcraft, demonology and heresy. Best of all, the fruits of that research have given us this dictionary which should prove a handy reference guide for any student of the discipline.

Bailey aims for a wide audience and acknowledges the problems that engenders: 'Anyone trying to understand witchcraft in a broad yet accurate historical sense must confront a number of problems, of which perhaps none is more basic than the difficult question of how to define exactly what elements constitute witchcraft' (p xxi). He makes an effort to do so and includes apparatus to help define the field. There is a chronology that highlights important touchstones from the ca. 1750 BCE Code of Hammurabi right up to Ronald Hutton's (1999) *Triumph of the Moon* . His 25-page introduction also tries to give a brief sense of the development of the study of witchcraft as well as an historical overview. The bibliography offers lists of essential readings in both primary and secondary texts, the latter arranged by historical periods, and then by region.

The entries themselves vary from detailed to curt. Cross-referenced terms appear in bold. Of course, Bailey's strength lies in the late medieval and early modern periods and the entries from that era show this depth. His entry for Nider is detailed yet concise, as are his entries for Bernard Gui, Demons and Demonology. Entries cover the whole of his chronology; however, his most thorough descriptions remain those related to his major period of study.

Earlier records, such as Hecate and the Witch of Endor, seem to be glimpsed through the lens of the Middle Ages. Later entries include people as varied as Margot Adler and Gerald Gardner, both well-situated within the modern witchcraft movements, and there is an attempt to address the current varieties of witchcraft, but readers would probably find greater information from Hutton, Adler and some newer scholars on the present situation. Nonetheless, Bailey's book will give a novice scholar on that topic plenty to get started.

The major issue in formulating this collection is the definition of witchcraft primarily as criminal. Bailey's focus throughout most of his work remains on *maleficium* and the more benign aspects of witchcraft can be neglected. There are no entries on charms, despite their popularity to this day both for healing and prognostication (there is a section, however, on healing). Charms serve as an important glimpse into the magic of the early Middle Ages in particular, as do the penitentials (for which there is no entry either, although penitentials provide much of our knowledge about forbidden magical practices prior to the canon *Episcopi*). Given its importance both historically and currently, there really ought to be an entry on ritual as an essential component of witchcraft.

Bailey's *Dictionary* is only a beginning, but it is a good one. Its limitations show how much more work is yet to be done in this rapidly growing field. This volume is an excellent acquisition for any research library.

KA Laity

Ithell Colquhoun, 2003, *Goose of Hermogenes*, Peter Owen, London and Chester Springs. 115 pages, ISBN 0-7206-1177-6, Paperback £ 9.95

'This was a monstrous country - even the parklands were alive with beings earlier than man. Tortured oak-trees stood or lay, piercing or hollow; a single ancient, near a Templar's site, reared a herd of ancestral horns and opened its side in a Gothick window. Does the Maiden sometimes look out? I wondered. Clumps of the druidic tree recalled that mysterious Nightingale who nested in nine oaks; the Russian 'Bylinay' sing of him, but whether he is a bird or hero or demon they do not say.'

And whether Ithell Colquhoun's *Goose of Hermogenes* is a gothic fantasy or dream-narrative or alchemical allegory I cannot say; perhaps it is all three. The heroine of this fantastical tale tells the reader of her visit with an eccentric uncle during which she discovers that he is a rather sinister character and deeply involved in black magic. The story takes place on the uncle's other-worldly island; a surreal setting that matches the dangerous and mysterious character of its ominous owner. The heroine, described in the first person, eventually discovers that her uncle's ambitious quest for the philosopher's stone involves the acquisition of her heirloom jewels.

Her attempts to thwart his intentions and save her sisters and brother, who have mysteriously arrived on the island, unwillingly trapped in a spiritual brothel, are futile. The heroine eventually comes to a sensible solution and ends the nightmare. This brief plot is barely distinguishable amidst the author's descriptions of the heroine's dream-like wanderings, musings, and encounters with bizarre characters on the equally bizarre island. Colquhoun's story and style lead the reader down an esoteric garden path through a landscape both beautiful and frightening and always intricately described.

Despite the inherent beauty of Colquhoun's descriptive manner and fantastical tale, the novel is confusing and exclusive in its use of esoteric and occult symbolism. At best, *Goose of Hermogenes* will delight and intrigue the average reader, while at worst, that same reader may leave its pages feeling confused and disinterested. The author's intended audience seems to be those 'in the know' or readers with some knowledge of occultism. While readers without such knowledge may well appreciate the novel for its surreal and gothic style, the book remains a bit mysterious.

The title itself evokes mystery and requires explanation. In a brief biography of Colquhoun at the beginning of the novel, Eric Ratcliffe tells the reader that Hermogenes was a Carthaginian painter and philosopher whose anti-Christian Gnosticism encouraged the early church father Tertullian to write a lengthy treatise denouncing both Hermogenes' philosophy and artistic abilities. Ratcliffe also informs us that the Goose of Hermogenes was a name used by medieval alchemists for the Philosopher's Stone. In keeping with this alchemical association, Colquhoun uses the names of different stages of the process of alchemy for her chapter titles.

It is obvious that the author was quite familiar with occult symbolism, alchemy, cabalistic and ritual magic. This familiarity is apparent in her references to some of the standard sources in occult and alchemical literature such as *The Book of the Sacred Magic of Abramelin the Mage* and *Atalanta Fugiens*. It is in this usage that one could argue for the academic merit of the *Goose of Hermogenes*. It provides insight into the occult texts that were in circulation during the author's day or that were at least accessible in certain circles. Colquhoun's strange tale provides evidence for the historian of magic of the continuity of a magical tradition established in the late nineteenth century by the Hermetic Order of the Golden Dawn, which drew on older medieval and renaissance sources in the formulation of its magical system. Such evidence can of course be discovered in less subtle places, yet its placement here also establishes a continued link between the occult and the artistic world.

The author's surreal and esoteric style are undoubtedly influenced by her other passions. Ithell Colquhoun was a well-known English surrealist painter whose works are now held in several major art galleries including the Tate Britain and the National Portrait Gallery. She was also active in esoteric and occult circles and her relationships with individuals associated with the Golden Dawn have been well-documented, primarily in her last publication in 1975, *Sword of Wisdom: MacGregor Mathers and the Golden Dawn.*

Colquhoun also published two unusual travel books prior to *Goose of Hermogenes*, one on Ireland, *The Crying of the Wind*, and the other on Cornwall, *The Living Stones*, both focusing on the myths and legends associated with these places. Her occult interests were manifested prominently in both her written and painted works. In this, Colquhoun follows in the footsteps of earlier artists such as William Blake, W. B. Yeats and Florence Farr, all of whom imbued their artistic endeavours with occult symbolism.

The *Goose of Hermogenes* was first published in 1961 by Peter Owen, the same publisher of this second edition and her two travel books. The first edition was a sell-out and no doubt the publisher has similar aspirations for this republication. With such a well-established market for esoteric and occult literature, it is indeed likely that Colquhoun's book will enjoy similar success to its first publication and become part of the esoteric canon.

Alison Butler

Savage-Smith, Emilie, ed., 2004, *Magic and Divination in Early Islam*. [The Formation of the Classical Islamic World 42, General editor Lawrence I. Conrad], Ashgate·Variorum, Aldershot. 394 pages, ISBN 0-86078-715-X Hardcover $149.95, £82.50

As is usual for Variorum, this volume consists of articles reprinted in facsimile, concentrated in this case on the subject of Islamic occultism.

The articles are mostly from the 1980s and 1990s, although one is a newly published summary of a recent monograph (C. Burnett, 2003, *Weather forecasting in the Arabic world*), and another is a revision of an article collaborated on by the editor (E. Savage-Smith and M. B. Smith, 2003, *Islamic geomancy and a thirteenth century device: another look*).

Savage-Smith provides an introduction which surveys the range of magical practices found in Islamic culture and a general bibliography which helps to update some of the more aged articles. There is also a useful index. The articles, and even the introduction, for the most part shy away from theoretical concerns (e.g. 'what is magic?' or 'is a definition of magic possible?'), and are interested instead in simply establishing the character of the entirely emic categories of *siḥ?r* and *kihâna* (roughly magic and divination) which do not necessarily correspond to Western categories or any categories familiar from anthropological research. Hence this collection shows Islamic studies to be in a somewhat preliminary phase of development compared to either the study of Ancient Graeco-Egyptian magic (which is the predecessor of much Islamic magic), or of Renaissance occultism or the Kabbalah, which received much from the Islamic world. A. Fodor (1978) in *The rod of Moses in Arabic magic*, on the other hand, presents a detailed study of the Islamic reception and expansion of a Jewish occult tradition.

The articles anthologized here express relatively little concern for either the social role or legal status of the occult practices discussed, except in the case of astrology. This science was generally forbidden and viewed as fraudulent, idolatrous, or foreign, but nevertheless enjoyed the same kind of social prominence as in the Roman Empire or Medieval West because it, to a degree, succeeded as representing itself as a part of the general Aristotelian framework of knowledge and science, in much the same manner as philosophy or medicine (G. Saliba, 1992, *The role of the astrologer in Medieval Islamic society*; Y. Michot, 2000, *Ibn Taymiyya on astrology: annotated translation of three fatwas*). F. E. Peters (1990) in *Hermes and Harran: the roots of Arabic-Islamic occultism* presents a view of the Arabic sources on the transmission of Greek philosophy to the Islamic world that more nearly repeats the received historico-mythologoical tradition than analyzes it. Rather, the idea that the 'Sabians' of Harran[1] (taking for themselves a title that ought to refer to the Mandaeans, one of the 'four peoples of the book' granted toleration by the Koran) created a Mesopotamian-Hermetic-Neoplatonic syncretism that became the source of Islamic occultism[2] can best be treated as a metaphorical acknowledgement of the work of the 'Sabians' in Baghdad as translators of Greek philosophical works.[3]

In particular the idea that Hermes Trismegistus (= *Idris* in Islamic tradition) was the original inventor and source of Greek philosophy (an idea of vital importance in its reception by the European Renaissance) probably owes much to his prominence within the alchemical tradition, and there was not much translation into Arabic of the philosophical, rather than the alchemical, Hermetica. Such Neoplatonic learning as was received by Islamic scholars need have no origin more mysterious than the translations of well known works such as those of ps-Dionysius the Areopogite or the epitome of Plotinus' Enneads (which circulated under an attribution to Aristotle, showing how little was understood of the context and history of Greek philosophy).

Savage-Smith delineates a taxonomy of Islamic occultism along these lines: magic proper, which consists most frequently of amuletic practices, compounded for the most part of either Koranic passages or abstract combinations of letters and numbers (naturally, given the Islamic prohibition on images—although these sometimes appear nevertheless), especially the magic square, a form infinitely more elaborated in Islam than in, say, the Roman Empire (T. Canaan, 1937-8, *The decipherment of Arabic talismans* [which is an indispensable reference for any work on the epigraphy of Arabic amulets]; V. Porter, 1998, *Islamic seals: magical or practical?*). Iatro-magical practices made extensive use of magic bowls, but in a form and manner markedly different from the older use of Aramaic magic bowls. The paradoxographical element (stories of wonders and miracles) of Islamic magic may be most familiar to a general audience from its prominence in the *1001 Nights*. The reputation in the West of the Arabic world as a center of ceremonial magic seems much exaggerated. Islamic divination mostly descended from Graeco-Roman practices, but techniques like divination from the flight of birds or animal entrails dwindled in importance compared to the sortilege of the Koran, numerology, and astrology and physiognomy. J. Henninger (1981) in *Belief in spirits among the pre-Islamic Arabs*, which is here translated into English for the first time, presents an extended bibliographical and historiographical discussion of the Arabic folk-belief in the *jinn* (not etymologically related to the Latin *genius* as many Western scholars suppose), and debates evolutionary theories of religious development long since (even in 1981) abandoned by modern anthropologists, underlining Islamic Studies' relative isolation in the Western academy.

However, Henniger does advance the helpful idea that: 'the private worship of spirits… and public and communal worship of deities… can exist alongside one another,' (p 39), paralleling the recent work of

Classical scholars[4] in making a meaningful distinction between magic and religion. M. Dols (1992) in *The theory of magic in healing*, suggests that Peter Brown's[5] analysis of late antique Christian saints would cast helpful light upon the problem of magic in Islamic society. He points out that just as Jewish scholars shunned the Kabbalah prior to Gershom Scholem's work, modern Arabic scholars tend to avoid Islamic magic as a source of cultural shame (magic is dismissed as an upwelling of decadent superstition from the 'masses', despite the scholarly character of Islamic magic). Dols looks for an emic model of magic in Islam, and finds one provided by Ibn Khaldûn (13th century) in his *Muqaddimah* or introduction to history, who adopted the ideas of the 'philosophers' (sc. Neoplatonists, especially Porphyry in bk. II of his *De abstinentia*), by which the different levels of supernatural activity were performed by individuals functioning at different psychic levels: 'magic' was the use of the mind to exercise sway over the natural word and spirits; 'theurgy' employed intellectual rituals such as astrology and the manufacture of mathematical talismans; 'prestidigitation' relied on phantoms and trickery to cloud men's imaginations. Yet Khaldûn rejects all of these (as well as the attempts of Sufis to gain miraculous powers through the practice of *dhikr* meditation) as alien to Islamic piety and associated them with Syriac and Coptic Christians (in the Islamic era Egypt maintained its reputation as the home of magic). Saints are quite distinct from all this because their miracles are effected directly by God and have nothing to do with spirits.

On the whole this book has a preliminary character that renders it more suitable as an aide to further research than as an introduction to Islamic magic. It should be noted that both alchemy, perhaps the most important occult science in the Islamic tradition, and the *Picatrix* are entirely neglected here: the former perhaps because it could easily support a volume of this type on its own, and the latter perhaps because this text is more central to Western rather than Islamic magic, as well as the almost complete absence of scholarly attention following the promising publications of the German translation[6] of the Arabic version and Pingree's edition of the Latin text.[7]

Bradley Skene

Notes

1. T. Green (1992) *The City of the Moon God: religious traditions of Harran*, E. J. Brill, Leiden, gives a more thorough exposition of the entire history of the religion of Harran, while A. Kuhrt (1990) 'Nabonidus and the Babylonian priesthood,' *Pagan priests and power in the Ancient world*, M. Beard and J. North, eds. Cornell Universe Press, Ithaca, 117-55, is especially good on Harran's prominence in the Neo-Babylonian period.

2. M. Tardieu (1986) 'Sâbiens coraniques et <<Sâbiens>> de Harran,' *Journal asiatique* 274, 1-44, and *idem* (1987) 'Les calendries en usage à Harran d'après les sources arabes et le commentaire de Simplicius à la Physique d'Aristote,' *Simplicius, sa vie, son oeuvre, sa survie: Actes du colloque International de Paris (28 Sept.-1er Oct. 1985)*, I. Hadot, ed., Walter de Gruyter, Berlin, 40-57, made similar suggestions working from Greek evidence.

3. J. Lamear (1997) 'From Alexandria to Baghdad: reflections on the genesis of a problematical tradition,' *The ancient tradition in Christian and Islamic Hellenism*, G. Endress and R. Kruk, eds., Research School CNWS, Leiden, 181-91

4. F. Graf (1997) *Magic in the ancient world*, Franklin Philip, trans., Harvard University Press, Cambridge, Mass; M. W. Dickie (2001) *Magic and magicians in the Greco-Roman world*, Routledge, London

5. 1972, 'Sorcery, demons and the rise of Christianity: from late Antiquity to the rise of the Middle Ages,' *Religion and society in the age of St.*

Augustine, Faber and Faber, London, 119-146. Cf. now: *Brown* J. Howard-Johnston and P. Hayward, eds., 2000, *The cult of saints in Late Antiquity and the Middle Ages: essays on the contribution of Peter*, Oxford University Press, Oxford

6 H. Ritter and M. Plessner, trans., 1962, *Picatrix: Das Ziel des Weisen von Pseudo-Magriti*, London

7 D. Pingree, 1986, *Picatrix*, Warburg Institute London

Mandrake

Mystical Vampire
The Life and Works of Mabel Collins
By Kim Farnell
ISBN 1869928857, £12.99/$25

The characters
Mabel Collins, theosophist, novelist, fashion columnist, and anti-vivisection campaigner

Madame Blavatsky the extraordinary Russian occultist founder of theosophy, and other eminent members of her Theosophical Society

Annie Besant, social reformer and theosophist

Robert Donston Stephenson, a candidate for Jack the Ripper and Mabel's lover

Frances Power Cobbe, social reformer, suffragist and anti-vivisection campaigner

Charlotte Despard, social reformer, and anti-vivisection campaigner

The story
Mabel Collins was an independent woman in the oppressive Victorian climate. She wrote many novels, but most will remember Mabel Collins for her best selling mystical text "Light on the Path" published by the Theosophical Society. After her fall out with Madame Blavatsky, she carried on with her life as an esotericist, traveller and writer. She was moved by the plight and suffering of helplesscreatures, and became a campaigner for the abolition of vivisection.

The author
Kim Farnell is a professional astrologer and writer. She is a contributor to the academic journal "Theosophical History" founded by Leslie Price and edited by Professor James Santucci. Her previous works include a biography of the influential esoteric astrologer Sepharial.

The Magical Dilemma of Victor Neuburg By Jean Overton Fuller

ISBN 1869928792, 334pp 152x229mm, 10 illustrations 13.99 in paperback original

Firstly a record of one man's extraordinary journey to magical enlightenment. Secondly the story of Aleister Crowley, the magus who summoned Neuburg to join him in the quest. The book opens with the author's entry into the group of young poets including Dylan Thomas and Pamela Hansford Johnson They gather around Victor Neuburg in 1935 when he is poetry editor of the *Sunday Referee*. Gradually the author becomes aware of his strange and sinister past, in which Neuburg was associated in magick with Aleister Crowley. Neuburg had been Crowley's partner in magical rituals in the desert and in rites even more dangerous and controversial.

The Bull of Ombos: Seth & Egyptian Magick II
by Mogg Morgan

£12.99, ISBN 1869928873, 356pp, 80 b&w illustrations

Naqada is town in Upper Egypt that gives its name to a crucial period in the prehistory of Egypt. In 1895, William Matthew Flinders Petrie, the 'father' of Egyptian archaeology, stumbled upon a necropolis, belonging to a very ancient city of several thousand inhabitants. Petrie's fateful walk through the desert led him to a lost city, known to the Greeks as Ombos, the Citadel of Seth. Seth, the Hidden God, once ruled in this ancient place before it was abandoned to the sands of the desert. All this forbidden knowledge was quickly reburied in academic libraries, where its stunning magical secrets had lain, largely unrevealed, for more than a century - until now.

This book is for all Egyptophiles as well as anyone with an interest in the archaic roots of magick and the sabbatic craft.

Contents: Gold in the desert / Sethians & Osirians / Cannibalism / Temple of Seth / Seth's Town / Bull of Ombos / Hathor / The names / Animals / the red ochre god / Seth and Horus / Opening the mouth / Seven / The Boat / Heka & Hekau / Magical activities / Cakes of Light / Magick and the funeral rite / Re-emergence of the Hidden God / Appendices / Extended bibliography / Glossary

Orders to: Mandrake, PO Box 250, Oxford, OX1 1AP (UK)
Tel +44 (01865) 243671
email Mandrake@mandrake.uk.net
secure online ordering:
www.mandrake.uk.net/books.htm

The Journal for the Academic Study of Magic (JSM)

Issue 1
ISBN 1869928 679, ISSN 1479-0750
€23 / £13.99 / $25 (airmail) postpaid
Academic libraries & departments request proforma invoice

A multidisciplinary, peer-reviewed print publication, covering all areas of magic, witchcraft, paganism etc; all geographical regions and all historical periods.

Issue 1
ISBN 1869928 679, £13.99, Airmail $25, 200pp
Beyond Attribution: The Importance of Barrett's Magus/Alison Butler * Shadow over Philistia: A review of the Cult of Dagon/John C. Day * A History of Otherness: Tarot and Playing Cards from Early Modern Europe/Joyce Goggin * Opposites Attract: magical identity and social uncertainty/Dave Green * 'Memories of a sorcerer': notes on Gilles Deleuze-Felix Guattari, Austin Osman Spare and Anomalous Sorceries./Matt Lee * Le Streghe Son Tornate: The Reappearance of Streghe in Italian American Queer Writings/ Ilaria Serra * Controlling Chance, Creating Chance: Magical Thinking in Religious Pilgrimage/Deana Weibel

Issue 2
ISBN 1869928 725,, £19.99, 420pp
Alien Selves: Modernity and the Social Diagnostics of the Demonic in 'Lovecraftian Magick': Woodman/Wishful Thinking Notes towards a psychoanalytic sociology of Pagan magick: Green/A Shell with my Name on it: The Reliance on the Supernatural During the First World War. Chambers/The Metaphysical Relationship between Magick and Miracles: Morgan Luck/Demonic Possession, and Spiritual Healing in Nineteenth-Century Devon: Semmens/ Human Body in Southern Slavic Folk Sorcery: Filipovic & Rader/Four Glasses Of Water: Snell/The Land Near the Dark Cornish

Advertisements

Information and Advertisements
Please refer to our website regularly for updated information, we intend to maintain a collection of useful links for researchers, covering resources, jobs, academic courses on magic, libraries, museums, special interest groups, publications, events, conferences, specialist book suppliers etc.

Advertisers for Issue 4: please contact Mandrake (address on back cover) for details, deadlines and rates.

111 Magdalen Rd
Oxford OX4 1RQ
Tel 01865 245301
Fax 01865 245521

mail@innerbookshop.com
Open 10-5.45 - **Mon-Sat**
Books for mind, body and spirit

*Alchemy & Chaos Magick
to Wicca & Zoroastrianism*

Thousands of titles
(new, secondhand & bargains)
search & orderable on our website

www.innerbookshop.com

Visit us (and the Magic Café next door) and see our **Noticeboards** for Oxford and National events or use our **Mail-Order Service** via telephone or fax as well

Lightning Source UK Ltd.
Milton Keynes UK
UKHW011308031222
413284UK00001B/64